Adult Learning and Education in International Contexts:
Future Challenges for its Professionalization

# STUDIES IN PEDAGOGY, ANDRAGOGY AND GERONTAGOGY

Founded by Franz Pöggeler

Edited by Bernd Käpplinger and Steffi Robak

## VOLUME 69

Regina Egetenmeyer / Sabine Schmidt-Lauff /
Vanna Boffo (eds.)

# Adult Learning and Education in International Contexts: Future Challenges for its Professionalization

## Comparative Perspectives from the 2016 Würzburg Winter School

PETER LANG
EDITION

**Bibliographic Information published by the Deutsche Nationalbibliothek**
The Deutsche Nationalbibliothek lists this publication in the Deutsche Nationalbibliografie; detailed bibliographic data is available in the internet at http://dnb.d-nb.de.

**Library of Congress Cataloging-in-Publication Data**
Names: Egetenmeyer, Regina, editor. | Schmidt-Lauff, Sabine, editor. | Boffo, Vanna, editor.
Title: Adult learning and education in international contexts : future challenges for its professionalization : comparative perspectives from the 2016 Wurzburg Winter School / Regina Egetenmeyer, Sabine Schmidt-Lauff, Vanna Boffo (Eds.).
Description: Frankfurt am Main : Peter Lang, 2017. | Series: Studies in pedagogy, andragogy, and gerontagogy, ISSN 0934-3695 ; Vol. 69 | Includes bibliographical references.
Identifiers: LCCN 2017001535| ISBN 9783631678756 | ISBN 9783653070460 (E-PDF) | ISBN 9783631718803 (EPUB) | ISBN 9783631718810 (MOBI)
Subjects: LCSH: Adult education—Cross-cultural studies. | Continuing education—Cross-cultural studies.
Classification: LCC LC5215 .A3486 2017 | DDC 374—dc23 LC record available at https://lccn.loc.gov/2017001535

This book has been fundet with support of the
Human Dynamics Centre of Julius-Maximilian-University Würzburg

Proofreading: Sandstone GbR

Cover: © Beate Derra

Printed by CPI books GmbH, Leck

ISSN 0934-3695
ISBN 978-3-631-67875-6 (Print)
E-ISBN 978-3-653-07046-0 (E-PDF)
E-ISBN 978-3-631-71880-3 (EPUB)
E-ISBN 978-3-631-71881-0 (MOBI)
DOI 10.3726/b11144

This publication has been peer reviewed.

www.peterlang.com

# Table of Contents

6 Table of Contents

Bernd Käpplinger, *series editor*

# Preface

The professionalization of adult educators is an ongoing project. Managing, planning, counselling and teaching are among the core tasks of adult educators, but there are some who take the view that professionalization is not really needed, or that the practitioners' intuition or experience are enough. In the Canadian discussion, for example, Selman and Selman disputed with Nesbit and Hall as to whether Canadian adult education is still progressing at all – that is, whether it can still be seen as a movement. In this Canadian controversy, some opponents discuss professionalization and scientific education rather as an obstacle than a support for learners. Teachers or trainers should be produced by movements, not academic training. The German discourse on this topic, as exemplified in Nittel's book published in 2000, maintains that adult education has, in many respects, changed from wanting to be a mission to wanting to create a profession. If professionalization is defined as a process, this term implies that there is still a long way to go and includes backlashes such as precarious working conditions. Voluntary engagement can also mean exploitation, especially when it is systematically used in lieu of good payment for good work. There are certainly similar discussions and struggles going on in other countries.

There are many advantages to having professionally trained staff. Professional staff are able to plan courses and events in such a way that many mistakes are at least less likely or can even be avoided from the outset before any teaching and learning take place. Unfortunately, programme planning is often rather neglected and not researched extensively enough by adult education research, which is sometimes too preoccupied with the analysis of political discourses. Professional staff should shield teachers and learners from unnecessary formalities and organizational pressures brought about by short-sighted administrators, intrusive financiers and biased advocates of various educational movements and trends. Professional staff are able to deal with complex learning situations, avoid painful learning experiences or be aware of poor group dynamics. Good intentions and activism are not enough. In 1968, the renowned Ivan Illic – who was certainly not an advocate of formal learning – stated in a famous speech to volunteers that the road to hell is paved with good intentions. People have to know and to reflect what they are doing in a professional way. Adult educators can also advise and guide learners in their educational decisions in private and vocational contexts. Learners and clients are now often burdened with information overload and thus increasingly need support to orient themselves; however, that support should not make decisions on their behalf or preach certainties. There is an ocean of knowledge and know-how that can be tapped into to configure good adult education. Approaches that are solely based on experience are subject to the accidental limitations of individual experience and frequently take place in an unbalanced organizational context shaped by unquestioned routines and rituals.

Nonetheless, professionalization should not be idealized, and it is important to take stock of the achievements, shortcomings and circuitous routes taken in the many different fields of adult education – nationally, internationally and transnationally. In this respect, this volume makes an extremely interesting contribution and has its inception in the innovative, international Würzburg Winter School. The introduction by its principal contributors Regina Egetenmeyer, Sabine Schmidt-Lauff and Vanna Boffo deals with these aspects in much greater detail.

This volume has three main chapters. The first is concerned with policy, since professionalization is often linked to political decisions. Unfortunately, recent political developments in North America have caused many adult educators to see the state as an opponent rather than a potential source of support for adult education that should be coaxed into playing a more active and supportive role. The second chapter discusses professionalization frameworks, which are an important source of orientation in a larger context. It is increasingly important to compare developments in different countries and perhaps even look for shared frames. The third and final chapter deals with the various different dimensions of professionalization in adult education.

I am delighted to have been given the opportunity to recommend this volume and the international Würzburg Winter School from whose work it has arisen, and I am certain that we will hear a lot more about both the school and its participants in the future.

## References

Nesbitt, T. & Hall, B. T. (2011): Canadian Adult Education: Still Moving. Conference Proceedings of the Adult Research Conference at OISE Toronto, pp. 489–495.

Nittel, D. (2000): Von der Mission zur Profession? Bielefeld.

Selman, G., & Selman, M. (2009): The life and death of the Canadian adult education movement. Canadian Journal of University Continuing Education, 35(2), pp. 13–28.

Regina Egetenmeyer, Sabine Schmidt-Lauff & Vanna Boffo

# Internationalization and Professionalization in Adult Education: An Introduction

**Abstract:** Adult education and lifelong learning are becoming international phenomena, which have a strong influence on its professionals. The 2016 Würzburg Winter School 'Comparative Studies in Adult Education and Lifelong Learning' analyzed this and identified influences on policy at local, national and international levels. It further analyzed the internationalization of adult education and identified the emergence of different dimensions of professionalism in adult education.

## Introduction

Over the last two decades, adult learning and lifelong education have become international phenomena. They represent an on-going process of globalization in education, which decades ago was mainly a national issue. This can be seen at the educational policy level of international organizations, such as UNESCO, the European Union, the OECD and the World Bank. International education policies have a strong effect on national education policies, extending to areas that are not formally connected, as can be shown by the impact of EU policies in South and Southeast Asia (Egetenmeyer 2016).

Beyond the policy level, these processes of internationalization can also be observed at the meso- and micro-level of adult, continuing and lifelong education. At the meso-level, adult and lifelong education organizations are working increasingly in transnational and international contexts. In Germany, for instance, vocational and continuing education will be promoted as an "export product", especially towards Asian countries (cf. BiBB 2015). This means that the structures, offerings and contexts of providers in adult and lifelong education are progressively becoming more international. At the micro-level, students are now expected to deal with international learning requirements, which concern not only language skills but also the rising number of students who have migrated to European countries seeking refuge from war, terrorism, climate change and economic and social turmoil. This trend can also be seen in India and China, where there are strong migration tendencies, especially intra-country migration and rural-urban migration (Schulze Plastring 2015; BPB 2012). Handling rising migration has been promoted within the European Union from early on in the context of labour mobility as well as in the context of the development of a European identity. It was most recently promoted with a special focus on young, highly-qualified people. This means that professionals in adult learning and education need to be able to interact with people who have migrated to Europe from various countries. This will allow these professionals to work in politically internationalized contexts and contexts that affect adult and lifelong education through global phenomena, such as temporal perspectives, individualization and globalization. The ability to reflect on global systems and to take intra-cultural and trans-cultural competencies into account can be described as inherent needs of professionalization in adult and continuing education. Adult learning and education in one's own context is far more understandable when viewed within the context of global developments, changes and continuities.

This book identifies these international developments and addresses the question of what these changes mean for professionalization in adult education. In this context, the editors foresee unique challenges for professionalization in adult education, which in the past was largely a national practice. The volume sheds light on the diverse range of European and international professional contexts in cultivating adult learning and education. This includes not only micro-level teaching and guidance of adult learning but also the development of a wide range of non-formal and informal learning in different contexts and institutions, as well as on the policy levels that deal with adult education and learning. It is therefore essential to reflect on the mega-, macro-, meso- and micro-levels and their correlations and interdependencies (Lima & Guimarães 2011).

The volume poses the following questions: How do current developments in society influence institutions, actors and the professionalization of adult educators? Which cross-national issues, (e.g., employability, acceleration and globalization), frames and dimensions offer the possibility for a joint understanding of professionalism?

In each country, professionalization and professionalism in the context of lifelong learning are marked by specific historical developments, actors, activities, institutions and curricula. This book summarizes articles and studies involving comparative research, which may enable reflection on a "modern" professional consciousness. What are the essential influences and key concepts? How do they differ between continents, countries and regions, and what are their similarities?

## On the ERASMUS+ Strategic Partnership: "Comparative Studies in Adult Education and Lifelong Learning"

These questions were addressed during the 2016 Würzburg Winter School, which was organized in the context of the ERASMUS+ Strategic Partnership "Comparative Studies in Adult Education and Lifelong Learning" (COMPALL) in February 2016. It centred on the international developments outlined above by focusing on supra-nationalinter-cultural, trans-cultural and comparative perspectives in adult education and lifelong learning. With its activities, COMPALL contributes to the development of international, trans-cultural and comparative competencies within the academic professionalization in adult education and lifelong learning. While the 2016 Würzburg Winter School on Comparative Studies in Adult Education and Lifelong Learning was the third installation of the event, the Strategic Partnership was started in September 2015 and allows the further systematic development of the initiative into a joint module, allowing for combined research activity.

The Strategic Partnership COMPALL is developing a joint module in "Comparative Studies in Adult Education and Lifelong Learning". There are seven partner universities from five European countries that are integrating the joint module into their master's and doctoral study programmes on adult education and lifelong learning. These include the Julius-Maximilian University Würzburg as coordinator, the University of Lisbon, the University of Florence, the University of Padua, the University of Pécs, the Helmut-Schmidt University in Hamburg and Aarhus University. Thanks to the exchange programme at the Julius-Maximilian University Würzburg with other international universities, namely the University of Delhi, the International Institute of Adult and Lifelong Learning in New Delhi, the Obafemi Awolowo University in Nigeria, and the University of Belgrade, participants from around the globe enrich this partnership. The joint module includes a preparatory phase, a two-week intensive phase at Campus Würzburg, Germany, and the possibility of publication for doctoral students and colleagues. The Winter School offers topics on international policies in adult education and lifelong learning as well as comparisons on selected issues within adult education and lifelong learning. The programme is augmented by field visits to adult and continuing education providers. During the preparation phase, students are educated through on-campus sessions on issues of adult education in their local and national contexts and sessions on European and international policies in adult education. They are also taught analysis strategies to facilitate undertaking comparative studies in the field of adult and continuing education. These sessions are supported by online tutorials, which are currently developed in a joint effort by all partner universities. These issues serve as preparation for the first week of the Würzburg Winter School. Additionally, all participants prepare by writing a transnational essay on one of the selected issues in adult and comparative education. This serves as the preparation for the second week, during which participants attend one comparative group session on a selected issue in adult education and lifelong learning. These include learning cities, learning regions and learning communities and competencies in formal, informal and vocational education. International experts in adult education and lifelong learning moderate these groups. Results gathered from these comparisons are presented at the end of the second week to the other groups. After the Winter School, doctoral students work together with the moderators on selected results arising from the comparative group sessions, allowing for deeper comparisons. The results of these comparisons are presented in this volume.

Furthermore, COMPALL is developing a professional online network for graduates and young researchers in adult education and lifelong learning. This allows the development of sustainable international networks among fellow students. Such networks provide opportunities for participants by helping to find appropriate partners for transnational studies and research. It further provides information on current international studies, research possibilities and international vacancies in adult education and lifelong learning. The professional network is located on LinkedIn and is open to anyone interested in adult education and lifelong learning (URL: https://www.linkedin.com/groups/8445381). Additionally, each year, a closed network is developed on LinkedIn, through which Winter School participants can connect with each other and with the fellow students they met during their stay in Würzburg. An information tool on the COMPALL homepage provides further study information on international and comparative adult education (URL: http://www.hw.uni-wuerzburg.de/compall/information_tool/). Topics are based on the information in the country reports on adult education available, datasets for comparative research in adult learning and education, international study offers in adult learning and education, online networking opportunities and information on preparation material for the Winter School.

In order to share the results of COMPALL with a wider public audience, the project is working on measures that will allow the results of projects to be presented and discussed. This will happen each year until 2018 at the end of the Winter School Multiplier Events. These events are organized in collaboration with international networks that have an emphasis on comparative and international studies in adult education and lifelong learning. Future related events include the International Society for Comparative Adult Education in 2017 and the ASEM

Hub for Lifelong Learning in 2018. This approach stresses the didactical focus of the Winter School, which intends to lead students from research-based learning to hands-on research.

*Table 1: Structure of the COMPALL Project.*

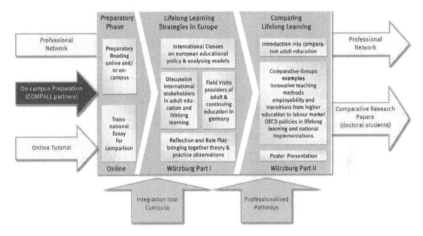

Source: COMPALL project

## Overview of the Book

All COMPALL activities are designed to support students in adult education and lifelong learning to develop international competencies and trans-cultural understanding. The contributions in this book analyze the influence of internationalization on the professional development of adult educators. It includes papers that compare adult education across different contexts, countries and projects, which were developed in direct relation to the 2016 Winter School. The book is divided into three different sections, outlined below.

The first section, *Adult Learning in the Context of International Policies,* introduces international education policy as it has emerged in countries from Europe to Asia. It particularly considers the extent to which these policies have influenced professionalization in adult education.

*Wei, Choi,* and *Doutor* analyze and compare policy documents designed to enhance young adults' employability in China, Portugal and the Republic of Korea. The paper focuses on current policies that have been implemented in the three countries, analyzing key documents from four perspectives: normative, structural, constitutive and technical. Despite the three countries' differences concerning ministerial responsibility for employability, economic circumstances and cultural values, the authors identify a common consensus that adult education contributes significantly to individual employability. The education policy documents selected also identify how societal tasks relate to adult education. With regard to professionalization in adult education, this paper offers a demonstration of how countries with varying educational and employment systems respond to employability as a common, current issue.

*Di Campo, Barany, Henning* and *Németh* compare three city/region student models in Germany, Hungary and Italy. They analyze policy interventions and elucidate the kinds of adult education and lifelong learning philosophies that these policies reflect. The comparison highlights substantial differences across the three regions but commonalities also emerge where in each case, it is the local context that guides the structure and the targets of the models. Furthermore, all three cases demonstrate that an important issue for professionals in adult education and learning is the capacity to develop networks and the opportunity to work together with those from other fields of education.

*Singh* and *Assinger* analyze elements of policy and general approaches to the governance of professionalization in adult education in India and Austria, two significantly different countries in terms of their size, location and socio-economic status. Through the lens of policy and governance, the authors discuss the ways in which professionalization is conceived, the varying definitions of competences, and participant structures and participant relations in the process of governing professionalization. Their comparison shows that as a policy and as a conceptual landscape, professionalization can prove flexible enough to encompass a broad range of tasks.

*Guimarães* and *Alves* concentrate on the development of formal regulations related to adult education occupations in Portugal from the late 1990s. These developments are discussed with reference to European Union guidelines, leading to the conclusion that European policies towards lifelong learning have substantially influenced those in Portugal. In particular, legislation has emerged to encourage occupations related to professional recognition and validation of competencies as well as the emergence of technicians for diagnosis and guidance, trainers and teachers for adult education and coordinators of adult education centres. The challenges that confront adult education occupations in Portugal are also discussed.

*Terzaroli* bases his chapter on the working context of adult education professionals in Italy, though he considers this against the background of European policies on adult education. Based on a country report that presents a review of policy, laws and scientific articles related to adult educators' professionalization, the paper offers a crucial discussion of the topic from the perspective of politics, culture and employment. Furthermore, it highlights new working opportunities within both the Italian public system as well as the private labour market.

The second section of this volume, *Frames of Professionalization in Adult Education*, offers research on contextual influences beyond the narrow policy focus that also affects professionalization in adult education. These four contributions show the extent to which 'frames of professionalization' can interrelate with international developments in the context of adult education.

*Kuhlen, Singh* and *Tomei* argue that drilling down to the level of university curricula is critically important for understanding the professionalization of adult education through higher education. The authors compare university contexts and university curricula in adult education and the impact of both elements on graduates' professionalization in three countries: India, Italy and Germany. Similarities are discerned between the two European countries, with commonalities between Germany and Italy, including similar terminology for educational management, a focus on research and teaching and the importance of national regulations on the development of curricula. Conversely, in India, the authors identify a greater emphasis on empowerment and uplifting marginalized groups through the use of fieldwork and experiential learning. Non-governmental agencies were also seen to exert more influence. The authors conclude that universities should introduce a combined approach integrating both research and fieldwork components into adult education curricula.

*Gioli* and *Ricardo* start from the premise that comparing adult education across different countries, and particularly at the PhD level, can aid in understanding and framing the concept of adult education itself. In particular, this chapter analyzes the impact of adult education PhD curricula on graduates' employability in Italy, Portugal and Malaysia. In the context of the current economic crises in Italy and Portugal, these countries' universities have only begun to recognize the need to ensure a smooth transition for PhD graduates from university to the labour market by facilitating the development of social and communicative skills, or 'soft skills'. The authors discuss this relatively new orientation towards employability in Italy and Portugal in reference to having less of a tradition in this respect, compared to the situation in Malaysia. The development of PhD curricula in adult education with a focus on strategies, methods and skills to ease the transition into the labour market thus seems to be a substantially new development for universities in Italy and Portugal.

*Pekeč, Mihajlovič* and *da Silva Castro* analyze the professionalization of adult education in Serbia and Brazil. They start by asking whether adult learning can, in fact, be considered a profession at all, given the wide range of activities undertaken by those employed in the field of adult education. They also engage with the question of the extent to which it may be possible, in future, for adult education to become a fully developed profession. Both questions are addressed using comparative research on adult learning and education. Despite the substantial differences between Serbia and Brazil in terms of their size, location and other factors, the authors identify categories through which they are able to analyze context, legislation and the opportunities for adult learning and educational practitioners. Complementary to the findings that emerged from the comparison of India and Austria described above, the results of this study indicate that there are differences regarding professional associations, formal preparation and the competences of adult educators between large countries, like Brazil, and smaller ones, like Serbia.

*Hösel* and *Terzaroli* focus on work transitions, particularly with respect to the pedagogical challenges involved in supporting adults who seek a different employment path. They develop a two-dimensional model, invoking the categories of identity, agency and structure, alongside a range of perspectives, namely that of the discursive, individual, institutional and professional. This model could be used as a possible tool for further comparative research on transitions in adulthood. With respect to professionalization in adult education, this means understanding the importance of providing sufficient support for individuals in transitions as an educational task.

The third part of this volume, *Dimensions of Adult Education Professionalism*, focuses on perspectives of adult education professionalization that emerge from the internationalization of societies. It contains five chapters that together consider the field of adult education across micro-, meso- and macro-levels.

*Schmidt-Lauff* and *Bergamini* compare modern conceptions of time and temporal influences on adult learning and education with particular focus on the contrast between Germany and Italy. They refer to legal frameworks in the two countries and to data arising from the OECD related to temporal perspectives of adult education. The chapter suggests that employment transformation processes should be mastered individually as well as within appropriate social structures. It further includes a plea about time-sensitivity as a central professional necessity in adult education across micro-, meso- and macro-levels.

*Nierobisch, Ergin, Tino* and *Schüßler* analyze subjective theories of adult teaching and learning in universities in Germany, Turkey and Italy that have adapted European policies and the UNESCO concept of lifelong learning. Based on an existing research project in Germany, they understand subjective theories as an implicit regulation of didactical actions in adult education. The authors show, with reference to the three contexts, that subjective theories of adult teaching and learning are closely connected to students' theoretical knowledge as well as to their practical experiences. Theories of learning and teaching in the context of adult education are thus highly relevant to the process of academic professionalization.

*Halim, Osman* and *Wan Nor Fadzilah* analyze the core competencies of Malaysian science centre facilitators who play a pivotal role in encouraging people to explore science and develop scientific literacy. Referring to international core competency studies, they analyze the set of competences that are needed by people who teach adults in the field of science and in informal contexts. They find that personal qualities, communication skills and evaluation of learning and learning assistance are all required in order to adapt to the learning needs of adults.

*Simeon-Fayomi* explores indigenous adult teaching methods in southwestern Nigeria and South Africa. Her analysis includes a discussion of music, dance, role-playing, oral tradition and storytelling. With this contribution, Simeon-Fayomi brings novel adult teaching methods into the discourse. Furthermore, her work illustrates the centrality of participant-orientation in adult education. She concludes that these methods are effective for teaching and learning and that incorporating African indigenous approaches into the Western tradition could be beneficial.

*Avramosvksa* and *Czerwinski* present Curriculum globALE, an international core curriculum for the training of adult educators worldwide. Developed by DVV International and the German Institute for Adult Education to encourage professionalization in the field of adult education, plans are underway to implement this global curriculum framework in 15 countries. The authors present the results from two pilot implementations of Curriculum globALE in Uzbekistan and Macedonia, countries with otherwise limited possibilities for the professionalization of adult educators and a strong demand for more resources for professional adult educators. In both contexts, Curriculum globALE contributed to the enhancement of professionals in the field, although several challenges were also identified.

## Internationalization and Professionalization in Adult Education

The contributions of this book indicate that insight into international developments in adult education is no longer knowledge that is just 'nice to know' and the ability to work in an international context in adult education is no longer simply 'nice to have'. Rather, recognizing the trends taking place in this field internationally is essential both for understanding one's own context and for advancing professional adult education more generally in a world of ongoing internationalization and globalization. When it comes to adult education, these two forces of internationalization and globalization thus do not become categories of 'good' vs 'bad' – but rather a reality that can be understood and developed in a highly differentiated way, according to learning opportunities that can be opened up for adults. In sum, continually seeking this knowledge and refining ideas and policies accordingly is inherently necessary for professionals engaged in adult education and lifelong learning.

With regard to the volume arising from the Winter School 2015, Egetenmeyer (2016, p. 19) outlined the target of developing "an attitude of further questioning one's own understanding in an ongoing endeavour to gain deeper understanding…to continue the never-ending journey of trying to understand each other." This set of comparative papers indicates that the contributing authors are following this vision of developing a joint understanding of adult education. This is especially the case when reading the papers that compare considerably different contexts, such as the governance of adult education in India and Austria or the professionalization in adult education in Serbia and Brazil. Despite these countries' substantial differences, the authors were able to identify points of commonality and categories for comparison. This adds considerable value to a heterogeneous field like adult education.

Comparisons of European and non-European countries provide important understandings of the similarities and differences arising in adult education research and the professionalization of its field of practice. With respect to Europe, in particular, the authors in this volume critically examine policies in adult education and lifelong learning. They also observe some degree of a common European identity of what is understood as adult education and how European policies – as well as national and regional policies – should further be developed for the benefit of learning possibilities for all adults in Europe. Considering the state of adult education in different European countries alongside what is taking place beyond its continental borders seems to make a common European identity especially visible. This is corroborated by a number of studies that consider country-specific outcomes alongside the broad European discourse on adult education. European policies on adult education thus seem to have strong implications for our collective understanding of adult education. In sum, while acknowledging that it is the differences that stand out when we compare European countries with non-European countries, this should not overshadow results that show a high, albeit somewhat implicit, impact of European educational policies on countries far beyond the European Union (Egetenmeyer 2016; Regmi 2016; Singh, Bora & Egetenmeyer 2016).

Finally, the comparisons make visible the importance of national professionalization structures in adult education, which seem to be better realized in smaller countries, notably Austria, Serbia and Switzerland, although the latter is not included in this volume. The reasons for this have not yet been analyzed, however, and it remains to be seen whether these types of systems can be realized in bigger countries with more people working in the field of adult education. Exploring this question in greater depth can be regarded as an important area for future research in the field of international adult education and its professionalization.

## Conclusion and Words of Thanks

This book presents the results of the discussion and research before, during and after the 2016 Würzburg Winter School. The contributions present and promote a didactical way from research-oriented learning toward research. This is only possible due to the support of the moderators at the Winter School. We are grateful for their enormous efforts with regard to the planning of comparisons, guidance of participants and teaching in the Winter School. We also deeply appreciate their further guidance of doctoral students by preparing the students to write comparative papers in joint authorships. Thank you very much to all moderators of the comparative groups. In addition to the editors, contributors to this volume include: Prof. Vanna Boffo (University of Florence), Tino Concetta (University of Padua), Prof. Soeren Ehlers (Aarhus University), Dr. Gaia Gioli (University of Florence), Prof. Marcella Milana (University of Verona), Prof. Balasz Nemeth (University of Pécs), Dr. Kira Nierobisch (University of Education in Ludwigsburg), Prof. Hajo Petsch (University of Würzburg), and Prof. Ingeborg Schüßler (University of Education in Ludwigsburg).

As outlined above, the 2016 Winter School is integrated into the Strategic Partnership Comparative Studies in Adult Education and Lifelong Learning (COMPALL). This volume has been produced outside of the project. It displays the strong interest of doctoral students in working together across international contexts and developing their networks. In order to make the 2016 Würzburg Winter School possible, hosting approximately 90 participants and 14 international lecturers, the support of several funders was necessary. For this, we are very thankful to ERASMUS+, the DAAD-Programme Summer Schools, the DAAD-Programme 'A New Passage to India', the Human Dynamics Centre of the Faculty of Human Sciences at the University of Würzburg and the Project Global Systems and International Competences at the University of Würzburg.

Thank you very much to all the reviewers (named at the end of this volume) who supported this volume with their feedback on the texts submitted. Overall, it was the dedicated Würzburg team that made for a successful and enjoyable 2016 Würzburg Winter School. A special thank you to Stefanie Kröner, who has, since the very beginning, done an excellent job as coordinator of all Winter School activities. Thank you very much to Monika Staab for her support of the COM-PALL project. Thank you to Clara Kuhlen, Beate Derra, Linda Williges, Alexander Mayer, Carolin Klass, Shalini Singh, Leonie Pampel, Vanessa Gärtner, Julia Molina, Antonia Lecht and Tini Masuch for your support.

The Würzburg Winter School is for educating young professionals so that they will be able to develop a diversified and international understanding of adult education and contribute to their local contexts. The School encourages an international network of young researchers to form, giving them the space in which to develop their future together. The participant feedback we have received thus far seems to indicate a shared appreciation for the widened understanding and increased open-mindedness that these students have gained. This may form the basis for the development of a new international generation in adult education with links within Europe and beyond.

## References

Bundesinstitut für Berufsbildung (BiBB) (ed.): *Jahresbericht 2014: iMove: Training – Made in Germany*. Bundesinstitut für Berufsbildung: Bonn. 2015, retrieved from https://www.imove-germany.de/cps/rde/xbcr/imove_projekt_ international/p_iMOVE-Jahresbericht-2014.pdf.

Bundeszentrale für politische Bildung (BPB): "Binnenmigration in China – Chance oder Falle?", *Focus Migration: Kurzdossier* 19, 2014, retrieved from http:// www.bpb.de/gesellschaft/migration/kurzdossiers/151241/binnenmigration-in-china?.

Egetenmeyer, R. (ed.): *Adult education and lifelong learning in Europe and beyond: Comparative perspectives from the 2015 Würzburg Winter School.* Peter Lang GmbH: Frankfurt am Main. 2016.

Lima, L.C. / Guimaraes, P.: *European strategies in lifelong learning: A critical introduction.* Barbara Budrich Publishers: Opladen & Farmington Hills. 2011.

Schulze Plastring, V.: *Das Potenzial der Migration aus Indien: Entwicklungen im Herkunftsland, internationale Migrationsbewegungen und Migration nach Deutschland.* Bundesamt für Migration und Flüchtlinge. Berlin. 2015, retrieved from https://www.bamf.de/SharedDocs/Anlagen/DE/Publikationen/Forschungsberichte/fb26-potenziale-migration-indien.pdf?__blob=publicationFile.

Singh S. / Bora, B. / Egetenmeyer, R.: "Adult education policies in India and international influences". In M. Schemman (ed.): *Current status of adult education regarding Millennium Development Goals and Education for All: Results and prospects from the perspective of South-, East- and Southeast-Asian states.* (International Yearbook of Adult Education 39). 2016, pp. 17–35.

# Adult Learning in the Context
of International Policies

Ge Wei, Eunyoung Choi & Catarina Doutor

# Initiatives to Support Employability of Young Adults: Comparative Policy Analysis of China, Portugal and the Republic of Korea

**Abstract:** This article takes a comparative look at national policies intended to support the employability of young adults in China, Portugal and the Republic of Korea. It finds that while countries carry out policies according to their particular political regime, economic circumstances and cultural values, the general consensus is that adult education is important for employability.

## Introduction

It is acknowledged that within market economies, employability is closely linked to shifts in the supply and demand of labour. Employees tend to hold themselves responsible for employment outcomes, which can be improved through the development of human capital (Allais 2014; Brown, Lauder & Ashton 2011). In the contemporary economic landscape, individuals are obliged to take care of their own employability, income and survival. In line with this rationale, Yorke (2004, p. 7) defines employability as a set of achievements that enable graduates to gain employment. Hillage and Pollard (1998) argue that employability involves the capability to move self-sufficiently within the labour market and realize one's potential through sustainable employment. For Schreuder and Coetzee (2006), employability refers to an individual's capacity and willingness to become and remain attractive to employers in the labour market as well as to the individual's capability to be successful in a wide range of jobs.

Versloot et al. (1998) propose three academic perspectives on employability: (a) the societal or national perspective, (b) the company level or organizational perspective and (c) the individual perspective. However, as a manifestation of political discourse, the (inter-)national policies on employability have received little attention. This article, a comparative policy study on 'employability' as it relates to adult education in China, Portugal and the Republic of Korea, addresses this omission. We carry out a textual analysis of key official policy documents, examining both the surface-level content and the common themes that emerge from the texts.

## Theoretical framework

In order to contextualize and theorize about the policy texts, we create detailed indicators to analyze the core elements based on four dimensions of policy studies (Cooper, Fusarelli & Randall 2004). With the help of a theoretical framework (see Figure 1), we are able to identify clearly the similarities and differences across the three countries' policy documents.

*Figure 1: A Comparative Framework for Policy Analysis (cf. Cooper, Fusarelli & Randall 2004).*

| | |
|---|---|
| **Normative**<br><br>*Objectives*<br><br>*Values* | **Structural**<br>*Federal/National*<br>*State/Provincial*<br>*Local* |
| **Constitutive**<br><br>*Adult Learners*<br><br>*Adult Educators* | **Technical**<br>*Resources*<br>*Instruments*<br>*Implementations* |

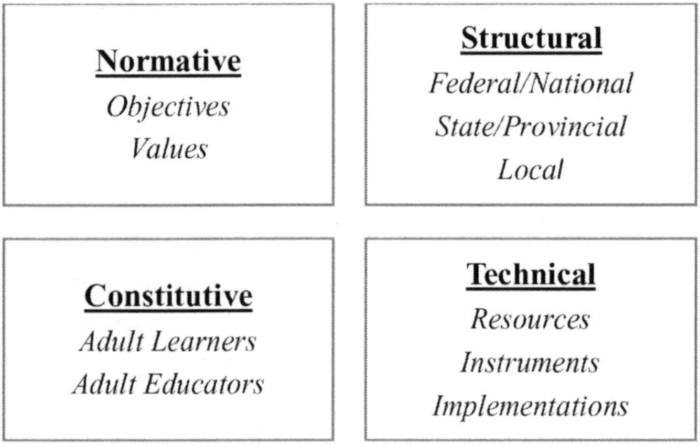

Understanding educational policy necessitates a consideration of the influence and intention of policies along the four dimensions of policy theory. By utilizing these four dimensions, namely normative, structural, constitutive and technical, we can examine the significant dimensions of each policy (Cooper, Fusarelli & Randall 2004). This framework enables us to understand policymaking in education from various perspectives.

## Policy Analysis across Three Countries

### China

Before the 1980s, China's economic system was a planned economy, which was predicated on a centralized labour allocation system for young adults. Young adults did not need to search for jobs because the state would allocate them to "appropriate" positions. During the transition from a planned economy to a socialist market economy, China's government found that the previous employment system was not suited to a dynamic labour market. It became increasingly impossible for the Chinese government to afford to find jobs for young adults, especially following the expansion of higher education enrolment in the 2000s. The Chinese government thus proposed several policy documents on "employability". In this section, three core official policy documents published in 2015 are analyzed, namely: Opinions of the State Council on Further Promoting Employment and Entrepreneurship in the New Situation (FPEE), Opinions of the General Office of the State Council on Deepening the Reform of the Innovation and Entrepreneurship Education in Higher Education Institutions (DRIEE) and Notice of the General Office of the State Council on Key Tasks of the Employment and Entrepreneurship in the New Situation (KTEE).

## Normative dimension

The stated objective of the FPEE is to promote young adults' employability. The undeclared, yet arguably more important, objective, however, is to boost the nation as a whole. In 2015, the unemployment rate was 4.05%, and in 2016, 150 million young people found employment after graduation. In the DRIEE policy, plans are presented for reforming innovation and entrepreneurship education for social and economic development at the macro-level. This builds upon an upper level policy called "Invigorating the Country through Science, Technology and Education", which has been in place since the start of the twenty-first century. In all three policies, the aim of "realizing the great rejuvenation of the Chinese nation and the Chinese dream" is strongly emphasized. From this perspective, nationalism is at the heart of policies for employability in China. Yet, according to the Chinese centralized political regime, this stance could be interpreted as the traditional social mechanism called communitarianism.

## Structural dimension

Governments, higher education departments and industrial organizations all have the responsibility to promote employability skills (Tasker & Packham 1994). In China, a ternary-level management system has been built to implement the policies. Firstly, the General Office of the State Council provides national level guidance. The Ministry of Finance, the Ministry of Education (especially the Department of Vocational Education and Adult Education) and the Ministry of Human Resources and Social Security cooperate to carry out specific policies targeting employability. Secondly, at the regional level, the government has the responsibility to supply funds and opportunities for networking based on economic circumstance. Thirdly, at the local level, Higher Education Institutes have been given increasing autonomy in domains such as enrolment size, curriculum development, teaching syllabi, course arrangements, teaching organization, evaluations and certificate insurance.

## Constitutive dimension

There are clear individual benefits to employability. It enables graduates to become productive workers and increases the likelihood of retaining a job. In terms of Higher Education Institutes, adult educators are responsible for holding entrepreneurial training camps as well as innovation and entrepreneurship competitions and for cultivating an entrepreneurial culture. With increased awareness of the importance of promoting students' employability, traditional disciplinary structures and training methods change, as does the willingness of educators to reform their pedagogical methods. The DRIEE maintains that new pedagogical methods, such as "heuristic teaching, seminars, participatory teaching, and apprenticeship" (DRIEE 2015)., need to be introduced into the adult education process.

## Technical dimension

The Chinese government is increasing its support for more employment opportunities for young adults. For example, in 2015, the government invested 40 billion RMB into advancing entrepreneurship. Furthermore, in order to promote young adults' employability, the local government introduced regulations for internships and training programmes (China State Council 2015b). Adult educators are an excellent resource for facilitating employability (China State Council 2015a). Mandate, inducement, capacity-building and system changes (McDonnell & Elmore 1987) are all used to implement the policies. Due to its major role in Chinese society, the government provides the main resources for advancing employability.

## Portugal

After the 2008 global economic crisis, the Portuguese economy entered a deep recession with high unemployment (Paiva et al. 2015). Since May 2011, Portuguese authorities have negotiated with the European Commission, the European Central Bank and the International Monetary Fund (IMF) for an Economic Adjustment Programme. Statistics show that Portugal's labour market remains strongly affected by the economic recession. In June 2016, the employment rate stood at 58.1%, up 0.2% from the previous month; for adults, the employment rate was

63.6%, while for young adults, it was 24.2% (National Statistics Institute 2016)[1]. To improve this, a range of programmes and measures specifically aimed at promoting youth employability has been instituted (Employment and Vocational Training Institute – IEFP). These include:

- *The Professional Internships Programme:*[2] This programme promotes initial and close contact with businesses and the world of work. An opportunity to display and develop work-based skills, this programme increases young people's employability and the likelihood of a successful career (Yorke 2004).
- *Employment-Integration Contracts:*[3] These contracts provide financial support to people receiving unemployment benefits. The contracts aim to reduce skill deterioration after long periods of unemployment, improve the employability of the long-term unemployed, and respond to local and regional labour market needs, especially for socially beneficial work activities.
- *The Stimulus Employment Programme:*[4] This programme uses incentives to induce the unemployed to return to the labour market. It is targeted at those who have had major difficulties and looks to match people's existing skills with available jobs and employer needs. Although individuals are responsible for what happens after gaining employment, their chance of long-term success can be improved through the development of employment skills (Allais 2014).
- *Active Youth Employment:*[5] This programme provides financial support to employers who are looking to hire young people on full-time job contracts. It aims to boost youth employment, reduce labour market segmentation and encourage the hiring of long-term unemployed youth.

## Normative dimension

The main aims of these programmes are to complement and develop the skills of young adults looking for a first or new job, support the transition between the education system and the labour market, create jobs in new areas, and promote the professional integration of unemployed people while enhancing their marketable

---

1   According to the National Statistics Institute, Portuguese unemployment rate declined to 10,5% in the third quarter of 2016. So, Portugal had the sixth highest unemployment rate in Europe. Concerning to youth unemployment rate (aged 15 to 24) dropped to 26.1%. For more information, see http://www.ine.pt
2   For more information, see https://www.iefp.pt/en/estagios
3   For more information, see https://www.iefp.pt/en/emprego-insercao
4   Approved by Ordinance No 149-A/2014, July 24
5   For more information, see https://www.iefp.pt/en/emprego-jovem-ativo

skills. These programmes encourage unemployed workers to acquire new skills through employability support measures and participation in the labour market. This also contributes to increased self-esteem and greater autonomy for these workers. Currently, policies tend to view the individual as solely responsible for his or her employment status; employers or companies are not considered in this regard (Hespanha, 2002).

## Structural dimension

According to Valadas (2013), the implementation of innovative employment policies has been encouraged by international organizations, such as the European Institution (European Council) and the Organization for Economic Co-operation and Development (OECD), and financing entities, such as the Human Potential Operational Programme (POPH). The Ministry of Solidarity and Social Security and the Employment and Vocational Training Institute (IEFP)are responsible for the regulation and administration of employment policies. In this context, companies, training entities and municipalities have a responsibility to promote employability (Paiva et al. 2015).

## Constitutive dimension

Many constituents and stakeholders are involved in the creation and evaluation of policy. Key interest groups, political parties, associations and unions generally have a personal and professional stake in how policies are implemented and evaluated and play a major part in assessing a policy's value and effectiveness. In the context of employability, the importance of formal education and training, as well as lifelong learning, has been growing (Valente, Soares and Fialho 2013). Some of these initiatives include providing learning systems, vocational training, education training courses for young adults, technological specialization courses, and new assets for schools.

## Technical dimension

In response to increasing youth unemployment at the end of 2013, Portugal adopted the European Commission's recommendation of a "youth guarantee". The guarantee, based on the commitment of each member state, seeks to ensure that all young adults enjoy better job opportunities, education, and the possibility of attaining apprenticeships or internships within four months of becoming unemployed or dropping out of school. The Active Youth Employment Programme's mandate is to facilitate the insertion into work of young adults who have not completed compulsory education. Specifically, the aim of the programme is:

*To promote peer learning and the development of professional, social and emotional skills...
and to collaborate with others and work autonomously. Participation in the programme
also aims to incentivize young people to return to formal education and training pathways
or the labour market*

(OECD 2015, p. 66)

## The Republic of Korea

Since the Asian Financial Crisis of 1997, Korea's promotion of adult education
and adult learning has become increasingly related to unemployment. Struggling
with a high youth unemployment rate, the Korean government has been replacing
supply-side employment policies with demand-side employment policies. Introduced in 2013, the "work-study dual system" is one of the key initiatives within Korea's youth employment policy that is broadly linked to Vocational Education and
Training (VET). [6] This policy is "a system that provides young adults with a long-
term and systematic, firm-centred, on-the-job training that recognizes equivalent
qualification by the state or industrial circles" (Nah 2013). Vocational Education
and Training programmes should be developed in accordance with the National
Competency Standards (NCS)[7]. In 2015, 5764 enterprises and 10,869 apprentices
participated in a work-study system (HRD-Korea, n.d.). The policy is expanding
from its focus on graduates to include currently enrolled students as well.

*Normative dimension*

The aim of a work-study system is to "increase the employment rate of young
adults and, in the long run, enable the making of a competency-centred society"
(Jeon, Lee & Lee 2015). In order to do this, the Korean government set goals of
10,000 enterprises and 70,000 apprentices by 2017 (Related Ministries 2014).
However, some scholars believe this objective is overly optimistic (Oh et al.
2015; Kang et. al. 2014). According to Kang et al. (2014), increasing the number
of firms to 10,000 in such a short period is highly unlikely. Furthermore, in the

---

6   A "work-study dual system" or "work and learning dual system" is a youth employ-
    ment policy adapted from apprenticeship in European countries, such as Switzerland
    and Germany. For more information, see http://www.bizhrd.net/dual/DU010101.
    do?cmd=Menu0101&type=3.

7   The National Competency Standard (NCS) is one of the main governmental entities
    involved in the building of a competency-based society. It measures the knowledge,
    skills and attitudes needed to perform one's job. Learning modules and training resour-
    ces are also developed in alignment with the NCS. For more information, see: http://
    www.ncs.go.kr/ncs/page.do?sk=index.

drive to achieve that target number, firms that fail to meet standards may be included in the total count.

## Structural dimension

Like the employment initiatives of China and Portugal discussed above, Korea's work-study system is a state-driven policy. The Ministry of Employment and Labour (MoEL) takes responsibility for the policy, and collaborates with HRD-Korea, the Korea Research Institute for Vocational Education and Training (KRIVET), the Sector Council, the Korea Polytechnic University (KPU) and Korea Technology. In December 2014, the Cabinet Council passed the Workplace Work and Learning Dual System Support Act and legislation to institutionalize a work-study system began to be enforced. The Act deals with criteria such as the recruitment of participants, education and training programme management and the protection of apprentices, among others (MoEL 2014).

While the central government plays an essential role, cooperation with municipal authorities has yet to be firmly established. This matters because, as the Act states, local authorities are responsible for ensuring that participation rates increase. At the local level, there are 24 Work-Learning Centres, 88 Learning Organizations and 13 Sector Council support firms. These organizations provide participating firms, 90% of which are SMEs, with services including apprentice recruitment, education and training programme development and apprentice evaluation (MoEL 2015).

## Constitutive dimension

In order to be able to participate in a work-study system, firms must first select in-company trainers from experienced employees. After a mandatory training course held at a training centre, they can start on-the-job training with apprentices. While on-the-job training helps to provide apprentices with tangible job experience, the in-company trainers still have their own duties outside of training, which can lead to difficulties with ensuring high quality training programmes. Additionally, because the trainers generally lack teaching experience, they rely on the training centres to help them to develop their own skills in this area (Jeon, Lee & Lee 2015). Young adults employed from the beginning of the apprentice programme can reduce the transition period between school and workplace. Moreover, their work-based learning experiences are qualified under the NCS system, improving apprentices' employability (Kim, Shin and Kang 2014). However, many SMEs are not as well-equipped as standard educational and training facilities and therefore, their learning environments might not be as secure or beneficial.

## Technical dimension

Firms and schools are the main resources for a work-study system. The vocational education and training programmes take two forms, namely, on-the-job training and off-the-job training. While on-the-job training takes place within the firm itself, schools, colleges and other learning organizations serve as sites for off-the-job training.[8] Firms provide in-company trainers and facilities while schools, including specialized high schools and Meister[9] high schools, provide graduates as apprentices.

Concerning implementation, employees involved with the process are often overburdened with complicated and redundant paperwork (Kang et al. 2014). Moreover, the work is made more complicated by VET programme criteria and evaluation systems that frequently change (Kang et al. 2014). The simplification and stabilization of the process would seem to be necessary to achieve more effective policy implementation.

## Discussion: A comparative analysis

In this section, we compare the national policies for employability in adult education in China, Portugal and Korea. It is important to highlight that these countries differ in terms of their history, culture and experience of capitalism, among other social elements. Examining policy documents from the three countries reveals the details of their similarities and differences.

## Normative dimension

China, Portugal and Korea all have the same objective: to promote the employability of young adults. However, Portugal and Korea are primarily concerned with developing young people's social and professional skills while China focuses mainly on the benefits that the state itself will derive from higher youth employment. Chinese citizenship is based on a communitarian model, which entails

---

8   Firms can join if they have enough resources for an academic programme. A "single firm-type" of work-study system means that both on-the-job training and off-the-job training take place in a single firm. However, a large number of firms operate using a "learning organization-type" in which off-the-job training is entrusted to schools, colleges or learning institutions (MoEL 2014).

9   Meister Schools or High Schools Tailored to Industrial Demand are one of vocational high schools designated by national government in 2008 and 2009 to secure graduates' career development as industrial technicians and support their continuing education (Jang, Kim&Min 2010).

control from the national government, rather than on a liberal or social democratic approach. The main goal of a communitarian society is to leave a legacy
for the community.

## Structural dimension

The structural dimension of policies for employability in adult education refers to governments, systems and agencies that support educational policies. In
terms of this dimension, the three countries' differences become most salient at
the federal/national level. In China, the most important actors are the General
Office of the State Council, the Ministry of Education and the Ministry of Social
Security. In Portugal, of critical importance are certain international organizations, such as the European Council, the OECD and the POPH. In Korea, the
Ministry of Employment and Labour takes a leading role at the national level.
At the level of state/province, all three countries emphasize the role of government. At the local level, in China, Higher Education Institutes have significant
autonomy while in the other two countries, specific entities are responsible for
promoting employability, namely "training entities" in the case of Portugal and
Work-Learning Centres in Korea.

## Constitutive dimension

In all three countries, adult learners tend to be young adults. However, concerning
adult educators, we observe the following differences. In China, adult educators have
the responsibility to hold entrepreneurial training camps and innovation and entrepreneurship competitions. In Portugal, the unstable employment situation of adult
educators has caused a disinvestment in their qualification process and in the field of
adult education more generally. In Korea, in-company trainers are the adult educators.
However, these adult educators lack teaching experience and thus must spend time
at training centres to learn pedagogical tools and approaches (Jeon, Lee & Lee 2015).

## Technical dimension

In terms of the technical dimension, the main resources in Portugal and Korea are
companies and schools, which create opportunities for young people who wish
to enter the labour market through traineeships or certified vocational training.
Portugal also adopted the European Commission's recommendation of a Youth
Guarantee, which strives to promote active youth employment. In Korea, various
"learning organizations" offer academic courses; however, employees are often
overburdened with complicated and redundant paperwork. In China, the resources

in this area come largely from the government. The instruments designed to implement employment policies include mandate, inducement, capacity building and system change. When it comes to implementation, certain programmes also exist for internships and training.

This discussion offers a comparative policy analysis of employability, presenting various cross-national initiatives related to adult education that are intended to support the employability of young adults. In the context of considerable, on-going change within labour markets, employability emphasizes the need for individuals to take responsibility for their professional opportunities and, in effect, make themselves more employable. In this sense, are individuals entirely responsible for their employability? Certainly, the individual must be adaptable and flexible to new and changing circumstances in the labour market as a way to remain employable. An individual's capacity to improve his or her knowledge and skills emerges as the key to employability.

## Conclusion: Lessons from each other

In order to investigate cross-national policies on young people's employability, this paper has focused on key policy documents related to employability in three countries, scrutinizing the documents along normative, structural, constitutive and technical dimensions. Based on this documentary analysis, certain themes emerged, which underpinned the discussion of the similarities and differences of policy values, designs, stakeholders and implementations across the three countries.

This paper also showed how employability is contextualized in each country. The comparative approach identified the diverse ways in which China, Portugal and the Republic of Korea have set goals and objectives concerning employability. Cross-national differences stem from each country's distinct social organization and political history. The analysis has also shown intra-national variation in terms of the implementation of employability policies. This variation reflects complex structural relations, stakeholders' interests and the resources available to increase the employment of young adults.

The overall result of this comparative analysis is a demonstration of how countries with varying educational and employment systems respond to employability as a common, current issue. Like most other policies, each country's policy for employability is constructed by complex social, political and economic dynamics. Along with a continued focus on this broader context, further comparative research is needed to refine our understanding and conceptualization of employability.

## Acknowledgements

All three authors contributed equally to this article. We are grateful to Professor Vanna Boffo for her careful supervision throughout the writing process. We also warmly thank Professor Regina Egetenmeyer and Professor Sabine Schmidt-Lauff for valuable comments on an earlier version of this article.

## References

Allais, S.: *Selling out education: National qualifications frameworks and the neglect of knowledge*. Sense Publishers: Rotterdam. 2014.

Brown, P. / Lauder, H. / Ashton, D.: *The global auction: The broken promises of education, jobs, and incomes*. Oxford University Press: Oxford. 2011.

Chinese State Council: *Opinions of the General Office of the State Council on deepening the reform of the innovation and entrepreneurship education in higher education institutions*. 2015, retrieved from http://www.gov.cn/zhengce/content/2015-05/13/content_9740.htm.

Chinese State Council: *Notice of the General Office of the State Council on key tasks of the employment and entrepreneurship in the new situation*. 2015, retrieved from http://www.gov.cn/zhengce/content/2015-06/26/content_9982.htm.

Cooper, B.S. / Fusarelli, L.D. / Randall, E.V.: *Better policies, better schools: Theories and applications*. Allyn & Bacon: Boston. 2004.

European Commission: *Commission staff working document: Lisbon strategy evaluation document*, SEC (2010) 114 final, 2010, retrieved from http://ec.europa.eu/europe2020/pdf/lisbon_strategy_evaluation_en.pdf.

Hespanha, P.: *Algumas questões de fundo para uma avaliação da nova geração de políticas sociais*. (VII Congresso Internacional del CLAD sobre la Reforma del Estado y de la Administración Pública). Lisboa. 8–11 October 2002.

Hillage, J. / Pollard, E.: *Employability: Developing a framework for policy analysis*. DfEE: London. 1998.

HRD-Korea (n.d.): *HRD Korea*, retrieved from http://www.hrdkorea.or.kr/3/1/6/1.

Instituto de Emprego e Formação Profissional (IEFP): (n.d.), retrieved from www.iefp.pt/apoios.

Jeon, S / Lee, S. / Lee, H.: *A study on the status of operation and improvement of apprenticeship*. KRIVET. 2015.

Kang, K. / Kim, J. / Park, C. et al.: *An analysis on socio-economic outcomes of apprenticeship*. KRIVET. 2014.

Kim, J. / Shin, S. / Kang, S.: *Survey of Korean dual system*. National Research Council for Economics, Humanities, and Social Sciences. 2014.

McDonnell, L.M. / Elmore, R. F.: *Alternative policy instruments.* Center for Policy Research in Education: Wisconsin. 1987.

Ministry of Employment and Labour: *Workplace work and learning dual system support act passed the cabinet council.* 2014.

Ministry of Employment and Labour: *Operation Manual for Korean Work-Study Policy.* 2014, retrieved from http://hrdc.hrdkorea.or.kr/hrdc/download/downloadFile.hrd?attachSeq=478234

Ministry of Employment and Labour: *Status of participating enterprises in apprenticeship,* 2015, retrieved from http://www.moel.go.kr/view.jsp?cate=3&sec=17&div_cd=&mode=view&bbs_cd=OP0315&seq=1420615329146&page=1&state=A&pimSeq=5&piSeq=295.

Nah, Y.: "Introduction of Korean work and learning dual system". *The HRD Review,* November 2013, pp. 114–119.

Oh, H. / Ra, Y. / Lee, S. / Ryu, J. *Analysis of youth employment issue and policy suggestion.* KRIVET. 2015.

Organisation for Economic Cooperation and Development (OECD): *OECD skills strategy diagnostic report: Portugal.* OECD: Paris, 2015, retrieved from http://www.oecd.org/skills/nationalskillsstrategies/Diagnostic-report-Portugal.pdf.

Paiva, J. / Pinto, L. / Monteiro, A. / Augusto, N.: *Empregabilidade na economia social: o papel das políticas ativas de emprego.* Rede Europeia Anti-Pobreza: Porto. 2015.

Related Ministries: *From school to work: Measures for young adults' employment.* 2014.

Schreuder, A. / Coetzee, M.: *Careers: An organisational perspective.* Juta & Co. Ltd: Claremont. 2006.

Tasker, M. / Packham, D.: "Government, higher education and the industrial ethic". *Higher Education Quarterly* 48, 1994 pp. 182–193.

Valadas, C.: "Mudanças nas políticas: Do (des)emprego à empregabilidade". *Revista Crítica de Ciências Sociais* 102, 2013, pp. 89–110.

Valente, A.C. / Soares, M.C. / Fialho, J.S.: "Empregabilidade, mercado de trabalho e políticas ativas de emprego". *Semana da Responsabilidade Social, Fundação Cidade de Lisboa.* 6 June 2013.

Versloot, A.M. / Glaudé, M.T. / Thijssen, J.G.L.: *Employability: een pluriform arbeidsmarktfenomeen* [Employability: A multiform labour market phenomenon]. MGK: Amsterdam. 1998.

Yorke, M.: *Employability in higher education: What it is – what it is not.* (Learning and Employability Guides, Series 1). LTSN-ESECT: York. 2004.

Julia Di Campo, Thomas Barany, Georg Henning
& Balázs Németh

# Capacities for Cooperation: Potentials for and Barriers to Adult-Learning Professionals in Learning City-Region Formations

**Abstract:** This paper aims at providing a comparative analysis of the relevance of learning city-region models that have been recently used in Germany, Hungary and Italy. Its authors will focus on the impacts of initiatives from these countries and highlight key insights for adult-learning professionals.

## Some Theoretical Frameworks for Learning and the Learning Economy

Learning city-region models first appeared after World War II, when heavy industries began to be engulfed by crisis after approximately two decades of economic recovery. More flexible forms of teaching and learning were claimed in both formal and non-formal structures in order to generate the new skills and competencies vital to a changing labour market and society. While the concept of the learning economy and educating and learning cities thus dates back to the 1970s (Longworth 2006), we will concentrate on how the learning city-region models have changed in the last twenty-five years.

In the 1990s, economic geographers conceptualized learning cities and regions and connected them to spatial innovations and contexts. It was Florida (1995) who invented the model of the learning region, and further researchers also identified this concept (Bokema et al. 2000) as the grounds for regional innovation systems. These narratives worked from the base assumption that learning should be promoted by reasonable learning infrastructures (i.e., a regional innovation system); more precisely, locales should learn to enforce locality in order to compete in a global economy. Through the foundation of this bridge, Allison (2001) widened learning's spheres of activity and effect to emphasize a learning communities approach towards local economic development. This approach builds a direct link between learning initiatives, partnerships and governance, social capital and the enhancement of local resources together with skills and economic growth.

The achievements of researchers in the field of educational innovations run parallel to this special approach to local economic development. Tooke (2000), for example, claims that the wider benefits of learning have been directly valued by those who are engaged in and concentrate on public education, lifelong learning and adult and community education. This traditional scholarly point clearly resembles a critical approach to the concept of learning regions, demonstrating the deep impacts of wider social and community development issues. The TELS (Towards a European Learning Society) Project (Longworth 1999) and the UK Learning Towns Project (Yarnit 2000) provide four obvious critical objectives for learning and learning initiatives, namely: (i) economic prosperity; (ii) social inclusion; (iii) sustainability; and (iv) governance. In this complex conceptualization, learning's dimension of action and value expands well beyond a narrow definition of industry clusters and issues of competitiveness and innovation (as important as these may be). As the progress of learning initiatives by Yarnit (2000), Longworth (1999), Longworth and Franson (2001), Allison and others (2001) describe, learning is embedded into the evolution of the community in many ways.

The examples below depict two basic aspects of the comparison of learning city-region models. The first indicates what layer of spatial/policy interventions they address, whether the macro-, meso- or micro-level; the second refers to the aspects of adult and lifelong learning they reflect, which may focus on performance, increasing participation and/or building partnerships.

## Local responses to global initiatives with the aim of community development: the Pécs Learning City-Region Forum in Hungary

Based on a decade-old international project partnership, the learning city-region model was developed in cooperation with PASCAL Observatory, the UNESCO Institute for LLL, the University of Pécs and its former Faculty of Adult Education and HRD. It was established in the context of the Pécs Learning City Region Forum in 2013, as a tool for pedagogical/andragogical work targeting the training of teaching staff, educators and facilitators of learning. The Pécs Learning City-Region Forum, accordingly, began its activities in the fall of 2014 in three major fields by accelerating partnerships and dialogues.

The first of these fields is "Atypical/Non-formal Learning". This platform tries to help cultural organizers, curators and managers organize more successful educational programmes for adults as well as to aid school teachers engaged in the development of cultural programmes for children. A collaborative framework such as this involves more than eight organizations/institutions and their representatives, working together to identify innovative learning methods, tools and methodologies with atypical contexts.

The second platform was labelled "School and Environment". It supports dialogue amongst professionals developing specific, environment-oriented programmes for local youth and their parents, to help them become more nature-friendly and conscious of the need to protect their environment. Around nine member organizations/institutions work actively in this Forum through delegates and professional experts, providing a platform-based exchange of ideas to make school pupils and their families more aware of nature and environmentally friendly and "green" ways of thought.

The third platform is called "Inclusion and Handicapped Situations". It helps teachers to engage in collaborative actions by providing dialogues on problems that emerge from working with young children with learning difficulties, e.g., autism.

The three dimensions of the Forum's platforms have enabled participating partners to recognize some key barriers to collecting and sharing good practices. The first of these barriers consists of the weak cultures of mutual partnerships and collaborative actions for sharing experiences and developing the professional skills and competencies of teachers, trainers and facilitators. The second set of barriers is the limited time available for educators/teachers, trainers and facilitators to develop skills and share their knowledge and experience. The third barrier identified is the small number of resources available, which constrains participation in the Forum's programmes, and the simultaneously heavy workload, which dominates the majority of working time.

Recent analyses have indicated some ways in which the Forum could attempt to increase the local and regional attention of stakeholder groups. Decision-makers and stakeholders exhibit a growing interest in developing and maintaining new and effective ways and methods for gaining useful and problem-based knowledge. In order to develop tailor-made programmes through the Forum to effectively meet these claims, we will need trained adult-learning professionals, cultural managers and trainers spread out among the institutions/organizations of the school sector, labour market, cultural organizations and institutions and other respected non-formal learning grounds and environments. The Forum will have to make better use of available EU-funds that are targeted towardseconomic development, innovation and social mobility. There is a clear need for a common identification of strengths, weaknesses, opportunities and threats for learning city-region development, whilst we must also concentrate on improving learning conditions and collaborative spaces for young people with learning difficulties, through inclusive learning environments.

The Forum's major goal is to involve more and more adults in lifelong learning in a micro-environment that is affected by both the meso- and macro-levels. Accordingly, it must continue to support recent platforms, potentially growing partnerships by headquartering the Forum in the House of Civic Communities. Finally, the Forum should work as a disseminating "device" between its locality and UNESCO's global initiative of learning cities (GLCN) (Németh 2016).

## LERNENDE REGIONEN and LERNENvorORT: Comprehensive structures in the educational system of Germany as a key to lifelong learning?

In Germany, the approach's national implementation has mainly focused on the institutional aspects of constructing region- and city-based models: the goal of lifelong learning for everyone (BMBF 2001) was introduced to "create new learning structures and learning cultures" and to further "provide and establish permanent and sustainable learning structures by mobilising and developing the entire potential of a region". The following projects can be understood as the national interpretation (macro-level) of the European policies concerned with lifelong learning, policies that are mainly represented by the European Union and UNESCO (mega-level). German policies that founded projects were established on the basis of Key Message 6 of the European Memorandum on Lifelong Learning, which declares "[…] bringing learning closer to home" (EU 2000) as one of the main objectives of national programmes, in order to provide a proper learning infrastructure. In contrast to the Hungarian model, the Pécs Learning City-Region Forum, German projects have focused on programmes for learners and the institutional and organizational structures surrounding them. While Hungary established the professionalization of adult educators and cooperating actors as a central aspect of working in learning city-region models, Germany has encouraged its already highly-institutionalized educational system to create new forms of educational networks between traditional educational actors, such as schools and universities, and non-educational actors, such as employment agencies, companies and regional administrations, which can all be related to meso-level structures. Germany's objectives have been two-fold: firstly, to mobilize educationally disadvantaged clientele by increasing the transparency of educational opportunities and increasing the quality and usability of lifelong learning activities; secondly, to strengthen the personal responsibility and creativity of the people in non-formal learning settings (micro-level). Furthermore, Germany has wished to promote access to new information and communication technologies in order to increase the individual competencies and testing of new teaching arrangements (Ambos et al. 2001). In developing its programmatic content, Germany has prioritized an interlaced and integrated form of education, with the aim of improving human capital.

LERNENDE REGIONEN placed its main focus on making the institutional and organizational boundaries of learning contexts increasingly permeable. As a result, networks of educational, economic and employment-related institutions presented a unique form of institutionalized education. The programme promoted a variety of new perspectives on networks and education in Germany. From 2001 to 2009, the programme experienced a long period of development and received extensive financial support that enabled it to work towards its goal of establishing sustainable network structures, implementing 76 networks in total. During this entire period of public funding, the construction of cross-link formations of transversal actors in the network was attended by academic support and programmatic reflection and discussion. As a spatial category, the programme defined a region fairly flexibly as a city, a separate district or even a federal state.

In 2009, the Federal Ministry of Education and Research (BMBF) funded the project "LERNENvorORT" (learning on the spot), which opened a different focus on, and discourse about, learning and its space-related conditions. It provided new interpretations for educational, political and scientific discussions. The focus now shifted from the extensively institutional structures of educational networks to the local aspects of learning settings. It emphasized the importance of local communities with concerted municipal structures and stakeholders in providing educational opportunities for local citizens and creating specific conditions for successful learning biographies (BMBF 2004). Citizens were brought into contact with learning and its support structures in a very direct way, e.g., in tramways in Dresden (Dresdner Bildungsbahnen). From 2009 to 2014, the BMBF brought 36 cities and counties into LERNENvorOrt. The programme's objectives were defined as categories of participation in education, aiming at strengthening individuals' employability by fostering locally organized networks. Increased transparency of educational opportunities and better transitions between the individual stages of education were especially meant to improve the individual's access to education. The BMBF also introduced political substantiations on the macro-level to strengthen the democratic culture and manage demographic change (BMBF 2014).

As an interim assessment of this German situation, we would like to highlight some interesting aspects, especially by pointing out the structure of participating stakeholders. First, the macro-level influence is outstanding. Germany not only referred to European policy strategies, but funded all projects with resources from the European Social Fund. When the funding periods ended, nearly all the projects of LERNENDE REGIONEN and LERNENvorORT were finalized concurrently. Secondly, Germany focused heavily on economic objectives: in both projects, regional and local educational networks were funded to improve the employability of educationally disadvantaged persons. Companies as well as labour-market administrations were central stakeholders on the meso-level. Both projects linked the economic and employment-related aspects directly to issues of social inclusion and citizenship as a concept of cultural participation in society and therefore focused on institutional network structures as a key to fulfilling these aims. Only a few projects have continued to exist after the cessation of public funding. Apparently, specific aspects of sustainability are crucial for establishing regional network structures that can survive the absence of such funding. The following chapter presents a good practice example of a learning region in Eastern Germany that still exists.

## PONTES – Learning in and for Europe. Building bridges in the Euroregion of Neisse

One example of a learning region in Germany is the PONTES network, a trilateral project composed of German, Polish and Czech regions (Gellrich 2008, p. 5). It generally operates across the borders of three countries: joint work that places it on the mega/macro-level. PONTES is one of the most peculiar learning regions. It is worth mentioning that the name "PONTES" derives from the Latin term for bridges. It is located in the geographical area that forms the triangle of the German-Polish-Czech Euroregion Neisse-Nisa-Nysa (ERNNN).

By bringing three different countries closer together, the ERNNN creates a learning centre that highlights the development of social, linguistic and intercultural competencies (Gellrich 2008, p. 5). From 2002 to 2007, the project and the programme connected to it were funded by the European Union and the BMBF, stakeholders acting on the mega/macro-level. Consequently, the programme developed a cross-border network that implemented innovative educational initiatives to promote the concept of lifelong learning. Within this network, the project promoted the joint work of various educational actors operating on the meso-level in the whole region. Initially, the network aimed not just at the proverbial construction of bridges between the educational actors of one region but also mediated between the different fields of action of the educational level and educational supply and demand (Gellrich 2008, p. 5). At the same time, it was considered to form a "bridge" between the educational infrastructures of the three countries constituting the Euroregion Neisse-Nissa-Nysa (ERNNN) and the people living there (micro-level). In this way, it helped promote the common process of lifelong learning (Gellrich 2008, p. 11).

The main goal of the PONTES project was, and still is, the development and establishment of a cross-border learning region in the ERNNN. Thus, the programme has primarily worked to develop and expand all educational and intermodal networks whose actors are developing innovative and lasting measures to promote lifelong learning. Among other actors, the programme's main coordinating partners include many different NGOs and the representatives of the German, Polish and Czech municipal communities of the ERNNN. The project mainly connects stakeholders at all levels, whether mega/macro, meso or micro. Because of its European dimension, the ERNNN has a unique potential as a learning centre. The project is therefore particularly concerned with exploiting these special potentials and opportunities in order to support the development of the local people and their skills. The cross-border cooperation of the actors on the meso- and the micro-levels is especially apparent. The main aim of a joint project of Polish and Czech citizens was described as "[...] *(euro)regionalspezifische Angebote für lebenslanges Lernen zu entwickeln*" [to develop (euro)regionally specific opportunities for lifelong learning] (Gellrich 2008, p. 12, translation by authors). This initiated, innovative PONTES network has mainly focused on qualitatively changing the structures, contents and methods of learning. The programme also emphasizes promoting the employability and permanent capacity to act of the people living in the ERNNN, taking into account the area's specific euro-regional educational and economic structures as well as the increasing identification with the border region (Gellrich 2008, p. 12). The one-year planning phase of the project led to the development of a new teaching and learning culture that has affected the entire region. Throughout the network's development, strong demands have been made of the contents of the partnership, which is clearly reflected in the programme's guiding principles.

PONTES is an "*Ideenschmiede und Motivator für Innovationen*" [think tank and motivator for innovations] (Gellrich 2008, p. 12) for developing a creative environment and a new teaching and learning culture in its region. The project is also committed to promising educational opportunities, promoting regional solidarity in new ways, gaining the support of the ERNNN's inhabitants for the concept of lifelong learning and establishing the region as an attractive business location (Gellrich 2008, p. 12). The overall objective of the network's activities was and still is to create a transparent, easily accessible and euro-regional educational structure as needed, which is also associated with the development of a new practical teaching and learning culture. Demonstrating all the particular steps of the implementation process would lie beyond the scope of this section of the paper. In conclusion, we would therefore like to offer only a short overview of PONTES's current situation and a brief outlook on the future of this notable project (and the learning regions in general). An essential result of the implementation stage of the project *PONTES – Learning in and for Europe* is the permanent establishment of the network in the ERNNN (Gellrich 2008, p. 66).

The trilateral network, PONTES, still acts for the benefit of the concept of life-long learning, the entire ERNNN and even Europe itself. PONTES represents an outstanding example of a learning region in Europe, as it is not country-specific but a transnational learning region that successfully achieves all of the BMBF's fixed objectives. Moreover, it still exists and operates to improve the quality of life of all the people living in the border region, even without financing from the German state. Ultimately, the success of this outstanding project, PONTES, rests on the great cooperation and mutual influence of various actors at the various different known levels: mega/macro, meso and micro.

## Policies and actions: macro-, meso- and micro-levels in Italy

In 2014, UNESCO used its 2013 Beijing Declaration to reassert the strategic role of cities in promoting social inclusion, economic growth, public safety and en-vironmental protection (UNESCO UIL – Beijing Declaration 2013). Recently, UNESCO reported that the proportion of the world's population living in cities would expand to over 60% by 2030. Local governments will increasingly face new challenges related to new technologies, the knowledge economy, cultural diver-sity, environmental sustainability and social inclusion. Cities will need to develop innovative strategies that allow their citizens, young and old, to learn new skills and competencies throughout life, thereby transforming their cities into learning cities (UNESCO UIl 2015).

According to town planner Charles Landry, education and training are the first steps to take towards "making a city". In place of a "city of knowledge" or a "smart city", he suggests calling it a "learning city": a creative city that learns continuously. A city that thinks by itself and learns from its mistakes is strategic, because it be-comes a "camp-school" (Landry 2009). Landry articulates a new vision: formal and non-formal spaces for learning should be everywhere – learning spaces may be in the streets, shopping centres, parks and in the prisons. This is a lifelong learning process that weaves its way into formal and non-formal settings. Multiple learning experiences offer everyone a way to personally improve their skills.

What are Italy's policies and actions regarding learning cities, learning regions and learning communities? The situation is articulated and complex, with different actors having different needs and aims. However, Italy has no specific policies for the development of learning cities, regions or communities. This is an important difference, as it stands in significant contrast to the German and Hungarian mod-els. Actions are extremely fragmented and local. Frequently, the term "learning cities" is confused with "smart cities". Italian policies are sectorial. They do not involve partnerships of formal and non-formal training places, for example, between universities, school and research or adult education centres. Italian policies also do not support the idea of an open community as a place where people can learn together with different tools. Several Italian smart city models consider education as a factor that can affect the quality of life in functional terms, such as by providing new skills and services. As Giovannella has indicated (2014), a smart context is a context in which human capital (and, more generally, each individual/citizen) not only possesses a high level of (possibly innovative) skills, but is also strongly motivated by continuous and appropriate challenges, while its needs are reasonably satisfied. However, in Italy several questions in this field do not find national answers: how should inclusive learning be promoted, from basic to higher education? How can learning in families and communities be revitalized and how can learning for and in the workplace be facilitated? How can the use of modern learning technologies be extended, quality and excellence in learning encouraged and a culture of learning promoted throughout life? How can the future be planned in a participatory way? How should collective learning strategies be defined? How can barriers between business, government and research be broken down?

There are several main actors involved in this process, distinguishable by their different levels of analysis. The first is the macro-level, composed of institutional partners such as the Ministry of Education University and Research (MIUR), which coordinates activities in the national context; the National Education Council, which assists the Ministry in planning and defining education policies; and the National Institute for the Evaluation of the Education System (INVALSI). Furthermore, MIUR is organized into three departments: the first is responsible for the general organization of the school system, the second for financial policy and the third for higher education. Another institutional actor is the Ministry of Economic Development, which, in 2015, created a new team of experts to promote the smart cities projects. Finally, the National Association of Italian Municipality (ANCI) has created a National Observatory of Smart Cities. The aim is to collect all projects realized by Italian cities focused on learning cities and smart cities and to present them in a "best practices" database. At the meso- and micro-levels, the regional institutional office (USR, extension of the MIUR) monitors minimum performance requirements and the observance of general educational provisions. The USR regional office is divided into local offices (UST) that operate at the provincial level. USTs are agencies that aid and support schools with administration, accounting procedures and innovatively planning their educational offerings.

They monitor students' participation and compliance with compulsory schooling. Other actors are trade unions, chambers of commerce, industry associations, NGOs, associations, private actors and companies, municipalities and local companies, local public administration and employment centres.

This is a short presentation of the institutional framework in Italy. To promote learning, it is crucial that communities commit to transversal actions that consider the European, national and local levels. To support a good quality of life for everybody, economic growth and equal and inclusive citizenship are very important, as is "active listening". The main objectives are the development of talents and human resources, social justice and citizenship. In the most inclusive sense of the term, active listening means taking people's differing needs as the starting point.

## "Active listening" to improve learning communities: the EDOC@WORK3.0 project

In 2012, the MIUR called for new ideas for smart cities and communities and social innovation, in three specific areas. One of these areas focused on educational actions to support the design of innovative devices for students. However, only one of the seventeen new projects promoted by MIUR focused on education.

EDOC@WORK3.0 – Education and Work on Cloud – is a research project funded by PON (National Operative Plan) that is currently underway. Its aim is to change educational systems, from primary schools to vocational training, with the support of new pedagogical and didactical models. The project intends to renew learning environments, languages, tools and content through the use of new technologies. It offers a range of proposals and solutions to bring the schools into the cloud, through innovative open source platforms. The project's strengths lie in the involvement of different stakeholders, its experimentation with new methodologies and the possibility it offers to identify best practices and new ways to build an open, territorial learning community.

The project team consists of a partnership between several different actors, including universities, companies and local organizations, and operates in the Puglia Region (that is, in Southern Italy). The main stakeholders are families, teenagers, companies and public administrations. It includes an experimental phase aimed at schools and training institutions. This experimental process involves all stakeholders: students, teachers and families who actively participate together. Its aim is to collect data and information about the use of different methodologies and the effects of the new, proposed educational models. Different educational technologies and services are being tested, such as MOOC (Massive Open Online Courses) and collaborative classrooms where people from all different geographical areas can share their experience, information and tools as if in a physical classroom. One interesting tool is a gamification platform that offers a change from classic learning methods and adds motivational tools, such as game mechanisms, in order to increase young people's involvement. Teachers, students and families can all use the instruments. The project allows networking and furthers the creation of a learning community. It uses mixed methods that combine formal and non-formal education with the support of digital media. The project is currently being implemented in classes, vocational schools and universities, which each include a set of different resources: different physical spaces, technological tools, documents, people and know-how.

While Italy recently introduced the EDOC@WORK3.0 project, its effort is in some ways lacking compared to the international context and, in particular, to Hungary's Pécs Learning City-Region Forum. At the moment, it does not inclusively make provisions for all those who have different learning needs, experience difficulties accessing learning opportunities or have a disability. For example, the tools used in the project do not consider the dimension of access for blind people. This is a crucial point, as it reveals a lack of "active listening" – in particular, a failure on the micro-level. In Italy, the question of learning cities is not a specific research area in and of itself. Instead, its projects are included in the field of "smart cities". Accordingly, there is a risk that the importance of education may be undervalued. Lifelong learning becomes a tool and strategy to improve policies and promote economic growth. Italy needs an "educational national transversal strategy" in research and in its social life that is interconnected between the macro-, meso- and micro-levels.

## Conclusion and perspectives for professionalization

A comparison of all three national studies reveals only a few commonalities. Hungary, Germany and Italy all define the spatial aspects of learning through network structures of local or regional actors with the objective of improving learning for individuals in a certain way. They exhibit significant differences in their histories, stakeholder interests, funding and specific objectives beyond the general category of the improvement of learning. While Hungary's concepts of learning cities/regions are long-term, matured ideas that are closely connected with social aspects of community-life and social inclusion within local areas, the situation in Germany is very different. Germany's highly institutionalized education systems were impacted by two publicly funded projects driven by a national policy between education and perspectives oriented on the labour market. In Italy, the "smart city" model has provided a framework for combining local-regional innovations for economic development amongst specific stakeholders and for providing a relevant platform for strategic development and planning in urban contexts. Finally, the examples from Germany, Hungary and Italy all underline the need for well-trained, adult learning professionals who are definitely able to improve the social dimension of learning city-region models in order to develop the new skills and competencies needed in our new economy and for more social and environmental awareness.

## References

Allison, J. / Keane, J.: "Evaluating the role of the Sunshine Coast University (USC) in the regional economy". *Local Economy* 16(2), 2001, pp. 123–141.

Ambos, I. / Conein, S. / Nuissl, E.: *Lernende Regionen – Ein innovatives Programm.* Deutsches Institut für Erwachsenenbildung: Bonn. 2002.

Bokema, F. / Morgan, K. / Bakkers, S. (eds.). *Knowledge, innovation and economic growth: The theory and practice of learning regions.* Edward Edgar: Northhampton, MA. 2000.

Bundesministerium für Bildung und Forschung (BMBF). *Die Strategie für das lebenslange Lernen verwirklichen.* 2004, retrieved 15.4.2016, from http://www.forschungsnetzwerk.at/downloadpub/lifelong%20learning%20%20strategie_lll_verwirklichen.pdf.

Bundesministerium für Bildung und Forschung (BMBF): *Lernen vor Ort.* 2014, retrieved 15.4.2016, from http://www.lernen-vor-ort.info.

Florida, R.: "Towards the learning region". *Futures* 27(5), 1995, pp. 527–536.

Gellrich, R.: "Lernende Region PONTES: Bildungs- und regionalentwicklung in der Euroregion Neisse-Nisa-Nysa", *Schriften des Internationalen Begegnungszentrums St. Marienthal* 9. IBZ: Ostritz. 2008.

Giovannella, C.: "Where's the smartness of learning in smart territories?". *Interaction Design and Architecture(s) Journal – IxD&A* 22, 2014, pp. 60–68.

Landry, C.: *City making: L'arte di fare la città.* Einaudi: Torino. 2009.

Longworth, N.: *Making lifelong learning work: Learning cities for a learning century.* Kogan Page: London. 1999.

Longworth, N.: *Learning cities, learning regions and learning communities.* Routledge: New York. 2006.

Longworth, N. / Franson, L. (eds.): *The TELS project towards a European learning society: Final report.* European Commission: Socrates Program, European Lifelong Learning Initiative. 2011.

Németh, B.: "Challenges and Opportunities for Innovations in Learning City – Region Developments in Pécs, Hungary. New Perspectives for Community Development and Co-operative Learning". In: A. Pejatovic, A. / R. Egetenmeyer / M. Slowey (eds.): *Contribution of Research to Improvement of Adult Education Quality*. University of Belgrade: Beograd. 2016, pp. 195–213.

Pécs Learning City-Region Forum, retrieved 10.4.2016, from http://www.tanulovaros-regio-pecs.hu/.

Tooke, J.: "Learning regions: The politics of knowledge at work". *Planning and Environment A* 32(5), 2000, pp. 764–768.

UNESCO (UIL): *Global Network of Learning Cities – Guiding Documents*. UIL: _Hamburg. 2015, retrieved 10.4.2016, from https://uil.unesco.org/fileadmin/keydocuments/LifelongLearning/learning-cities/en-unesco-global-network-of-learning-cities-guiding-documents.pdf.

UNESCO (UIL): *The Beijing Declaration on Building Learning Cities. Lifelong Learning for All: Promoting Inclusion, Prosperity and Sustainability in Cities.* 2013, retrieved 10.4.2016, from http://learningcities.uil.unesco.org/fileadmin/content/Publications/Conference/Beijing_Declaration_EN.pdf.

Yarnit, M.: *Towns, cities and regions in the learning age: A survey of learning communities*. DEE: London. 2000.

Shalini Singh & Philipp Assinger

# Policy and Governance for the Professionalization of Adult Education

**Abstract:** Governance through adequate policy will be essential in order to meet future challenges for professionalization. This paper provides evidence from Austria and India. As will be shown, in theory and in practice, professionalization, policy and governance form a wide conceptual landscape.

## Introduction

Adult education (AE) as an occupation is generally characterized by a high degree of diversity, heterogeneity and individualized career pathways. Developing professional structures is therefore of major importance to advance the performance of both individuals and the sector. Consequently, evidence-based policies and functioning governance structures are needed to create, implement and evaluate measures for professionalization. In so doing, adult education will be prepared to meet future challenges.

This paper presents a comparison of two unequal countries: Austria and India. While the Austrian system of professionalization is regarded as one of Europe's role models (CEDEFOP 2013; Egetenmeyer & Käpplinger 2011, p. 25), a high degree of professionalization is still missing in India. Policies and governance, however, play an important role in both countries, in spite of their very different characteristics. Drawing on this initial assessment, the paper examines the following research question: what are the central elements of professionalization in Austria and India with regard to a) governance approach and b) policy focus? The authors attempt to provide evidence on the theoretical and practical aspects that condition professionalization. Such evidence is of equal relevance for practitioners, researchers and policy makers. Choosing policy and governance as categories for comparison allows for observing the macro-level of professionalization. Moreover, policy and governance are all-encompassing devices to drive developments in the public realm.

The authors proceed as follows: first, they construct theoretical links between the concepts of professionalization, policy and governance. Subsequent case studies provide evidence for the comparison. Finally, the authors discuss findings and their relevance for the objectives of the book. For reasons of efficiency, the paper cannot elaborate on cultural or historical differences between the countries. Data for the Austrian case study were gained by way of literature review and analysis of web content. For India, the authors drew on personal conversations with state functionaries, university scholars and NGO representatives.

## Theoretical links between professionalization, policy and governance

The term *profession* refers to a community of highly regarded, specifically qualified members who have followed a determined pathway of education in order to access a professional community (Nuissl 2009, p. 127). The scholarly discussion on adult education practice is more precise. It defines two conceptions: professionalization as a process of developing a profession, and professionalization as a process of achieving professionalism (Egetenmeyer & Käpplinger 2011, p. 22). Giesecke (2011, p. 385) defines professionalization as programmatic support for work in AE. Conversely, professionalism refers to pedagogically competent action, regardless of occupational standards. Moreover, Heilinger (2012, p. 67) emphasizes the pertinence of contingent understandings of quality and standardization. Whether pedagogical competences, programmatic support or quality and standardization, all three approaches have the common factor of hinting at issues that require intervention.

According to Garraud (1990, p. 20, quoted in Knoepfel et al. 2011, p. 153), public policy is public administration's answer to problems in the public domain emerging from stakeholder claims, interest groups or individuals directly affected by unpleasant developments. In other words, public policy refers to the concrete content of political discussion created in reaction to a pending problem. The answer might be to disseminate a new strategy, implement a programme or institutionalize administrative structures and thereby govern progress (Blum & Schubert 2009, p. 13).

Governance "most commonly denotes an action aiming [sic] at purposefully directing developments" (Schrader 2010, p. 44). As opposed to government, governance implies that various actors participate in developing the system. Enabled by the processes of globalization, market liberalization and new forms of public administration, diversity among the actors involved in AE has increased. Brüsemeister (2011, p. 13) adds that – in contrast to a single actor – an institutionalized field acts to gain or maintain influence over developments. The state, NGOs and the free market all have interests at stake, and all the more so because adult education is embedded in societally functional systems such as educational, scientific, economic, political or legislative ones (Schrader 2010, p. 47).

It is widely agreed that the professionalization of AE requires educational courses for professionals (university programmes, non-formal further education, etc.); legislation regulating funding, contractual agreements and social security; initiatives making professionals and the profession visible; and evidence-based strategies (see Nittel 2014). Essentially, the need for judicious implementation of strategies and consensus politics links professionalization, policy and governance. The paper proceeds with examining the central elements of professionalization in Austria and India with regard to a) the governance approach and b) policy focus.

## Case studies

Each case study comprises four sections: an overview of the initial problem, information on professional profiles, a description of the governance structure and, finally, a discussion of the policy focus exemplified by the Austrian Academy of Continuing Education (Wba), and of a clear policy shift in the Indian case. The case studies end with a conclusion.

### *Austrian governance and policy for professionalization*

Initial problem: In 2014, the Austrian Conference of Adult Education Institutions (KEBÖ) reached a total number of 87,703 employees, with 57,042 taking over pedagogical tasks. This number is divided into three groups. They comprise full-time employees: 6,103 overall, of which 2,132 are pedagogical staff members; part-time employees: 56,320 overall, 42,474 pedagogical; and volunteers numbering 25,280 in total, including 4,483 with pedagogical tasks (Vater & Zwielehner 2015). Gutknecht-Gmeiner provides further information (2008, pp. 13, 15). On average, 40% of adult educators held an academic degree, 30% had graduated from secondary school and just one quarter of the total had an actual pedagogical qualification.

Profiles: Adult education is a non-regulated occupation, and is therefore open to all individuals. Originating in the 1867 constitution, freedom of teaching and learning (Art. 17, 18) as well as the right to free association (Art. 12) are legislative points of reference in this respect (Platzer 2009, p. 57). Employment contracts govern full-time and part-time positions in public as well as private institutions, and cover project posts and freelance engagements. Depending on the contractual classification, the job description stipulates work duties and competences. More illuminating, though, are the widely acknowledged, evidence-based Wba qualification profiles. They catalogue and describe outcome-oriented competences in the four main practice areas: training, counselling, management and librarianship. In addition to specific competences in these four areas, the profiles include key competences such as knowledge of general education theory, didactical skills and social (communication, conflict management, feedback) and personal competences (self-reflection, time management, self-promotion). The Wba model is linked to both the traditional understanding of professionalism and the European Qualifications Framework (Egetenmeyer 2011, p. 6).

Governance structure: The centre of governance is the Cooperative System of Austrian Adult Education, a joint initiative of the ten KEBÖ associations, complemented by the Bifeb (Federal Department for Adult Education) and supported and coordinated by the Adult Education Unit within the Ministry of Education. The main task is strategic planning of quality assurance and professionalization (erwachsenenbildung.at). The KEBÖ, the central organ, is a forum for the nine largest non-profit AE associations, joined by the Association of Public Libraries. Member representatives assemble at an annual conference to discuss pending issues, with the chair rotating biannually. There is no budget, nor are there employees or an office (Filla 2014, p. 172). Organizationally and administratively, the KEBÖ defines itself as a self-sufficient, free working group, with no legal form and the advantage that expenses can be limited to a minimum. In shaping policies, the government recognizes KEBÖ as its official and primary partner. Bifeb is the centre of competence for adult education. Its three main tasks are development and professionalization on the basis of the Adult Education Promotion Law (1973), a strengthening of the Cooperative System and an active contribution to implementing lifelong learning guidelines (Bifeb). It offers part-time courses, seminars and other programmes for adult educators and librarians. In line with the Adult Education Promotion Law the Ministry maintained Bifeb financially, infra-structurally and administratively (Lenz 2005, p. 25). Since the integration of new modes of public administration in 2013, Bifeb has been administrating its business self-sufficiently, although it is still subordinate to the Ministry (erwachsenenbildung.at).

Policy focus: A study on the qualifications of adult educators (2001) revealed that their career pathways were highly diverse and heterogenous, and reinforced the demand for a common reference framework. In 2003, planning for an Austria-wide reference framework started off, supported financially by the European Social Fund, with the explicit task of improving quality and professionalization and developing a European best-practice model (Heilinger 2005, p. 82). Five competence profiles were developed, termed Curricula: one entry-level certificate plus four specific diplomas for the main areas of adult educational work in Austria (ibid.). Moreover, the implementation structure was designed (Ocenasek & Reisinger 2012, p. 86). Shortly after, discussions on a national qualifications framework started. In a consultation process with the governing authorities, the Wba adapted all curricula to an outcome-oriented description of the competences. By the end of 2011, the redefinition was completed (Reisinger & furt Wagner 2011, p. 2) and in 2013, the new outcome-oriented qualification profiles were put into practice. In 2015, a further adaption was necessary to meet the demands of the EQF. Given the multitude of opportunities for acquiring qualifications and competences, Wba is intended as a new approach to coordinate, systematize and standardize the educational pathways of adult educators (Filla 2014, p. 205). Central to this is that the "Wba acknowledges prior learning results and offers guidance as far as the acquisition of missing skills is concerned" (Wba). It sets common standards allowing for transparency and the comparison of qualifications, and contributes to professionalization, quality assurance and opening up the formal education system. However, it does not provide educational programmes.

Conclusion: This case study shows that policy measures such as validation and accreditation of the Wba build on an elaborate governance structure whose work is regulated and legitimated. Furthermore, the close relationship between the federal level, adult education associations, agencies and academia facilitates interaction between policy, administration, practice and research. The measures implemented (Wba) comply with European Union policy by furthering the validation of competences and the quality assurance of the sector. Based on this, they are able to exert a certain degree of influence at the national level and offer expertise for cooperation at the international level.

## Indian governance and policy for professionalization

Initial problem: Policy analysis suggests that professionalization does not preoccupy the governing authorities in India (Singh et al. 2016). The vagueness of meaning and establishment of AE as a profession (Shah 2010, p. 2), the voluntary nature of adult educators' work, the absence of qualifying exams to become a professional adult educator (Shah 2010, p. 2), inadequate training (Karlekar 2004, p. 1–19) and a short-term governance approach (Shah 2010, p. 2) reflect this assessment. Professionalization is neither affordable nor a viable option, because the primary responsibility of adult educators is to address the problems of the marginalized population in the form of a mission. Resources for the professional training of adult educators are lacking. Consequently, the sector can hardly meet the expectation of acting professionally, efficiently and effectively without, for instance, an appropriate payment in return. Productive engagement with communities directly through governmental or non-governmental programmes is therefore merely hypothetical (Ehlers 2016, personal communication)[1].

---

1    This paper benefits from communication with the following experts in adult education and lifelong learning: Prof. Søren Ehlers, Aarhus University; Prof. S.Y. Shah,

Profiles: Adult education officials in government positions are themselves usually contracted from other departments (Sura 2016, personal communication), which supports the assumption that there is no need for any specific professional competence as an adult educator and that key competencies are not a concern. The governance focus is on quantitative output rather than qualitative outcome. In other words, adult education officials provide literacy to as many people as possible. Moreover, a narrow conception of adult education focusing on basic literacy skills rather than other aspects aggravates the situation (Krishankumar 2016, personal communication; Shah 2010, p. 1). Adult educators operate with a dual professional identity, where their professional identity for acting in other fields is stronger than their role as professional adult educators (Sura 2016, personal communication). Policy documents, provisions for funding, evaluating or monitoring, but also expected outcomes and even the content of training for adult educators at the grass-roots level, reflect this dual identity.

Governance structure: Governing intervention in India is directed at four areas: the formal education sector, including universities; skill development by means of public-private partnerships; the emerging labour market; and traditional missionary and literacy activities. Since governance approaches have distinct characteristics, the four different areas will be examined separately for the sake of precision.

The formal education sector is strongly influenced by regulations guiding financing and decision-making at a higher level (appointments to higher university positions, such as vice-chancellors or heads of department). Concerning the role of adult educators, personal conversations revealed that, apart from research, such professionals participate rather in an advisory and soft form of policy formation. In particular, they operate through their participation on boards or committees and at meetings (Shah 2016, personal communication). Adult educators mainly take over the role of policy implementer (Kumar 2016, personal communication).

A second area of intervention is in skill development. As Kumar (2016, personal communication) confirmed, in order to meet the needs of society adequately, this area builds on a public-private partnership model. However, the government's control over policies and decision-making is still strong. According to Shah (2016, personal communication), adult education representatives can influence

---

International Institute for Lifelong Learning and Education; Prof. Ajay Kumar, Jawaharlal Nehru University; Prof. Rajesh, University of Delhi; Dr. Rama Krishna Sura, Director Adult Education Ministry of Human Resource and Development, New Delhi; V. Balaji, Director, State Resource Centre, Chennai; and K.K Krishnakumar, Former Director Kerala Saaksharata Samithi, Trivandrum, State of Kerala and former Vice President, Bharat Gyan Vigyan Samiti, Kerala.

the governance processes, again predominantly through participation in meetings and on boards and committees.

An interesting role is performed by the labour market. In private corporations, departments for corporate social responsibility most commonly deal with AE issues. In this area, the government transformed from being a controlling authority to acting as a regulator and facilitator (Rajesh 2016, personal communication) thereby enabling the private corporates to act more autonomously (Shah 2016, personal communication). Government regulation provides the backdrop for relationships between AE and the market. The relationships are, however, regulated by market principles. In this context, the market indirectly influences policy formation.

Adult education as missionary work is traditionally the primary area for AE. Central actors are national and international NGOs as well as the government, which intervenes and imposes checks with regard to financing and policy formation (Balaji 2016; Krishnakumar 2016, personal communication). This leads to the fact that adult education professionals are contingent on a strict top-down model of policy implementation. The government tends to disregard feedback from the practitioners and neglects any incorporation (Shah 2016, personal communication).

Policy focus: Before the Indian Knowledge Commission's report (2006), AE policy was primarily a social policy and targeted at bringing the marginalized population into the mainstream development process. Additionally, policy included provisions for sustainable and balanced economic growth (Singh 2015, p. 238–240). Since then, the focus has shifted. India's transition towards an inclusive and sustainable knowledge economy, the need for bridging the labour market demand-supply gap and taking advantage of the demographic dividend and constantly increasing marginalization led to an incorporation of economic elements into AE policies (Singh 2015, pp. 250–255). In 2013, funding of adult education departments in universities was cut (Shah 2015, p. 21), while attention moved to skill development and vocational training. As stipulated in the 2013 Corporate Act (Government of India 2013, p. 80), the government directed the private sector towards contributing to inclusive growth and balanced, sustainable development by establishing departments for corporate social responsibility. In 2014, a new ministry for skill development and entrepreneurship was established and, in 2015, the government formed its new policy on skill development and entrepreneurship (Singh et al. 2016). The transition from a social to an economic policy focus draws a dividing line between the old and the new role of adult educators. However, a new education policy dealing directly with AE is still awaited. Set in motion by this policy shift, the profiles of adult educators started transforming from missionary to professional; they are now characterized by research and management, and are based on performance and quality indicators.

Conclusion: In a nutshell, professionalization is a neglected part of adult education. Due to scarce resources and diverging conceptions of the demands of AE work, professionalization remains a marginal issue. The governance structure, however, shows sector division regarding conceptual and practical approaches as well as participants. A relationship with the shift observed in policy focus is apparent. The more market-oriented areas contribute to an initial transformation of adult educators' profiles towards professional management and quality. In the traditional areas, however, the government remains dominant in defining policy and the profile in line with missionary tasks.

## Comparison

Figure 1: Comparison of governance approach and policy focus (Source: authors' own).

| Categories | Austria | India |
|---|---|---|
| Governance approach | Cooperative in creating measures and decision-making; centralized coordination; backed up by legal act; supported by academia | Sectorial division of tasks, participants and influence; opposition of government and market; governance by regulation |
| Policy focus | Professionalization through VPL; standardization and reference frameworks; quality in AE; compliance with international guidelines | Professionalization and key competences are formally marginalized; market-initiated shift towards professionalization away from missionary work |

The comparison reveals that Austria operates on the basis of a well-developed and participative governance approach, with cooperation between coordinating institutions and executive institutions. The Indian scenario is characterized by the government's central position, influenced by NGOs and INGOs as additional actors. However diverse the sector, Austria provides key competences, frameworks and validation to intervene proactively. In India, on the contrary, the promotion of pedagogical competences and professionalism is more neglected. While supranational developments, predominantly the EU, influence the policy focus in Austria, India is struggling through indifference and myopic conceptions, from coping with illiteracy and marginalization to skills development and inclusion.

## Implications

The subject of this paper was to examine core elements of policy for, and general approaches to, the governance of professionalization, with the intention of rendering the reader conscious of the factors that condition the advancement of professionalization. Policy and governance proved to be useful categories of comparison because they revealed significant differences in the way professionalization is conceived, the definition of competences as well as participant structures and participant relations in the process of governing professionalization. Moreover, the comparison shows that professionalization is a policy that has come to demarcate a conceptual landscape, furnishing space for very distinctive tasks like VPL or missionary work. The same inference is applicable to the role of governments and agencies, or the impact of the free market in the context of governance.

Writing this paper confronted the authors with the issue of contextual factors. Excluded in advance, the social and historical contexts proved to be too specific and influential, so the results are certainly hamstrung by this restriction. For the reader interested in research, it is therefore advisable to keep in mind that AE is embedded in societally functional systems. Focusing on global developments of professionalization, Dales Globally Structured Agenda for Education approach (2000) could be beneficial in this respect. On the contrary, if maintaining a national focus, Nittel, Schütz and Tippelt's (2012) approach to the comparison of pedagogical occupational groups might be an option, as might be a quantitative study. Concerning future challenges for professionalization, the comparison emphasized once again that the economic and political architecture in which the professionalization of adult education is included demands specific approaches to professionalization.

## References

Blum, S. / Schubet, K.: *Politikfeldanalyse*. Verlag für Sozialwissenschaften: Wiesbaden. 2009.

Brüsemeister, T.: "Educational governance: Aufriss von Perspektiven für die empirische Bildungsforschung". In C. Hof / J. Ludwig / B. Schäffer (eds.): *Steuerung – Regulation – Gestaltung*. Schneider: Hohengehren. 2011, pp. 7–16.

Dale, R.: "Globalization and education: Demonstrating a 'common world educational culture' or locating a 'globally structured educational agenda'?". *Educational Theory* 50(4), 2000, pp. 427–448.

Egetenmeyer, R.: "Zwischen europäischem Qualifikationsrahmen und erwach-
senenpädagogischer Professionalität. Drei Fallbeispiele zu einem Spannungs-
verhältnis". *MAGAZIN Erwachsenenbilding.at* 14, 2011, retrieved from http://
erwachsenenbildung.at/magazin/11-14/meb11-14_07_egetenmeyer.pdf.

Egetenmeyer, R. / Käpplinger, B.: "Professionalization and quality management:
Struggles, boundaries and bridges between two approaches". *European Journal
for Research on the Education and Learning of Adults* 2(1), 2011, pp. 21–35, retrieved from http://www.rela.ep.liu.se/issues/10.3384_rela.2000-7426.201121/
rela0058/10.3384rela.2000-7426.rela0058.pdf.

European Centre for the Development of Vocational Training: *Trainers in continuing VET: Emerging competence profile*. Publications Office of the European Union: Luxembourg. 2013, retrieved from http://wba.or.at/ueber_uns/
studien_zur_wba.php.

Filla, W.: *Von der freien zur integrierten Erwachsenenbildung: Zugänge zur Ge-
schichte der Erwachsenenbildung in Österreich*. Peter Lang: Frankfurt am Main.
2014.

Giesecke, W.: "Professionalisierung in der Erwachsenenbildung/Weiterbildung".
In: R. Tippelt / A. von Hippel (eds.): *Handbuch Erwachsenenbildung/Weiter-
bildung*. Springer: Wiesbaden. 2011, pp. 385–403.

Government of India: "Companies Act 2013 Section 135". *The Gazette of India
Extraordinary Part II*, 2013, retrieved from http://www.mca.gov.in/Ministry/
pdf/CompaniesAct2013.pdf.

Gutknecht-Gmeiner, M.: "Die statistische Erfassung des Erwachsenenbildungs-
und Weiterbildungspersonals in Österreich". *MAGAZIN erwachsenenbildung.
at* 4, 2008, retrieved from http://erwachsenenbildung.at/magazin/08-4/
meb08-4_06_gutknecht_gmeiner.pdf.

Heilinger, A.: "Von der Landschaft zum Markt: Erwachsenenbildung – ein Berufs-
feld qualifiziert sich". In: W. Lenz (ed.): *Weiterbildung als Beruf. "Wir schaffen
unseren Arbeitsplatz selbst!"*. Lit: Wien. 2005, pp. 157–182.

Heilinger, A.: "Professionalisierung mit Kompetenz steuern am Beispiel der
Weiterbildungsakademie Österreich". In: E. Gruber / G. Wiesner (eds.): *Er-
wachsenenpädagogische Kompetenzen stärken: Kompetenzbilanzierung für
Weiterbildner/-innen*. Bertelsmann: Bielefeld. 2012, pp. 59–82.

Karlekar, M.: "The total literacy campaign: An overview". In: M. Karlekar (ed.):
*Paradigms of learning: The total literacy campaign in India*. Sage Publications:
New Delhi. 2004, pp. 1–19.

Lenz, W.: *Portrait Weiterbildung Österreich*. (2nd edition). Bertelsmann: Bielefeld.
2005.

Nittel, D. with support of Siewert, A. / Wahl, J.: *Professionalitätsentwicklung als Element der (kollektiven) Professionalisierung! - Anforderungen und Ausblick.* Presentation GEW-Kongress Halle. 25 October 2014.

Nittel, D. / Schütz, J. / Tippelt, R.: "Notwendigkeit des Vergleichs! Der Ansatz einer komparativen pädagogischen Berufsgruppenforschung". *Erziehungswissenschaft* 23(45), 2012, pp. 87–100.

Nuissl, E.: "Profession and professional work in adult education in Europe". *Studi sulla Formazione. Metodologia della Ricerca Pedagogica: Modelli a Confronto* 1(2) (Anno XII), 2009, pp. 127–132, retrieved from http://dx.doi.org/10.13128/Studi_Formaz-8591.

Ocenasek, C. / Reisinger, K.: "Weiterbildungsakademie Österreich: Erfolgskriterien und Risikofaktoren eines Kooperationsprojektes der österreichischen Erwachsenenbildung – ein E-Mail-Dialog". In; E. Gruber / G. Wiesener (eds.): *Erwachsenenpädagogische Kompetenzen stärken: Kompetenzbilanzierung für Weiterbildner/innen.* Bertelsmann: Bielefeld. 2012, pp. 83–96.

Patel, I.: "Policy on adult and lifelong learning: International and national perspectives". *Participatory Lifelong Learning and Information and Communication Technologies (PALDIN),* Course 1 (Unit 2). Group of Adult Education, School of Social Sciences, Jawaharlal Nehru University (JNU) and Aladin-India: New Delhi. 2009, pp. 21–30.

Platzer, K.: *Weiterbildung als komplexe Rechtsmaterie.* WiKu-Verlag: Duisburg and Köln. 2009.

Reisinger, K. / Wagner, G.: "Die lernergebnisorientierte Beschreibung der wba-Curricula". *MAGAZIN erwachsenenbildung.at* 14, 2011, retrieved from http://erwachsenenbildung.at/magazin/11-14/meb11-14_12_reisinger_wagner.pdf.

Schrader, J.: "Governance in adult and further education". *European Education* 41(4), 2010, pp. 41–64, retrieved from doi 10.2753/EUE1056-4934410403.

Shah, S.Y.: *Teaching and training in adult and lifelong learning in India: Need for professionalisation,* 2010, retrieved from www.iaea-india.org/journal/oct-dec10/sy-shah.html.

Singh, S.: "India towards a knowledge economy: Alternatives for the global demographic challenge and inclusive development in India". In: R. Egetenmeyer (ed.): *Adult education and lifelong learning in Europe and beyond: Comparative perspectives from the 2015 Würzburg Winter School.* Peter Lang: Frankfurt am Main. 2015, pp. 237–260.

Singh, S. / Bora, B. / Egetenmeyer, R.: "Adult education policies in India and international influences: Current status of adult education regarding millennium development goals and education for all: Results and prospects from the perspective of South-, East- and Southeast-Asian states". *International Yearbook of Adult Education* 39, 2016.

Vater, S. / Zwielehner, P.: 'Konferenz der Erwachsenenbildung Österreichs'. In: Projektgruppe Statistik Erwachsenenbildung Österreichs (eds.): KEBÖ-STATISTIK 29 (Arbeitsjahr 2011). Wien, 2015, retrieved from http://www.adulteducation.at/de/struktur/keboe/druck/auswertungen/116.

## Online sources

Academy of Continuing Education – Wba: http://wba.or.at/

Federal Institute for Adult Education – Bifeb: http://www.bifeb.at/

Open access platform and journal – erwachsenenbildung.at: http://erwachse nenbildung.at/

Paula Guimarães & Natália Alves

# Adult Educators in Portugal: From the European Guidelines to a National Public Policy of Lifelong Learning Technicians

**Abstract:** this article focuses on clusters of activities in formal regulations of new adult education occupations within recognition of prior learning established since the late 1990s in Portugal. The challenges of the emergence of lifelong learning technicians are debated.

## Initial remarks

The discussion on adult educators (who they are, which formal and non-formal pathways they have followed etc.), as well as on their work features, can be found in several pieces of research. Nuissl and Latke (2008), Research voor Beleid (2008, 2010), Jütte, Nicoll and Salling Olesen (2011) and Egetenmeyer and Schüßler (2014), among others, aimed at analyzing different aspects of the work developed by these practitioners. The debates included arguments about the professionalization process that can be found in some countries and shed light on national and regional similarities and differences. These differences were justified since the field of adult education differs considerably across countries.

In Portugal, Canário (1999), Rothes (2003), Lima (2006), Loureiro and Cristóvão (2010) and Bernardes (2013), among others, have discussed the sociographic aspects of adult educators, and the formal education pathways and activities these practitioners have pursued. These debates were often part of public policy analysis for basic education and vocational training in adult education. The studies highlighted the work of these practitioners within the different domains of adult education, such as local development, vocational training and social and cultural animation.

In recent times, namely after the end of the 1990s, new forms of provision were established, such as the recognition of prior learning. As a result, the debate on adult educators benefited from new insights, owing to the establishment of new professional areas in adult education. These studies have emphasized innovative work methods centred on adult learners and on learning itself (Cavaco 2009), the impact of the European Union (EU) lifelong learning guidelines on adult educators' work (Guimarães 2009; Guimarães & Barros 2015) and informal learning in the workplace developed by these practitioners (Loureiro & Cristóvão 2010;

Paulos 2015). These stress the fact that adult education higher education pathways do not exist in Portugal.

This article aims to discuss new activities introduced by adult educators, particularly those related to the recognition of prior learning (*Reconhecimento, Validação e Certificação de Competências*, in Portuguese). This paper's analysis emphasizes the possible effects of the EU policy notion of professionalization (Jütte, Nicoll & Salling Olesen 2011) on practitioners working in centres of adult education in terms of promoting the recognition of prior learning. The interpretation of adult educators' work is based on clusters of activities presented by Research voor Beleid (2010). This article stresses the individualization of learning that these practitioners support. It also refers to the (weak) emergence of adult educators' professionalization in formal policy documents (formal regulations) between 2001 and 2016 in Portugal, and how specific clusters of activities are valued when they relegate adult educators to lifelong learning technicians following EU guidelines.

## The debate on professionalization based on adult educators and their jobs

As Dausien and Schwendowius (2009) noted, "There is no such thing as 'the' adult educator." In fact, *adult educator* is an analytical category used in this article to identify a multitude of jobs in quite different domains that can be broadly included in the UNESCO definition (1977, 2009) of adult education. According to Knox and Fleming (2010), professionalization depends on the characteristics of an educational field. Adult education is characterized by the diversity of practice and the complexity and heterogeneity of the organizations, actors and domains of intervention involved (Canário 1999). Somehow, this field involves an "incomplete professionalization" of adult educators, expressed by the distinction between traditional professions and incomplete professions that lack some of the requisite markers such as professional organizations and entry through academic qualifications (Jütte, Nicoll & Salling Olesen 2011). This situation challenges the traditional understanding of a profession, which includes elements such as the possession of special knowledge and skills to carry out a job, training at a higher level, social recognition of a professional seen as an expert and a high level of self-esteem experienced by the professionals themselves (Nuissl 2009). It also challenges the understanding of a professional occupation as a specialized and unified domain of intervention (Sava 2011). These circumstances therefore suggest challenges for the professionalization process of educators in adult education. The scope of the field of practice covered by educators in this field suggests that participants may be very different. Organizations that promote adult education activities also vary greatly. Finally, the aims of the initiatives developed, and participants' (that is, adult learners' or adult educators') objectives, are very diverse as well (Knox & Fleming 2010).

Additionally, several authors have argued that apart from a field of practices, adult education is also a domain of scientific problematization (Canário 1999) and an area of theoretical discussion in countries in which adult education is considered a scientific discipline. Egetenmeyer and Schüßler (2014) and Egetenmeyer (2014) discussed the concept of professionalization as a process of specialization and academization of professional knowledge. This debate stresses the features of initial higher education pathways and the continuing education of staff.

Owing to the variety of contexts in adult education in different countries (Jütte, Nicoll & Salling Olesen 2011), another debate has focused on the profiles and activities developed by adult educators, supported by a theoretical model of the division of labour (Dausien & Schwendowius 2009). Nuissl and Pehl (2004) indicated four main profiles of adult educators: teaching staff/course teachers; adult education managers; pedagogical staff members; and administrative staff members. Several authors identified and analyzed clusters of activities understood as sets of tasks, skills and competencies that are related to each of the domains of adult education. Following this approach, Nuissl (2009) proposed six clusters of activities: teaching, management, counselling and guidance, programme planning, support activities and media. This debate has also been driven by the importance the European Commission (EC) assigns to the quality of adult learning staff. Claiming that the quality of adult learning professions is a condition of ensuring the quality of lifelong learning, the EC has funded several research projects concerning adult learning activities, competencies and skills (Research voor Beleid 2008, 2010). Within these studies and based on empirical findings, Researcher voor Beleid (2010) presented thirteen clusters of activities:

- Needs-assessment activities (identification of needs, possibilities, potential and capacities of adult learners; identification and assessment of entry levels, prior learning and experience of the adult learners);
- Preparation of course activities (identification of learning resources and methods; planning and organizing the learning process; setting, negotiating and communicating the objectives of the course and informing adult learners of the structure of the learning process);
- Facilitation of learning activities (relating the learning process to the living world and practice of the adult learner; empowering, activating, motivating and encouraging the adult learner; creating a positive learning environment; making content accessible; managing group process and dynamics, etc.);

- Monitoring and evaluation activities (providing support and feedback to the learners; evaluating the context, the process and the outcomes);
- Counselling and guidance activities (offering career information and other information on work environments; obtaining information on careers for adults; offering guidance and counselling);
- Programme development activities (curriculum design; development of programmes);
- Financial management activities (managing resources and budgets; preparing applications for funding; determining and elucidating benefits);
- Human resources management activities (managing staff, staff professional development; recruitment of staff; monitoring and evaluating staff performance);
- Overall management activities (working in accordance with existing procedures; monitoring and evaluating programmes; building relationships with other organizations; lobbying and negotiating, etc.);
- Marketing and public relations activities (marketing of programmes; assessment of demand for existing provision and for new programmes; establishing relationships with external communities);
- Administrative support activities (dealing with administrative issues; informing staff and learners of administrative issues);
- ICT support activities (supporting the design of ICT-based and mixed-mode programmes; delivering ICT-based programmes; conducting and facilitating assessment within on-line environments, etc.,);
- Overarching activities (working with others; linking to social contexts, networks, stakeholders and the wider community; coaching new staff; reaching target groups).

## Adult educators in the context of public policies in Portugal and the influence of EU guidelines on lifelong learning

Due to the intermittent and discontinuous nature of adult education policies since the Democratic Revolution in 1974 (Lima 2008), by the end of the 1990s, adult educators had formed a strongly heterogenous group in terms of education pathways, professional experience, professional status, work contracts, etc. (Lima 2006). Many were teachers in second-chance education while also teaching children and young people in regular education, and others were trainers in vocational training. Some had been involved in social movements for autonomic and emancipatory progress; others were involved in non-formal activities such as social and cultural promotion and local development. The diversity of contexts of intervention and the heterogeneity of practices indicated that these practitioners developed quite a significant variety of roles and tasks. It also suggested that these practitioners did not see themselves as adult educators. According to their professional activity, they defined themselves as teachers, trainers or sociocultural promoters (Paulo 2015). As argued in some research work (Nuissl 2009; Sava 2011), this situation suggested the non-existence of a profession (if criteria that allow the characterization of a profession were used to recognize a field of practice such as teaching, social work, etc.) and the lack of an occupation clearly identified and supported by a body of knowledge and specific activities.

Since 2000, with the Memorandum of Lifelong Learning (European Commission 2000) and further policy documents concerning adult education, the EU guidelines on lifelong learning and its policy notion of professionalization have had an impact on adult education in Portugal both from a policy discourse perspective and in terms of encouraging action. As a result, the situation for adult educators changed dramatically with the introduction of adult education and training policy after 2000. This favoured the establishment of new job descriptions and new clusters of activities. This policy had different aims from the previous one, centred on second-chance (formal) education. One of its pillars was the valuing of educational methods, stressing experiential learning and knowledge and skills developed throughout life in non-formal and informal contexts through recognition of prior learning (Cavaco 2009). The writing of a learning portfolio by adult learners was a significant outcome for recognition of prior learning. It had to include evidence of key competencies developed throughout life, according to a Standard of Competencies. In order to receive a school-leaving certificate at the end of the recognition-of-prior-learning process, adult learners had to attend up to 50 hours of education and training sessions. Another relevant pillar was the strong link established in policy discourses between the qualification of human resources, in which recognition of prior learning played a fundamental role, and the development of the Portuguese economy in the context of the EU and globalization (Lima & Guimarães 2011; Guimarães & Barros 2015).

Formal legislation since 2000 has favoured the emergence of several occupations and the (weak) building of a labour market for adult education practitioners. These practitioners – namely professionals able to recognize and validate competencies, trainers and, after 2007, also technicians for diagnosis and guidance – were dealing with a dramatic increase in adult learners enrolled in recognition of prior learning schemes. Between 2000 and 2005, 153,719 adult learners were enrolled in such schemes, and out of these, 44,192 received formal (education) certification.

Due to the New Opportunities Initiative (2005), between 2006 and 2010, 1,163,236 adult learners were enrolled in recognition of prior learning courses in adult education centres. Out of these, 365,449 (CNE 2011) received formal certification (school education and/or professional). In 2010, there were 11,611 practitioners in employment in adult education centres (ANQ 2011).

One of the first aspects researchers noted concerned the fact that a higher education degree (especially in the social sciences) was a requirement for the majority of adult educators in adult education centres. Therefore, several researchers (Guimarães 2009; Guimarães & Barros 2015) argued that these practitioners were more qualified than other adult educators working in other domains, such as social and cultural animation or local development, and the number included a larger percentage of women (in 2010, 73.9% were women) (CNE 2011). With regard to professional associations, after 2008 the National Association of Professionals of Adult Education and Training and the Portuguese Association of Adult Education and Training were established. However, few developments were observed concerning the adoption of ethical codes or even a statement of professional autonomy, namely accountability and professional responsibility (Afonso 2008).

In 2012, the suspension of the adult education and training policy involved the dismissal of practitioners working in adult education centres. From 2013 onwards, new adult education centres have been established and (a few) adult educators (technicians for guidance, recognition and validation of competencies, as well as trainers and teachers) have been hired to develop more or less the same clusters of activities that previous adult educators offered in the centres mentioned above.

## "New" and "old" jobs, "new" and "old" clusters of activities: data analysis

Since 2000, adult education centres have been regulated by formal legislation. In the legal field, the expression "adult educator" was nowhere to be seen. Instead, practitioners were called "professionals" (for recognition and validation of competencies) and "technicians" (for diagnosis and guidance or for guidance, recognition and validation of competencies). This situation was also evident in policy discourse (Guimarães & Barros 2015), as it was impossible to find such a designation in other policy documents.

The legislation selected for analysis in this article mentions several clusters of activities to be performed by adult education practitioners. The professionals for recognition and validation of competencies (Portaria n.º 1982-A/2001, 5/09; Portaria n.º 370/2008, 21/05), who only had temporary employment contracts, had to carry out the following activities:

- Needs assessment through the recognition of prior learning and experience of adult learners;
- Facilitation of learning processes through empowering, activating, motivating and encouraging adult learners;
- Monitoring and evaluating adults' learning process, namely when writing material for inclusion in the portfolio, by providing support and feedback, evaluating the recognition of prior learning process and the portfolios when finished and participating in the jury for the certification of competencies

In 2008, a new job concerned technicians for diagnosis and guidance (Portaria n.º 370/2008, 21/05). These people also held temporary employment contracts and had the following clusters of activities:

- Needs assessment (identification of learners' needs; possibilities, potential and capacities of adult learners; identification and assessment of education and training entry levels);
- Counselling and guidance, as well as providing education and training and/ or work/career information

After 2013, professionals for recognition, validation and certification as well as technicians for diagnosis and guidance were substituted with technicians for guidance, recognition and the validation of competencies (Portaria n.º 135-A/2013, 28/03). These practitioners also work on temporary employment contracts, and have to inform, guide and counsel adult learners, perform needs assessments and support adults as they seek to gain recognition of prior learning. The work of these practitioners is complemented by trainers and teachers who support the recognition of prior learning and writing of learners' portfolios. These adult educators now have to fulfil these clusters of activities that were previously developed by professionals (for the recognition and validation of competencies) and technicians (for diagnosis and guidance).

   Other practitioners mentioned in legislation (since 2000) include trainers (Portaria n.º 1982-A/2001, 5/09; Portaria n.º 370/2008, 21/05) and, since 2013, teachers (Portaria n.º 135-A/2013, 28/03). These practitioners are hired to fulfil very specific training and teaching tasks. The job descriptors include activities that are less innovative in the sense that the tasks to be performed are quite similar to those of other (vocational) trainers and regular education (basic and secondary) teachers:

- The preparation of course activities (selecting the most appropriate learning resources and methods in order to foster the recognition of competencies in accordance with the existing Standards of Competences; planning and organizing the adult learning process through the support of adult learners' portfolio writings; etc.);

- The facilitation of learning (creating good learning environments in education and training sessions concerning a specific area of the Standard of Competencies; supporting adults in relating their learning to their day-to-day life, namely when writing their portfolios; making the content of the Standard of Competencies accessible; managing individual and group processes and dynamics in education and training sessions);
- The monitoring and evaluation of the learning process (providing support and feedback to the learners when writing portfolios; providing a link between the Standard of Competencies experience and adult learning; evaluating the process and the outcome of the recognition of prior learning, i.e., the portfolio)

Another job quite similar to the one that can be found in many other learning and education organizations has been devoted to co-ordinators of adult education centres (Portaria n.º 1982-A/2001, /09; Portaria n.º 370/2008, 21/05; Portaria n.º 135-A/2013, 28/03). Like trainers and teachers, these members of staff also do not enjoy a permanent contract in adult education centres. They develop the co-ordination and management activities. These practitioners are in charge of the formal representation of adult education centres and of the centres' strategic plans of intervention, with responsibility for the work achieved by the centre, financial management, human resources management activities (including the training of staff), overall management, marketing and public relations and overarching activities such as activities concerning the needs assessment of the local community in which the centre is based, the establishment of partnerships and evaluation of the centre (internal, and providing support to external evaluators).

In summary, data analysis (formal regulations published after 2000) allowed the identification of several jobs in the adult education and training field. Apart from "old" (traditional) adult education jobs, such as adult education co-ordinators, teacher and trainers, "new" ones were created, such as technicians for guidance, recognition and validation of competencies (as well as technicians for diagnosis and guidance and professionals for recognition and validation of competencies). These practitioners' activities included needs assessment; facilitation of learning; monitoring and evaluation; and counselling and guidance. These were similar to those developed by practitioners of the "*ingénérie de la formation*" (among others, Caspar 2011). However, several activities were simultaneously different in the sense that they were centred on the adult learners, and on their (non-formal and informal) experience and learning according to EU guidelines for lifelong learning. In fact, new clusters of activities developed by adult educators emphasized both learning and the link between adult education and training and the labour market since 2000. These adult educators developed activities that allowed the certification of "competencies to compete"; this made them human resources managers (Lima 2008; Cavaco 2009), facilitators of learning useful to economic development and promoters of "learning to learn" in work contexts. These practitioners could, therefore, be considered life-long learning technicians who favoured knowledge relevant for work performance and who were able to anticipate problems and promote adaptive solutions for adult learners (Guimarães 2009).

## Final remarks

In this article, we have followed the lead of the EU lifelong learning guidelines and understanding of the professionalization of adult educators. By these means, we have tried to comprehend the impact on adult education policies and on the work of practitioners hired in centres of adult education since 2000. This attempt was made using the analysis of clusters of activities adult educators achieve. We have noted that recent developments in adult education policies raise several challenges to professionalization.

A first challenge to be noted is that adult education is characterized by diverse contexts and by the heterogeneity of the professional terrain. However, the diversity of adult educators and the variety of roles they achieve makes it difficult to talk about a single professionalization process. Additionally, neither adult education practitioners working in adult education centres, as Paulo (2015) has noted, nor those involved in other adult education organizations represent themselves as adult educators. From 2000 onwards, we have observed an attempt at professionalizing a specific sector of adult education, owing mainly to the legislation published for centres of adult education and to specific occupations' regulations. The establishment of job descriptors of occupations in adult education (in line with a functional approach to professions) analyzed in this article only allows for reference to a (weak) professionalization process based on a debate on the activities, competencies and skills (Research voor Belied 2010) needed by people working in certain roles in adult education.

A second challenge concerns the existence of "new" and "old" jobs in adult education and training policy adopted after 2000. While some "new" jobs were created, many activities to be developed were characteristic of "*l'ingénerie de la formation*". These were complemented by innovative activities related to learning (within recognition of prior learning) and to the connection between adult education and training policy. Therefore, the real innovative character of these new occupations must be questioned. On the other hand, apart from "new" jobs, the "old" ones are still important. These include teachers, trainers and adult education centres coordinators. When considering the professionalization process across adult education, teachers must be highlighted. Even in the context of uncertainty that has character-ized the Portuguese education and training system in recent times, these practition-ers have more stable work conditions; established rights and duties; and the power of teachers' trade unions to negotiate with state authorities. Adult educators were never completely recognized as "professionals" and "technicians" (professionally or socially), mainly due to a general economic, social and political context marked by state deregulation, job insecurity and a fragile legal status heavily dependent upon intermittent and discontinuous adult education policies.

A third challenge relates to the fact that practitioners working in adult education centres have temporary employment contracts or are hired to develop very specific tasks. This situation is most relevant when we consider the discontinuous character of public policies in Portugal that has brought more insecurity to working in adult education. This systemic trend has also had an impact on the changing nature of the designation of jobs and occupations, as we have already stressed. The reliability of public policies, organizations and jobs in adult education is a relevant precondition for any successful professionalization process (Dausien & Schwendowius 2009).

A fourth challenge concerns the non-existence of specific paths in adult edu-cation at a higher education level such as one leading to a first degree (a bach-elor's). The practice of hiring practitioners to work in adult education centres who have a degree, without taking into consideration the specific scientific character of working in adult education, can be seen in different ways. For some, these circumstances are an opportunity to develop knowledge and skills (Loureiro & Cristóvão 2010) and learning contexts (Paulos 2015). But for many others, these circumstances can also be problematic, as they constitute the devaluing of adult education as a specific and complex domain of practices and a theoretical field. The heterogenous character of qualifications for practitioners in centres of adult education raises questions concerning expertise. Owing to this, the quality of work achieved by practitioners can be more than questionable. In fact, if qual-ity management systems have been developed at all since 2000, they have very much centred on the technical dimensions of the work of adult educators due to the formalization of work in adult education centres. Quality management has not, therefore, emphasized the specific knowledge and skills these practitioners need to possess when hired or could develop when working as adult educators. In addition, the lack of continuing education programmes for staff focused on adult education (Guimarães & Barros 2015) has failed to allow any possibility for debate on the general and technical dimensions of the work achieved, and especially on educational and political issues relating to public policies and adult education programmes.

# References

Afonso, A.J.: "Políticas educativas contemporâneas: Dilemas e desafios". In: N. Cunha (coord.): *Pedagogia e Educação em Portugal Séculos XX e XXI*. Museu Bernardino Machado: Famalicão. 2008, pp. 59–80.

Agência Nacional para a Qualificação (ANQ): *Linhas orientadoras para o futuro da iniciativa novas oportunidades*. Agência Nacional para a Qualificação: Lisboa. 2011.

Bernardes, A.: *Políticas e práticas de formação em grandes empresas: A dimensão educativa do trabalho*. Porto Editora: Porto. 2013.

Canário, R.: *Educação de adultos: Um Campo e uma problemática*. EDUCA: Lisboa. 1999.

Caspar, P.: *La formation des adultes: Hier, aujourd'hui, demain…* Eyrolles: Paris. 2011.

Cavaco, C.: *Adultos pouco escolarizados – políticas e práticas de formação*. EDUCA – UI & DCE: Lisboa. 2009.

Dausien, B. / Schwendowius, D.: "Professionalization in general adult education in Germany – An attempt to cut a path through a jungle". *European Journal of Education* 44(2), 2009, pp. 183–203.

European Commission (EC): *Memorandum on lifelong learning*. European Commission: Brussels. 2000.

Egetenmeyer, R.: *Academic professionalisation in adult and continuing education in Germany and beyond: From theory to research*. James Draper Memorial Lecture at the International Institute for Adult and Lifelong Learning. 29 August 2014.

Egetenmeyer, R. / Schüßler, I.: "Academic professionalization in master's programmes in adult and continuing education: Towards an internationally comparative research design". In: S. Lattke / W. Jütte: *Professionalization of Adult Educators: International and Comparative Perspectives*. Peter Lang Edition: Frankfurt. 2014, pp. 91–103.

Guimarães, P.: "Reflections on the professionalisation process in the framework of public policies in Portugal". *European Journal of Education* 44(2), 2009, pp. 205–219.

Guimarães, P. / Barros, R.: "A nova política pública de educação e formação de adultos em portugal: Os educadores de adultos numa encruzilhada?". *Educação & Sociedade* 36(131), 2015, pp. 391–406.

Jütte, W. / Nicoll, K. / Salling Olesen, H.: "Editorial: Professionalization – The struggle within". *RELA – European Journal for Research on the Education and Learning of Adults* 2(1), 2011, pp. 7–20.

Knox, A.B. / Fleming, J.E.: "Professionalization of the field of adult and continuing education". In: C. Kassworm / A. Rose / J. Ross-Gordon (eds.): *Handbook of Adult and Continuing Education*. SAGE: Los Angeles. 2010, pp. 125–134.

Lima, L.C.: "A educação de adultos em Portugal (1974–2004)". In: R. Canário / B. Cabrito (orgs.): *Educação e formação de adultos: Mutações e convergências*. EDUCA: Lisboa. 2008, pp. 31–60.

Lima, L.C. (org.): *Educação não escolar de adultos: Iniciativas em contextos associativos*. Universidade do Minho/Unidade de Educação de Adultos: Braga. 2006.

Loureiro, A. / Cristóvão, A.: "The official knowledge and adult education agents: An ethnographic study of the adult education team of a local development-oriented non-governmental organisation in the north of Portugal". *Adult Education Quarterly* 60(5), 2010, pp. 419–437.

Nuissl, E.: "Profession and professional work in adult education". *Studi sulla Formazione* 127(132) (Year XII, I/II), 2009, retrieved 15.6.2016.

Nuissl, E. / Lattke, S.: *Qualifying adult educators in Europe*. W. Bertelsmann: Bielefeld. 2008.

Nuissl, E. / Pehl, K.: *Portrait Weiterbildung Deutschland*. Bertelsmann: Bielefeld. 2004.

Paulos, C.: "Qualification of adult educators in Europe: Insights from the Portuguese case". *International Journal for Research in Vocational Education and Training* 2(1), 2015, pp. 25–38.

Research voor Beleid: *ALPINE – Adult Learning Professions in Europe: A study of the current situation, trends and issues – Final report*. Research voor Beleid: Zoetermeer. 2008.

Research voor Beleid: *Key competences for learning professionals: Contribution to the development of a reference framework of key competences for adult learning professionals*. Research voor Beleid: Zoetermeer. 2010.

Rothes, L.A.: "A formação dos educadores de adultos em Portugal: Trajectos e Tendências". *Forum* 34, 2003, pp. 35–62.

Sava, S.: "Towards the professionalization of adult educators". *Andragoske Studije* 2, 2011, pp. 9–22.

UNESCO: *Recomendação sobre o desenvolvimento da educação de adultos aprovada pela conferência geral da UNESCO na sua décima nona reunião*. Universidade do Minho/Projecto de Educação de Adultos: Braga. 1977.

UNESCO: *Global report on adult learning and education*. UNESCO Institute for Lifelong Learning: Hamburg. 2009.

Carlo Terzaroli

# Work Opportunities for Adult Educators in Italy: A Challenge for Professionalization

**Abstract:** The paper is based on a country report focused on the topic of professionalization of adult educators in Italy. In particular, it concentrates on the political framework of the adult education field, with specific attention paid to work issues and opportunities in the public system and in the social economy sector.

## Introduction

During recent years, the topic of professionalization has developed into a huge debate in adult education. The European policy statements and programmes that bolster the development of skills for responding to societal and economic challenges, and the transformation of the labour market, have all called for reflection within the entire field. From this perspective, this paper deals with the debate about the professionalization of adult education with relation to the Italian system. The paper is based on a country report that presents a review of policy documents, laws and previous scientific articles on the topic. Its purpose is to provide an overview of the current situation in Europe and in Italy to support the development of a comparative analysis at the international level. Moreover, the following paragraphs aim to analyze the challenges of adult educators' professionalization in relation to opportunities provided by the public system and the private labour market at the state level.

In order to outline these topics, the paper introduces the European framework that constitutes the broad context within which national states develop their own agenda. Indeed, the recent reforms at the national level directly refer to European lifelong learning strategies. The other parts of the paper highlight the policy level in Italy for adult education, alongside issues for adult educators' entrance into the public system and the new emerging opportunities in the social economy sector. The final aim of the paper is to discuss critically the professionalization of adult educators from political, cultural and employment perspectives.

## Professionalization of adult educators in the European framework

In recent decades, adult education has become more and more relevant in educational fields. Awareness of its importance, promoted by international institutions (such as UNESCO and the European Union) in numerous policy documents, has supported the dissemination of adult education in many countries. Despite the conceptual shift from education to learning, and its consequent process of individualization, we can notice "a boom in adult learning" (Bélanger & Federighi 2000, p. 5) all over the world. This process has also been fostered by European institutions, which highlight adult learning "as a vital component of lifelong learning" and define it as "all forms of learning undertaken by adults after having left initial education and training, however far this process may have gone (e.g., including tertiary education)" (European Commission 2006, p. 2).

The importance attributed to adult learning derives from the Memorandum on Lifelong Learning (2000) that sets the strategic goal for the European Union "to become the most competitive and dynamic knowledge-based economy in the world" (Council Resolution, SEC (2000)/1832). From this perspective, the challenge of professionalization in the field of adult education has been addressed since 2006–2007 in two documents: Adult learning: It is never too late to learn (European Commission 2006), which "draws a broad picture of quality in adult education, including teaching methods, staff, providers and delivery aspects of quality in adult education" (Egetenmeyer & Käpplinger 2011, p. 22); and Action Plan on Adult Learning. It is always a good time to learn (European Commission 2007), which "identifies the staff involved in delivery as 'the key factor' for the quality of adult education" (Egetenmeyer & Käpplinger 2011, p. 22).

In the same vein, the European Agenda for Adult Learning of 2011 invites EU member states to implement measures "aimed at enabling all adults to develop and enhance their skills and competences throughout their lives" (Council Resolution 2011/C 372/01). In essence, the European Union policy process started stressing the importance of adult education for "the dual function of contributing to employability[1] and economic growth, on the one hand, and responding to

---

1   According to Cedefop's definition in *Terminology of European education and training policy*, the term "employability" is defined as "the combination of factors which enable individuals to progress towards or get into employment, to stay in employment and to progress during their career. [...] Employability of individuals depends on (a) personal attributes (including adequacy of knowledge and skills); (b) how these personal

broader societal challenges, in particular promoting social cohesion, on the other" (Federighi 2013, p. 7). That is why adult learning, as a way to support skills development, has grown into a matter of primary discussion in the field of education. This leads us to consider the role of professionals in the field of adult education and the discussion on how professionalization could be implemented at the European and national levels. As a matter of fact, the theoretical definition of the term "professionalization" reveals an approach that firstly intends to point out the attention paid to initial training of adult educators. It then goes on to consider continuing education and lifelong learning from the perspective of employability. In this sense, the term can be understood

> *[...] as a process [...] focused on two different perspectives: one perspective refers to professionalization as the process for developing a profession (e.g., adult education); and the other perspective understands professionalization as a process of developing professionalism for people working in a specific field.*

(Egetenmeyer & Käpplinger 2011, p. 22)

The first conception clearly refers to the historical development of the professions between the Middle Ages and the Modern Age (Egetenmeyer & Käpplinger 2011, p. 23). Until recently, this concept has been discussed with reference to professional groups and ways in which it is possible to belong to them. From this perspective, the meaning directly relates to "special knowledge and skills [that] are needed to carry out a job in this field", but states that "special training or education [...] is formally required to get access to the profession" (Nuissl 2009, p. 127). This is the case for traditional professionals in the fields of law, medicine and primary education, for instance.

The second conception, according to the perspective of Egetenmeyer and Käpplinger, concerns "professionalization" as situated in a specific context that requires adequate personal and professional competences. In other words, professionals should be able "to put on professional glasses through which they can see situations clearly from the perspective of adult education. [...] Professionalism in this sense means understanding the situation in which professional acting is taking place" (Egetenmeyer & Käpplinger 2011, p. 25). In this approach, the concept, which is conceived from a broader and more open perspective, suggests investigating adult education to discover the characteristics and opportunities of this occupational field. Looking at the situation at the European level, we could state

---

attributes are presented on the labour market; (c) the environmental and social contexts (i.e., incentives and opportunities offered to update and validate their knowledge and skills); and (d) the economic context" (Cedefop 2008, p. 70).

that this field is "the educational sector most closely connected with many other societal actors" (Nuissl 2009, p. 127). Despite this, professionalism in adult education has not yet been clearly defined. This is why "in no country [in Europe] the access to a job in adult education is regulated for the whole field of adult education" (Nuissl 2009, p. 128) and there is often an overlap with other professional groups.

The factors that cause this situation in the adult education field are multiple. Institutional articulation of responsibilities at the macro-level, for example, usually "does not lie with one particular ministry but is spread over various ministries, such as education, the labour market, social affairs, culture or science" (Nuissl 2009, p. 128). It could represent the result of a low awareness of the added value of adult education across different sectors. Another factor can be observed in the fragility of adult educators' identity. As a matter of fact, "many adult education staff members do not even see themselves as adult educators but rather as belonging to a certain social or business context" (Nuissl 2009, p. 129). That is why we could assert that a public debate about adult education professionalization in Europe is not yet widespread. The case of Italy, presented in the following paragraphs, underlines this long-term process, but with some issues and progress that have been observed in recent years as well.

## The political framework for professionalization in adult education in Italy

The implementation of a national system of adult education in Italy has not been linear. In fact, it did not originate from a comprehensive framework of policy measures in education, training and culture. On the contrary, it developed within the actions of movements that supported broadening access to education within civil society (ISFOL 2008, p. 177). Over the decades, this has produced contradictions and tensions within the field that can still be identified even now, in modern times.

Historically, adult education started diffusing after World War II with associations for democratic education. In the 1970s, workers also became important in the spread of adult education, through the recognition of their rights to schooling (ISFOL 2008, p. 177). As a matter of fact, Law 300/1970, better known as the "Workers' Statute" (*Statuto dei Lavoratori*), enunciated for the first time, within Article 10, the right to obtain time in order to attend educational courses. During the '70s, many national collective contracts introduced time allowances for workers to participate in education, and granted 150 hours per year for additional education and flexible working time to enable this. This principle was specified more precisely by Presidential Decree 395/1988, which applied the "Right of 150 Hours" per year to public workers as well.

The most important event of the last decade of the twentieth century is Law 53/2000, which places a specific focus on the right to care and education. Law 300/1970 states the right to educational leave "to complete compulsory education or to obtain a secondary or higher education degree"[2] and the right to continuing educational leave "to increase knowledge and professional skills"[3] for a period not exceeding eleven months.

Over the same period, Ministerial Order No. 455 of 29 July 1997 of the Ministry of Education, University and Research established local permanent centres for adult education (CTP - *Centri Territoriali Permanenti*) that offered education and guidance services, basic skills courses and language and information technology courses. The aims were to foster adults' participation in formal learning and professional activities, and to support skills development connecting to work and social life (ISFOL 2008, p. 179). The CTP system was reformed by Presidential Decree 263/2012, which triggered a reorganization of the centres, now called provincial centres for adult education (CPIA - *Centri Provinciali per l'Istruzione degli Adulti*). The CPIAs

> *provide programmes corresponding to initial education up to the completion of compulsory education as well as language courses for immigrants. [...] All courses provided by CPIAs have a flexible organization, allowing for personalized study paths and the recognition of prior learning.*

(Eurydice 2015)

Another important political stage of the development of adult education is the Joint Conference for State Regions (*Conferenza Unificata Stato-Regioni*) of 2 March 2000, which approved the reorganization and strengthening of continuing education for adults. This document defined the field of adult education as "the set of opportunities at the formal level (school education and certified professional training) and at the non-formal level (culture, health education, social education, associations, physical education)".[4] The idea of continuing learning for adults has been further developed by Law 92/2012, which concerns the provisions for a growth-oriented reform of the labour market. Art. 4 defines lifelong learning as "all learning activity formally, non-formally and informally undertaken throughout life with the aim of improving knowledge, skills and competences in a personal, civic, social and/or employment-related perspective" (Eurydice 2015).

---

2   Own translation from Law 53/2000.
3   Own translation from Law 53/2000.
4   Own translation from Joint Conference State-Regions of 2 March 2000, http://archivio. pubblica.istruzione.it/dg_postsecondaria/allegati/acc020300.pdf.

The law also provides, for the first time, the definition of formal, non-formal and informal learning at the Italian level (Eurydice 2015), according to the European lifelong learning framework.

## Work fields for adult educators in Italy: challenges and opportunities

Italy has recently started developing the issue of professionalization in the adult education field. The profile of the adult educator was established only after World War II, when Italy faced the issue of re-building the country through popular education. With this aim, adult educators started operating "in associations, in religious contexts and in schools for adults" (Boffo, Kaleja & Fernandes 2016, p. 122) for "promoting basic literacy and numeracy skills" (EAEA 2011, p. 4). The qualification of the profile was established some decades later, in 1997, through Ministerial Order 455/1997, which implemented the Permanent Territorial Centres for Adult Learning and Training (CTP).

Over the same period, initial training for adult education at a higher level of education was also established. As a matter of fact, the study programme in adult education was implemented in 2001, when "the new policy on the length of degree programmes in higher education completely changed the face of the Italian university" (Boffo, Kaleja, Sharif-Ali & Fernandes 2016, p. 104). Law 240/2010 then implemented two different levels for initial training in adult education: a bachelor's course – "Education and Training Sciences" – and a master's course – "Adult Education and Continuing Training Sciences" (Boffo, Kaleja, Sharif-Ali & Fernandes 2016, p. 104). In this sense, the definition of the professional field of adult education

> only includes those profiles from whom adult learning constitutes the primary or most significant source of income. Adult learning includes activities aimed at recovering educational skills also within professionalization pathways.
>
> (Boffo, Kaleja, Sharif-Ali & Fernandes 2016, p. 105)

When it comes to the fields of adult educators, the Italian context presents opportunities for both the public and private sectors. In terms of the public sector, as stated above, the CTP scheme has represented the main development of adult education in recent decades. Nevertheless, the centres were replaced in 2012 by the CPIAs (Presidential Decree 263/2012), which focus more on delivering formal basic and secondary education. In fact, the provincial centres for adult education and upper secondary school are now "responsible for organisation and teaching in second level adult education pathways" (Eurydice

2015). Indeed, the CPIAs provide autonomous educational provision for adults and young adults "with specific and organisation structures [...] organised in territorial service networks, generally at the provincial level" (Eurydice 2015). They provide "first-level courses (divided into a first and second teaching term) and literacy or Italian language pathways [...]; – second level courses (divided into three teaching terms)" (Eurydice 2015*).*

The first-level pathways aim to lead to the achievement of the first cycle of educational qualification and the certificate of basic skills in compulsory education. On the other hand, the second-level education pathways aim to help participants obtain "certificates of technical, vocational or artistic education" (Eurydice 2015). The particular characteristic of this formal education is the personalization of pathways. In fact, "they can be personalised according to individual formative agreements upon recognition of the adult's knowledge, formal, informal and non-formal competences" (Eurydice 2015). There are now 126 CPIAs distributed throughout the nation.

Professionalization in the public sector is an important issue for adult educators, because "the profile of an adult educator is the same as that of a teacher (7 EQF)" (Boffo, Kaleja & Fernandes 2016, p. 123). In fact, CPIAs are formally considered public schools for adults and access to work is regulated. This produces a shift from adult "education" to "schooling", which is also exemplified by formal requirements for the teaching profession. The analysis of formal qualifications and degrees for access in CPIAs provides an impression of how adult education is conceived in Italy. In fact, Ministerial Decree 92/2016 stipulates the requirements for teaching Italian language to the L2 level. Through in-depth analysis, we can point out that there are specific mentions of language and literature studies, with specialization in L2 teaching, but there are no requirements that refer to adult education degrees.

For this reason, we can state that the reform that took place in 2012, from CTP to CPIA, represents a huge step back from the broad concept of adult education as "an educational sector most closely connected with many other societal actors" (Nuissl 2009, p. 127). The Italian pathway is heading towards a fixation on schooling, equating adult learning to that of school pupils. For this reason, formal requirements concentrate on basic knowledge and language degrees for high schools, with no attention paid to the soft and educational skills that are needed when working with adults.

On the other hand, adult education in Italy is represented by the private sector and the social economy. The term "social economy" is defined as:

*a specific part of the economy: a set of organizations (historically, grouped into four major categories: cooperatives, mutual, associations, and, more recently, foundations) that primarily pursue social aims and are characterised by participative governance systems.*

(European Commission 2013, p. 12).

In the sector, "education and training are one of the main fields" (Federighi 2015, p. 121) "aimed at boosting the knowledge, competences and capacities of both the people to whom the services are aimed, and the people who operate within the social enterprises" (Federighi 2015, p. 125). From this perspective, education and training cover:

*at least 75% of the social economy services:*
*– Social assistance services (e.g., childcare, eldercare, disability support);*
*– Education and training;*
*– Culture and recreation;*
*– Work integration, employment;*
*– Economic, social and community development[.]*

(Federighi 2015, pp. 123–124)

Such a rich labour market provides many employment opportunities for adult educators, especially for those with a degree in adult education and continuing training. As a matter of fact, the analysis of educational provision in the social economy[5] reveals many types of action. Educational events and services, the organization of learning processes and training management, policies and strategies (Federighi 2015, pp. 125–126) are just some examples that could involve adult educators at the micro-, meso- and macro-level in the social economy.

In recent years, the increasing "demand from social enterprises for qualified workers seems to be accompanied by a progressive improvement in working conditions" (Federighi 2015, pp. 129). In fact, the phenomenon of expansion in the social economy and the consequent opportunities for employment contribute to the "professionalization of the staff working within the social enterprises" (Federighi 2015, p. 129). If the initial phase of the social economy has been characterized by volunteers, recent developments have produced "the start of qualification requirements […] for internal processes" (Federighi 2015, p. 129).

---

5   The arguments refer to the SALM research project *Skills and Labour Market to Raise Youth Employment*, which aims "to contribute to the development of innovative approaches and specific instruments to reduce youth unemployment, equipping young people with the right skills for employment […] considering for instance senior tourism and social services" (Carneiro, Chau, Soares & Sousa Fialho 2015, p. 7).

Even though some research projects identified "a mismatch between the professionalism that is demanded on the one hand and supplied on the other" (Boffo 2015, p. 160), there is a high demand for people with specific skills in the adult education field. In spite of this, in terms of professionalization, adult educators in Italy are still considered "weak professions from the viewpoint of establishing a specific category, with defined competences and a definite and recognized profile" (Boffo 2015, p. 161). Nevertheless, social enterprises present:

> *the need for workers with transversal didactical-educational and communication-relational skills, but above all with competences in planning, accounting, needs analysis of the local area and of the companies involved in education and training.*

*(Boffo 2015, p. 161)*

According to this overview of the national situation in the adult education field, we can state that the private sector expresses, in ways either implicit or explicit, a growing demand for workers with specific professionalism in adult education. On the one hand, the challenge for these workers lies in the managerial and organizational skills that are also required in the workplace; this issue will be significant for the future of a closer relationship between higher education and the labour market.

## Conclusions

At the end of this brief country analysis, some challenges for adult education in Italy can be highlighted. In fact, the issues and opportunities presented above underline some elements for a broad analysis of the field in the whole country. First of all, the social recognition of the value of the professionalization of adult education seems strictly influenced by the recent development of the field at the higher-education level. The fact that Italy has established a broad legal and policy framework for adult education only in the last two decades represents an issue for the development of this professional sector. The fragmented institutional framework of adult education therefore reflects, in some ways, a low awareness of the field's identity. The conceptual shift from education to schooling, initiated through the introduction of the CPIA (Presidential Decree 263/2012), shows how the concept is conceived at the institutional level and sometimes generates misunderstanding among stakeholders.

Accordingly, an unclear understanding about what adult education is, and what skills are required to work in the field, affects the private sector directly, too. In fact, employers in the social economy really need workers with hard and soft skills that could be developed in adult education degree courses. Nevertheless,

they do not always recognize adult education graduates as candidates that meet
these requirements. In a certain way, this represents one of the biggest challenges
in the field. Moreover, issues for professionalization can be found at the micro-
level. Even though adult education is related to many non-formal and informal
contexts (as enterprises, cultural and non-profit associations, etc.), they often do
not perceive themselves as adult education professionals, but just "as belonging
to a certain social or business context" (Nuissl 2009, p. 129).

From this national analysis, we can therefore conclude that the challenge for
adult education in Italy is closely linked to cultural and political recognition of
the whole field. The absence of a public debate, policy understanding based largely
on the school-level process and the mismatch between private employers and the
demand for degrees reveal the great challenges that adult education professionals
in the country face.

## References

Bélanger, F. / Federighi, P.: *Unlocking people's creative forces.* UNESCO Institute
for Education: Hamburg. 2000.

Boffo, V.: "Employability for the social economy: The role of higher education". In:
V. Boffo / P. Federighi / F. Torlone: *Educational jobs: Youth and employability
in the social economy.* Firenze University Press: Firenze. 2015, pp. 147–168.

Boffo, V. / Federighi, P. / Torlone, F.: *Educational jobs: Youth and employability in
the social economy.* Firenze University Press: Firenze. 2015.

Boffo, V. / Kaleja, K. / Fernandes, J.: "Regulations and working conditions for
trainers in adult education: A comparative glance". In: R. Egetenmeyer (ed.):
*Adult education and lifelong learning in Europe and beyond. Comparative per-
spectives from the 2015 Würzburg Winter School.* Peter Lang GmbH: Frankfurt
am Main. 2016, pp. 103–120.

Boffo, V. / Kaleja, K. / Sharif-Ali, K. / Fernandes, J.: "The curriculum of study programmes for adult educators – the study cases of Italy, Germany and Portugal".
In: R. Egetenmeyer (ed.): *Adult education and lifelong learning in Europe and
beyond. Comparative perspectives from the 2015 Würzburg Winter School.* Peter
Lang GmbH: Frankfurt am Main. 2016, pp. 121–132.

Carneiro, R. / Chau, F. / Soares, C. / Sousa Fialho, J.A.: "Introduction: The aims
of the study". In: V. Boffo / P. Federighi / F. Torlone (eds.): *Educational jobs:
Youth and employability in the social economy.* Firenze University Press: Firenze. 2015, pp. 1–8.

Council of the European Union: *Council resolution on a renewed European agenda for adult learning*, Ref: 2011/C 372/01, 2011, retrieved March 2016, from http://eur-lex.europa.eu/legal-content/EN/TXT/PDF/?uri=CELEX:32011G1220(01) &from=EN.

Egetenmeyer, R. (ed.): *Adult education and lifelong learning in Europe and beyond. Comparative perspectives from the 2015 Würzburg Winter School*. Peter Lang GmbH: Frankfurt am Main. 2016.

Egetenmeyer, R. / Käpplinger, B.: "Professionalisation and quality management: struggles, boundaries and bridges between two approaches". *European Journal for Research on the Education and Learning of Adults* 2(1), April 2011, pp. 21–35.

European Association for the Education of Adults: *Country report on adult education in Italy*, 2011, retrieved March 2016, from www.eaea.org/country/italy.

European Commission (EC): *A memorandum on lifelong learning*, Ref: SEC (2000) 1832 final, 2000, retrieved March 2016, from http://arhiv.acs.si/dokumenti/Memorandum_on_Lifelong_Learning.pdf.

European Commission (EC): *Adult learning: It is never too late to learn*, Ref: COM (2006) 614 final, retrieved March 2016, from http://eur-lex.europa.eu/LexUriServ/LexUriServ.do?uri=COM:2006:0614:FIN:EN:PDF.

European Commission (EC): *Action Plan on Adult Learning: It is always a good time to learn*, Ref: COM (2007) 558 final, retrieved March 2016, from http://eur-lex.europa.eu/legal-content/EN/TXT/?uri=CELEX%3A52007DC0558.

European Commission (EC): *Social economy and social entrepreneurship: Social Europe guide*. European Union: Luxembourg. 2013.

Eurydice: *Italy: Adult education and training*, 2015, retrieved March 2016, from https://webgate.ec.europa.eu/fpfis/mwikis/eurydice/index.php/Italy: Overview.

Federighi, P.: *Adult and continuing education in Europe: Using public policy to secure a growth in skills*. Publications Office of the European Union: Luxembourg. 2013.

Federighi, P.: "How to solve the issue on mismatch between demand and supply of competences: Higher education of education and training professionals in the social economy". In: V. Boffo / P. Federighi / F. Torlone: *Educational jobs: Youth and employability in the social economy*. Firenze University Press: Firenze. 2015, pp. 121–146.

Federighi, P. / Torlone, F. (ed.): *Policies for regional cooperation in the field of lifelong learning*. Firenze University Press: Firenze. 2010.

ISFOL: *Sostenere la partecipazione all'apprendimento permanente*. ISFOL: Roma. 2008.

Nuissl, E.: "Profession and professional work in adult education in Europe". *Studi sulla Formazione* 1(2), 2009, pp. 127–132.

Presidency of the Republic: "Decree of the President of the Republic No. 263 of 29 October 2012: Regulation laying down general rules for the reorganization of teaching in adult education centers". *Gazzetta Ufficiale* 48 (general series), 25 February 2013.

Thöne-Geyer, B.: *Benefits of lifelong learning – BeLL: Final Report – Public Part*, 2014, retrieved July 2016, from http://www.bell-project.eu/cms/wp-content/uploads/2014/06/Final-Report1.pdf.

# Frames of Professionalization
# in Adult Education

Clara Kuhlen, Shalini Singh & Nicoletta Tomei

# The Higher Education Curriculum for the Professionalization of Adult Education

**Abstract:** The authors argue that the role of research, as a component of curricula, should be central in promoting professionalization in adult education, with strong international collaboration through networks, reflective practices and open, participatory academic interactions.

## Introduction

This article analyzes the role of curricula in shaping the professionalization of adult education through the comparison of curricula offered at the master's level in adult education in Germany, India and Italy. The authors seek an answer to the question: *which aspects of curricula contribute to the professionalization of graduate adult educators in different contexts?*

Content analysis of scientific texts, combined with a descriptive and critical approach, has been used to compare and draw inferences. Due to the lack of academic literature on the topic in the Indian context, oral interviews were carried out to supplement the scientific sources and policy documents. Relevant contextual aspects of the various curricula have been described and considered along with challenges and prospects regarding the process of professionalization of adult education as it emerges in different contexts.

Adult education is a special field where skills to educate adult learners are important and adult educators take on the role of facilitators. As such, the learning environment becomes an important factor in shaping the competencies of adult educators, and the authors use the term "curriculum" to refer to the formal and non-formal content that are used to help participants develop the competencies necessary to act as adult educators in different professional and national contexts.

## The higher education curriculum for the professionalization of adult education in India

The professionalization of adult education in the Indian context can be seen as "a long process by which a profession succeeds over a period of time in meeting the criteria of a professional gamut. It includes an enhancement in status and professionalism of knowledge and skills involved in the professional practice." (Shah 2009, p.10)

Knowledge and skills in adult education may be gained by pursuing professional programmes in a particular discipline. In India, adult education as an academic
discipline is often conceptualized as a field of knowledge that is supposed to bring
about a direct social transition. Professionals in the field of adult education are
usually assumed to be more engaged with marginalized sections of society, rather
than spending most of their professional career in an "ivory tower" (Kumar 2016,
personal communication)[1]. Even if they are engaged in research or work as professional master trainers, the content and subject matter they deal with is related
largely to impoverished and vulnerable members of society. Owing to the size of
the population that is increasingly being pushed to the margins, the profession of
adult education has become quite challenging and not so attractive in terms of job
satisfaction and professional gratification (Shah 2016, personal communication).

Master's programmes help participants to understand the discipline compre-
hensively and offer opportunities for specialization. Universities design curricula
autonomously for the courses in accordance with the guidelines provided by the
government. In general, the structure of curricula in India is highly interdisciplinary and lectures offering exposure to the field and experiential learning are used
as transactional methods. The mode of evaluation includes exams at the end of
each semester coupled with assignments, dissertations, paper presentations and
reports. Unlike in Europe, where adult education caters to the needs of all adults,
the thrust of adult education in India comprises dealing with marginalized sections of society and forms the core component in the curriculum. Contextual
components supersede statistical and theoretical components in research, while
policy studies and the study of evolutionary aspects of the discipline command the
least attention. Specializations like counselling, human resource management and
skill development and extension are offered in many universities, which, in a sense,
is a good practice as it offers variations and broadens the scope of the programmes.
However, it also makes the basis of the discipline rather loose and unstructured.

A critical evaluation of the curricula shows that in order to achieve professionalization in the discipline, several changes in the current curricula are required.
Outcomes of experiential learning need to be research-oriented rather than intended to merely expose learners to fieldwork (Rajesh 2016, personal communication). Furthermore, research should promote the development of theoretical

---

1   This paper benefits from communication with the following experts in adult education
    and lifelong learning: Prof. Søren Ehlers, Aarhus University; Prof. S.Y. Shah, Internatio-
    nal Institute for Lifelong Learning and Education; Prof. Ajay Kumar, Jawaharlal Nehru
    University; Dr. V. Balaji, Director, State Resource Centre, Chennai; and Prof. Rajesh,
    University of Delhi.

paradigms, models and frameworks that could provide a strong base for the discipline as well as for professionalization in adult education. Adaptability in the curricula according to the needs of the current job-market is also required. Better career prospects after pursuing adult education programmes will attract talent and contribute to creating a pool of quality resources that could lead the discipline towards more professionalization (Shah 2016, personal communication).

Lifelong learning and skill development initiatives have offered enormous scope for the expansion of the discipline and its professionalization, but there is a need to include more individuals trained professionally in the field with exposure to research and international best practice (Rajesh 2016, personal communication). International collaboration will give the discipline additional strength by providing practical options for mobility, exposure to best practice, standardized research opportunities, a solid foundation to the discipline and new information. On the other hand, collaboration with India can enrich theoretical research abroad and practical aspects of research could be tested through reflection on the Indian experience. This will enable the current collaboration between countries to attain a truly global character, promote professionalization of adult education in a more integrated, transnational manner and provide adult educators with tools for countering and acting beyond the structural constraints imposed by their own contexts in favour of opportunities to influence those contexts in the long run.

## The higher education curriculum for the professionalization of adult education in Italy

The low relevance that Italian policy has traditionally assigned to educational issues is preventing the development of clear indications about the pathways through which it is possible to acquire professionalization in adult education. A master's qualification is just one of many pathways through which it is possible to develop the competences demanded by the labour market. Adult and continuing education graduates in fact develop sector-oriented professional skills and also fulfil the prerequisites for acquiring the national qualification to work in provincial centres for adult education (INDIRE 2006, p. 75; ISFOL 2014, p. 51).

Master's programmes in adult and continuing education were introduced after the implementation of the Bologna Process (1999). As Alberici recalls, it "is with the academic reform [...] that curricula for the professionalization of adult education professionals has found – for the first time – a recognition and a specific position in the university structure" (Alberici & Orefice 2007, p. 29). Master's programmes in Italy indicate the willingness to develop professional profiles able to perform management, planning, implementation and evaluation of educational and training actions in the different sectors of adult and continuing education. Since the implementation of Law 270/2004, "*Regulation and norms for the didactical autonomy of the Universities*", which was introduced to rationalize academic training on offer for a better marketability of university degrees, graduates who hold a degree in adult and continuing education must possess certain competences which can be developed through the following groups of activities:

- Basic activities, aimed at providing a solid expertise in educational, methodological and didactical subjects
- Characterizing activities, aimed at providing advanced knowledge about training needs analysis at the individual and organizational level
- Additional activities, aimed at providing technical and professional competences related to ethics, economy, law and policy
- Research activities, often combined with internships, aimed at producing the ability to problematize, conceptualize and argue about the field of adult education in a scientific and reflective way

After the implementation of the new regulation, eleven universities have started master's programmes in adult and continuing education. While one of them closed the programme in 2013, nine of the original programmes implemented are still under way. Since the academic years of 2015/2016, a tenth university has built up its own programme, as well. The curricula defined by these universities can be examined based on the scientific sector, which is assigned to each of their teachings. For the purpose of this paper, the scientific sectors, defined by the Ministry with the ministerial decree of 18 March 2005, can be grouped into five categories: pedagogical teaching, psychological teaching, sociological teaching, technical teachings and humanities.

The change in regulations should have contributed to triggering an innovation process of academic curriculum design in adult and continuing education, but in general, all the curricula remain closely linked to a pedagogical approach that brings together the humanities, sociology and psychology. With the significant exception of one university, which allows psychology only as an elective course, technical teachings are residual almost everywhere and internships are still missing at two universities. Only the presence of a variable amount of ECTS left to student choice seems to guarantee the strengthening of methodological dimensions and technical competences as requested by the Ministry. Nevertheless, the epistemological perspective of each university is crucial for defining the eligible training activities that can be accredited (Alberici & Orefice 2007, p. 114).

Due to these considerations, the Italian pathways to the academic professionalization of adult and continuing education seem to be characterized by a large amount of autonomy given to institutions and students. This confirms the pluralistic and even non-systematic approach of the entire Italian system of professionalization in adult and continuing education (Boffo 2010, p. 45). It also supports the idea that if "what unites the family of education and training professionals is the function of providing services and opportunities to increase people's skills in various moments of their lives and to develop the organizations' possessed knowledge" (Federighi 2015, p. 33), then professionalization through higher education can be understood in two senses: firstly, as the initial pathways through which someone becomes a professional in the field, where they start to acquire skills and competences that ensure the ability to perform a wide range of roles (educators, teachers, tutors, service managers, HR managers, etc.); secondly, as the processes that allow/qualify professionals to move through the different levels at which they perform their duties (operational, management, strategic level), further developing their professionalism.

## The higher education curriculum for the professionalization of adult education in Germany

Since the Bologna Process has been initiated and its main objectives have been transferred to the German higher education system, a wide range of recommendations for action has been materializing in this particular field of education. In the case of adult education, the development of master's programmes plays a crucial role when it comes to the education and training of future professionals (Egetenmeyer & Schüßler 2013). The following section aims to provide an insight into processes of professionalization for adult educators through these master's programmes, structured by a legislative framework and the higher education institutes (HIEs) themselves.

Through the so-called "Framework Act for Higher Education", the German Rector's Conference (2007) is influencing the structures of HEIs to prepare students for future careers within their disciplines. Furthermore, the statement includes the importance of imparting field-related knowledge, skills and methods to foster scientific or artistic work within a liberal, democratic and social constitutional state (HRK 2007, pp. 3–4; HRK 2013, pp. 3–9). This assumption about the role of HEIs is worded in general terms and originated in the lack of an overall legislative background concerning access to the field of adult education in Germany. Given the sovereignty of the federal states, the *Länder*, the federal government does not influence processes of professionalization. Hence, the professionalization of adult educators appears to be a wide field and is thus hard to survey in Germany as a whole (Research voor Beleid 2010, p. 209).

As a reaction to the lack of a comprehensive framework, the German Society for Educational Science (2006) developed a core curriculum for both bachelor's and consecutive master's level studies in adult education, consisting of nine study units in total. It is based on the further development of former recommendations, such as core curricula in educational science or suggestions for basic curricula in adult education that were published in 2004/2005. The implementation of a core curriculum aims to make studies at different institutions comparable, to enhance the student's mobility and to facilitate the understanding and agreement of graduates within different occupational areas. The "core curriculum" itself only includes a compulsory minimum of contents that are considered central and overarching. They are derived from the field of educational science and adult education. The universities hold the responsibility for specifying modules, volumes and their delivery within the institutions themselves. Whereas bachelor's-level studies focus on attaining basic knowledge about adult education, master's studies imply an explicit specification in the field of adult education (DGfE 2006, pp. 1–6). The following list outlines a model of the four study units for master's studies (DGfE 2006, pp. 5–6).

- Study Unit 6 (from core curriculum ed.sc.) *Educational research and methodological basics*: qualitative and quantitative methods, theoretically relevant approaches from educational science, educational research
- Study Unit 7 *Theory, research and frame conditions of adult and continuing education*: historical basics, theoretical and actual developments, state of research and future perspectives, political, legal and economic framework conditions
- Study Unit 8 *Professional competences in adult education*: introduction to educational management, development of competences in the field of educational management, staff development/HR, quality management, controlling, evaluation, programme planning, marketing, teaching, organization of didactical and methodological setting for learning and teaching
- Study Unit 9 *Study-research project*: research question from the field of adult education; can be combined with internship

The core curriculum for master's students highlights the importance of a basic body of knowledge, scientific reflection on this knowledge and specified educational competences. As Egetenmeyer and Lattke (2009) argue, professionalization is closely linked to competences and can be defined as the visible, repeatable articulation or performance of them, within the framework of a professional's work. For the development of this professionalization, the scientific and reflexive character of higher education can be considered crucial, since competences are being continuously developed and reflected on in this context (Egetenmeyer & Lattke 2009, pp. 1–11). The body of knowledge that these assumptions are based on is structured by the curriculum (Egetenmeyer & Schüßler 2013, pp. 17–34). In line with this rationale, the core curriculum for master's-level studies in adult education in Germany is rendering major contributions to processes of academic professionalization of adult educators within HEIs.

## Comparison between India, Italy and Germany

Since comparative studies are not just juxtapositions of mere data, similarities and differences were identified in order to extract meaningful information from national databases (Reischmann 2009). From this perspective, the curricula were analyzed according to the relevance of certain categories: 1) terminology related to curricula and 2) the concept of professionalization as perceived in higher education.

### Terminology used in higher education curricula

Comparison shows that terminology and concepts used in higher education curricula for adult education are contextual rather than standardized. Commonly used names for curricula are "adult education (and continuing education)" or "lifelong learning". While in Europe terms show an economic lineage ("Educational Services Management and Continuing Education" in Italy or "Educational Management" in Germany), in India a social lineage is visible ("Development Extension"). German universities, highly influenced by the Ministers' Conference and the Bologna Process, mostly use terms such as competence, research, management, learning or teaching. Though prevalent in other countries as well, they are supplemented with other catchphrases such as training needs and autonomy in Italy, as stated by Law 270/2004. In India, terms like empowerment, marginalized, skills, community engagement, development and literacy are mainly used, due to the importance of non-governmental organizations that are often closely related to community work. Concept analysis points out that Italy and Germany prioritize research and teaching, while India prioritizes fieldwork and experiential learning. There are some common tenets such as the interdisciplinary approach, as well as the recognition of experiential learning such as internships and fieldwork.

### Professionalization through higher education curricula

Comparison reveals that professionalization processes within higher education are often affected by labour market trends and policy influences. In India, government policies influence the development of curricula as well as non-governmental organizations. In Germany, professionalization through higher education curricula is influenced by legal frameworks, but also by professional national networks (e.g., DIE) and international ones. In Italy, where the autonomy of universities is relatively new, ministerial regulations still have a deep impact on the professionalization of adult education (Ministerial Decree 2007, p. 4). In all three countries, the professionalization of adult educators is characterized as a process through which individuals in the field perform to fulfil the needs of their profession.

Despite the provision of academic schooling, adult educators can enter the field through various study paths, which 1) leads to a mild polarization between graduate and non-graduate professionals in Italy, 2) prevents the possibility of accessing high-income jobs in India and 3) distinguishes between the professionalization of the field and professionals in Germany. Moreover, adult education professionals are identified by their roles as teachers, HR managers, trainers or community workers rather than by their function as reflective practitioners and facilitators of human potential. Through professionalization, they are building up certain sector-oriented competencies whilst using a specialized body of knowledge in their specific contexts (Boffo 2010, pp. 45–46; Egetenmeyer & Schüßler 2013; Shah 2016, personal communication). In all three countries, professionalization may be understood as both the development of the profession of adult education and the development of professionalism among adult educators as individual actors. Following the comparison of curricula, a reflective approach to both research and fieldwork is a crucial aspect in all countries, as it offers the basis for building up new curricula, further developing existing ones and providing professionals with a shared body of knowledge.

## Conclusion

Aspects of curricula that help to develop the competencies of adult educators as practitioners are a crucial element of professionalization through higher education. While it is not possible to compare detailed contents of curricula because they are often contextually bound and country-specific, commonalities were revealed through analyzing terminology and the aspects of professionalization through higher education. Though curricula in all three countries focus on the development of individual competencies, the curricula of the two European countries show an economic lineage, while those of India show a social lineage. The influence of government regulations in European countries was shown mainly through the Bologna Process and thus the supranational institution, the European Union. In India, national and non-governmental actors are more influential.

As an overall result, curricula that promote professionalization in various settings differ due to their contexts, and so does the role of professional adult educators, fostered through higher education curricula. For a more common understanding of professionalization of adult education, international networks may help to develop a strong body of knowledge for the discipline. Furthermore, reflective mind-sets and the exchange of expertise from both research and field-work could challenge structural constraints that often restrict professionalization processes in the context of higher education.

## References

Alberici, A. / Orefice, P. (eds.): *Le nuove figure professionali della formazione adulta: Profili e formazione universitaria.* Franco Angeli: Milano. 2007.

Beleid, R.V.: *ALPINE – Adult Learning Professions in Europe: A study of the current situation, trends and issues: Final Report.* Zoetemeer. 2010, rerieved 13.1.2016, from http://www.ginconet.eu/sites/default/files/library/ALPINE.pdf.

Boffo, V.: "Training and professionalisation pathways: A comparative analysis". In: A. Strauch / M. Radtke / R. Lupou (eds.): *Flexible pathways towards professionalism: Senior adult educators in Europe.* W. Bertelsmann Verlag: Bielefeld. 2010, pp. 39–53.

DGfE, D.G.: *Kerncurriculum für konsekutive Bachelor/Master-Studiengänge im Hauptfach Erziehungswissenschaft mit der Studienrichtung Erwachsenenbildung/ Weiterbildung.* 2006, retrieved 10.4.2016, from http://www.dgfe.de/fileadmin/ Ord-nerRedakteure/Stellungnahmen/2006 KCE_EB-WB_konsekutiv.pdf.

Egetenmeyer, R. / Lattke, S.: "Professionalisierung mit internationalem Label". *Bildungspolitische Statements und akademische Praxis* 63(73) (REPORT), 2009, pp. 63–73, retrieved 13.1.2016, from http://www.die-bonn.de/doks/ report/2009-internationale-erwachsenenbildung-01.pdf.

Egetenmeyer, R. / Schüßler, I.: "Zur akademischen Professionalisierung in der Erwachsenenbildung/Weiterbildung". In: R. Egetenmeyer / I. Schüßler / R. Arnold (eds.): *Akademische Professionalisierung in der Erwachsenenbildung/ Weiterbildung.* Schneider: Baltmannsweiler. 2013, pp. 17–34.

Federighi, P.: "How to solve the issue on mismatch between demand and supply of competences: Higher education of education and training professionals in the social economy". In: V. Boffo / P. Federighi / F. Torlone (eds.): *Educational jobs: Youth and employability in the social economy: Investigations in Italy, Malta, Portugal, Sain, United Kingdom.* Florence University Press: Firenze. 2015.

HRK, H.: *Hochschulrahmengesetz (HRG),* 2007, retrieved 9.3.2016, from http:// www.gesetze-im-internet.de/bundesrecht/hrg/gesamt.pdf

HRK, H.: "Hochschulrektorenkonferenz Entschließung des 124. Senats der Hochschulrektorenkonferenz". Berlin, 11 June 2013, retrieved 20.4.2016, from http://www.hrk.de/uploads/tx_szconvention/Entschliessung_Perspekti-ven_11062013.pdf.

INDIRE: *L'educazione degli adulti in Europa: I quaderni di eurydice* (25). Istituto nazionale per la documentazione, l'innovazione e la ricerca educative: Roma. 2006.

ISFOL: *Istruzione degli Adulti: Politiche e casi significativi sul territorio*. Istituto per la formazione professionale dei Lavoratori: Roma. 2014.

European Ministers of Education: *The Bologna declaration of 19 June 1999: Joint declaration of the European Ministers of Education*. The European Higher Education Area. 1999, retrieved from http://www.magna-charta.org/resources/files/text-of-the-bologna-declaration.

Kumari, P.V.: "Adult/Continuing education in Indian universities". *Journal AED: Adult Education at Universities* 56, 2001, retrieved 1.5.2016, from https://www.dvv international.de/adult-education-and-development/editions/aed-562001/adult-education at-universities/adult-continuing-education-in-indian-universities/.

Law 270/2004: *Regulation and norms for the didactical autonomy of the universities*, 22 October 2004, retrieved 22.5.2016, from http://www.miur.it/0006Menu_C/0012Docume/0098Nor-mat/4640Modifi_cf2.htm.

Ministry of Education, University and Research: "Ministerial acts: Determination of degree classes: 16 March 2007". *The Official Journal of 9 July 2007*, n. 155, retrieved 22.5.2016, from http://attiministeriali.miur.it/anno-2007/marzo/dm-16032007.aspx.

Peters, R.: "Erwachsenenbildungs-Professionalität: Ansprüche und Realitäten". In: W. Tietgens / DIE (eds.): *Theorie und Praxis der Erwachsenenbildung*. Bertelsmann: Bielefeld. 2004.

Reischmann, J.: *ISCAE-International Society for Comparative Adult Education*, 2009, retrieved 21.7.2016, from htttp://www.ISCAE.org.

Semrau, F. / Vieira, N.G. / Guida, E.: "Academic professionalisation in adult education: Insights into study programs in Germany, Italy and Portugal". In: R. Egetenmeyer (ed.): *Adult education and lifelong learning in Europe and beyond: Comparative perspectives from the 2015 Würzburg Winter School*. Peter Lang: Frankfurt am Main. 2015, pp. 133–146.

Shah, S.Y.: "Mapping the field of training in adult and lifelong learning in India". *Teachers and trainers in adult education and lifelong learning: Professional development in Asia and Europe*. German Institute for Adult Education: Bergisch Gladbach (Germany). 29–30 June 2009, retrieved 1.5.2016, from https://www.die-bonn.de/asem/asem0921.pdf.

UNESCO: *Glossary of curriculum terminology*. International Bureau of Education: Genf. 2013a.

UNESCO: *Second global report on learning and education: Rethinking literacy*. UNESCO Institute for Lifelong Learning: Hamburg. 2013b.

## Data used for comparison of university programmes

*Germany*

*Hochschulkompass* (2016): *Erweiterte Studiengangssuche. Studientyp: weiterführend; Fachsuche: Erwachsenenbildung.* Accessed on 22.05.2016: http://www.hoch schulkompass.de/studium/suche/erweiterte-suche/search/1/studtyp/ 2.html?tx_szhrksearch_pi1%5Bxtend%5D=1&tx_szhrksearch_ pi1%5Bfach%5D=erwachsenenbild-ung&tx_szhrksearch_pi1%5Bsit%5D=1&tx_ szhrksearch_pi1%5Bsitena-bled%5D=0&tx_szhrksearch_pi1%5 Bmas-ter%5D=0&tx_szhrksearch_pi1%5Bpointer%5D=0.

*Italy*

Universitaly-Web portal of the Ministry of Education, University and Research (2015). Accessed 22.05.2016: http://www.universitaly.it/index.php/.

*India*

North Eastern Hill University (Meghalaya) (2015–16): *M.A. Adult and Continuing Education*

SNDT Women's University (Maharashtra) (2015–16): *M.A. Non-formal Education and Development*

HNB Garhwal Central University (Uttarakhand) (2015–16): *M.A. Extension Education* •

Sri Venkateswara University (Andhra Pradesh) (2015–16): *M.A. in adult education*

The Global Open University (2015–16): *M.A. adult education*

Indira Gandhi National Open University (2015–16): *M.A. adult education*

University of Delhi: *M.A. Lifelong Learning and Extension*

Gaia Gioli & Rute Ricardo

# Employability and Phd Curricula. The Case Studies of Italy, Malaysia and Portugal[1]

**Abstract:** This paper departs from the basic question about which skills PhD programmes are offering in adult education and which are those required by the labour market. How can these skills sustain the PhD holders' employability? The paper compares examples from Italy, Portugal and Malaysia.

## The Theoretical Framework

Recent research (Schulz 2008; Vieira & Marques 2013) shows that new and higher levels of soft skills[2] will be needed in society and that education and training play a role in achieving this end. As a matter of fact, the Bologna Process called for an urgent reform of the higher education system so universities could become sources of change and innovation.

Institutions of higher education across Europe are being forced to create a new relationship with the labour market, and to increase the employability of their graduates. This implies a commitment for universities to redesign their curricula based on the analysis and re-interpretation of the demands of businesses. The most pressing of these seems to be providing people with soft skills that can be applied in working contexts, as some national and EU-funded projects demonstrate (e.g., Tuning, Modes, SALM[3], PRIN EMP&Co.[4]).

---

1 The paper represents the work of all authors, although Part 1, 3, 5 are written by Rute Ricardo and Part 2, 4, 8, 9 are written by Gaia Gioli.

2 We will refer to skills, although there are several possible objections to the use of this term, as Holmes (2001) has highlighted.

3 The SALM – Skills and Labour Market to Raise Youth Employment – is a European Project (527690-LLP-1-2012-1-PT-LEONARDO-LM SALM Project – 2012–2014) (aiming at defining soft skills for the development of professional profiles in the Social Economy).

4 The Project PRIN EMP&Co. Employability & Competences – Curricula innovativi per creare nuove professionalità PRIN 2012 LATR9N – is an Italian national project financed by the Ministry of Education, University and Research and focused on the development of educational actions and curricula that can foster the employability of Italian graduates in the new professions.

Over recent decades, the social economy[5], which has been considered the major actor in matching social needs and the main fields of work for graduates in adult education, has experienced a significant increase in social workers in contrast to other economic sectors that have been suffering from the financial recession. As a consequence, the social economy requires higher levels of qualification and specialization. Starting from these points of observation, we try to analyze the characteristics of the demand for competences in the social economy in order to draw the indicators for an employability-oriented curriculum.

It is important to focus on three important concepts in the field of soft skills that will help us to understand this topic: *soft skills, employability and transitions.*

## Soft skills

Various lists of skills are discussed in the literature and, since the 1980s, a very important role has been played by "transferable" or "general" and "soft skills". More recently, they have been presented as generic skills by Yorke (2006a) when referring to the work of Bennett (2000) and all the skills required in the wider economy in all professional contexts.

Nowadays, as a response to increasing social demands, higher education is expected to produce innovative, collaborative and interdisciplinary knowledge (Holley 2015). However, we consider that there are some main transferable skills that are very important in every working context, and especially for educators: namely, listening and communication skills (see the following paragraph).

## Employability

Many interpretations (Yorke 2004; Watts 2006) define employability as the propensity for graduates to get a job and progress in their career. Employability can be seen as a lifelong process that is complex and involves a large number of interconnected aspects; it is "about supporting students to develop a range of knowledge, skills, behaviours, attributes and attitudes which will enable them to be successful not just in employment but in life" (Cole & Tibby 2013, p. 5).

Harvey (2003, p. 3) has also contested that employability is not just about getting a job, but "about learning and the emphasis is less on 'employ' and more on 'ability'. In essence, the emphasis is on developing critical, reflective abilities, with a view to empowering and enhancing the learner".

---

5   The authors identified the Social Economy according to the classification adopted by the European Commission (2011) and taken up by CIRIEC (2012).

Some of the conclusions of Harvey's work are that employability is not something different from learning and pedagogy, but something that grows and improves with good learning; employability is not just about gaining the skills to get a job. Harvey (2002, 2003, 2006), together with Yorke and Knight (2002, 2004, 2006), has developed a new idea of employability, in connection with higher education and relevant curricula. In their opinion, employability is essential for society, and higher education institutions must consider the nature of employability in their educational vision. Modernizing didactics, increasing traineeships and creating curricula with embedded employability are the tools they possess that can be shared with businesses, entrepreneurs and private/public institutions. Indeed, the development of employability is very important not only for the self, but also for all of society, since it can influence social, economic and political well-being (Boffo 2016) through the well-being of the individuals.

## Transition

Since the 1960s, it has been possible to refer to studies in the field of transitions. But it was the unemployment and economic crisis of the 1970s that increased the visibility of this concept. It is to be noted that although transitions are part of everyone's life, they are much more evident when the focus is on youth (Fragoso et al. 2013).

When looking at the concept of "transitions", a first approach argues that transitions are a process of multiple changes that bring individuals into contact with new contexts or life circumstances. Bernard Gazier and Jérôme Gautie (2011, p. 2) define transition along these lines. They identify the phenomenon as an "*Übergang*" in the transitional labour market approach (TLM). Some other authors highlight the importance of reflecting on the factors that bring people to experience a transition, which go beyond individual and psychological ones (Fragoso et al. 2013). In recent decades, some researchers have identified a new reflexive model based on the link between structure and agency (Fragoso et al. 2013).

According to Harvey (2003), transitions do indeed tend to be hard. From the perspective of this author, successful transitions from higher education to work require the use of tacit knowledge related to everyday skills and learning.

## Listening and communication as basic skills for adult educators

So what does building up a hidden curriculum for adult educators mean when talking about employability and transitions?

In the opinion of the authors, the pedagogical dimension of curriculum design lies at a micro-level. Thus, we cannot talk about a doctoral curriculum in adult education without considering the competences that PhD students should acquire in order to be able to manage their professional paths.

Nowadays, communication is important at every level and utilizes every possible tool; we live in a society full of social media posts, tweets, images, sounds and rumours, where the said and the unsaid have been replaced by the tools of communication, and where the content has become less important than the context. On the contrary, an educational relationship based on empathy (Stein 1985) still has an important message to give, and it is one that needs to be heard. It is precisely in the capability to listen carefully and pay attention to others (Rogers 1980) that the role of the adult educator finds its basis.

To become professionals in adult education, PhD students must thus receive an *ad hoc* education that enables them to develop their active listening and communicative skills and to analyze the contexts of education critically. For all these reasons, we believe that active listening and communication are central aspects of the hidden curriculum for employability.

As a consequence, the design and creation of a curriculum is not just a technicality, but uses *formation* as an educational dimension that will be built upon by the future professionals and their educational relationships. These will be relationships where others feel, e.g., comfortable, understood, not judged and free to express their opinions (La Rochefoucauld de F. 2001).

## Case studies of Italy, Portugal and Malaysia

Nowadays, the learning and quality of professionals should correspond to the often messy and complex nature of real-world problems (Elias & Purcell 2004; Holley 2015). In spite of their relevance, PhD programmes have been criticized for not preparing graduates to function effectively in a global, complex and interdisciplinary environment (Manathunga, Lant & Mellick 2006, in Holley 2015).

According to the ESRALE project,[6] doctoral studies as "the way to building up the European knowledge society in a globalized economy" should be "able to link the political goals of increasing the quality of postgraduate programs, meet the needs of a wider employment market, and combine tradition and innovation" (ESRALE). In this sense, the connection between doctoral work, higher education and adult learning is very important (Communiqué of the Conference of European Ministers Responsible for Higher Education 2009).

---

6   The ESRALE project is developing a model of a master's degree and PhD programme in adult education with a partnership between 10 European universities and research institutes that are working towards the creation of a joint master's degree and joint PhD.

The following chapter adopts a qualitative research methodology based on the comparison of three case studies regarding the PhD curricula in adult education in Portugal, Italy and Malaysia.

## The case of the PhD School in Education and Psychology of the University of Florence, Italy

The Italian doctorate is characterized by a very flexible structure that has been developed over the last 10 years as a consequence of the harmonization process that took place at the European level,[7] and was implemented at a national level.[8]

Italian providers[9] of doctoral education can adopt a light structure that fosters the development of a research mindset, flexibility of thought, creativity and intellectual autonomy through contribution to the creation of new knowledge in research and didactics, and in connection with the labour market or within civil society with the support of high-level professionals.

Although the introduction of a doctoral school – as a substitute for the old PhD courses – dates back a while, the absence of a specific definition of "doctoral school" presented an obstacle to the homogenous development of a national third tier of higher education. Italian universities, in accordance with the autonomy principle, have developed very varied PhD programmes.

Looking at the University of Florence, for example, the PhD in Education and Psychology is organized into four main curricula: The History and Theory of the Learning Process; Quality of Knowledge; Research Methodology for the Socio-Educational Services; and Psychology for Education, Organizations and the Labour Market (PhD in Education and Psychology, University of Florence 2015).

This division has been developed in the awareness that a PhD study programme represents not only the pinnacle of higher education of future skilled professionals in the pedagogical and psychological spheres, but also forms the link between pedagogics and educators with other professionals within a

---

7    We refer to the 2005 "10 Salzburg Principles" and to the 2009 Communiqué of the Conference of European Ministers Responsible for Higher Education that stated the necessity to create a curriculum tailored to individuals' learning needs through the creation of flexible and high-quality paths.

8    The Italian ministerial decree No. 262/2004 for the planning of education for the years 2004–2006 introduced a new model of PhD through the creation of doctoral schools as autonomous organizations.

9    According to the ministerial decree No. 45/2013, the institutions that can offer PhDs are both private and public universities and consortia of universities.

labour market that recognizes – and encourages the recognition of – the skills possessed by experts in education.

Therefore, the course is driven by the need to recognize the learning and relevant practical experience that allow the acquisition of knowledge and skills needed by researchers and practitioners who will be employed inside and outside of academia. It is divided into four parts in order to ease the acquisition of specific epistemological and methodological skills, disciplinary expertise and soft skills that fit the specificity of the research field. The format for delivery includes lectures, international experiences and interactive workshops, as well as other learning activities that can be intentional or not (Jarvis 2010).

## The case of the adult education PhD programme at the University of Lisbon, Portugal

In the case of the PhD programme in the field of Education at the University of Lisbon, the main aim is to develop theoretical and methodological tools that allow students to develop research projects in that field.

The PhD programme offers a variety of specialization paths, such as the education of adults, teacher training, the psychology of education, supervision in education, administration and educational politics, the didactics of maths and sciences, the philosophy of education, the history of education and technologies and communication in education.

When taking a look at the adult education programme, we can see that it is oriented towards the interrelationship between education, training and work. The main themes are related to public policies for education and training for young adults and adults; policies and practices of professional training in enterprises; the relationship between education, training and work; employment and professional insertion; experiential learning; the recognition, validation and certification of knowledge acquired throughout life; and popular education and social emancipation, etc. (Education PhD programme 2014).

This PhD programme is organized in two separate phases. The first phase includes mandatory classes in the first year, which consist of four seminars in the first semester (thematic seminar I, research seminar I, project seminar I and transdisciplinary seminar I) and four seminars in the second semester (thematic seminar II, research seminar II, project seminar II and transdisciplinary seminar II).

These seminars represent three different pedagogic modalities: the presentation of fundamental topics related to the field of adult education and work with research methodologies; moments for analysis and discussion about relevant authors and scholars; and the individual support work/projects of the students.

These sessions enable students to consolidate new knowledge and, at the same time, improve their theoretical and methodological knowledge. They are based on debate, discussions and analysis. At the end of the first year, students should be able to present their PhD project. This project is a complete work that includes the research question, the main aims, the principal theoretical topics, the methodology and the chronology of the PhD research. In other words, this project forms the basis for research and will be evaluated as a solid starting point for future work. In the second and following years, students study and work autonomously.

It could be stated that this pedagogical option for the PhD demands the active participation of students, some basic knowledge and a good deal of personal investment for the construction of a subject with deep theoretical-methodological knowledge. We can say that this PhD, through research activities, conference and seminar participation and informal conversations with peers and faculty, demonstrates an awareness of the skills inherent to interdisciplinary work and practice in debate, critical thought, discussions, reflection and the development of the ability to employ these emerging skills. According to Holley (2015), interdisciplinary work is a crucial domain for preparing individuals in their personal lives and social and research fields.

## Case study of the PhD programme in education in Malaysia

The PhD programme at the National University of Malaysia (Universiti Kebangsaan Malaysia – UKM) is managed by the UKM Graduate Centre, which provides higher education courses for the country. Indeed, it leads the education of future researchers trying to develop their sense of belonging to the country. The most important document for this aim is that containing the national guidelines. In a certain way, the UKM graduate centre works for the reproduction of the national educational system. In that sense, it is responsible for guiding the transfer of knowledge between generations of researchers.

Malaysia is characterized by the absence of a PhD programme specializing in adult education, yet it has a wide curriculum in education. PhD candidates are able to choose a course in adult education in accordance with their interests, as the programme offers them freedom of choice.

According to the UKM guidelines, PhD students should develop some specific soft skills by participating in formal, non-formal and informal learning activities (such as support programmes, formal teaching and courses or campus life) that are organized in accordance with a clearly defined didactical model created in conjunction with the Ministry of Higher Education.

According to Malaysia's Ministry of Higher Education (2006), the main soft skills that a PhD student should develop are the abilities to:

- demonstrate a systematic comprehension and in-depth understanding of the theory and practices of the education discipline as a whole, and mastery of skills and research methods relevant to the field of specialization;
- demonstrate capabilities to generate, design, implement and adopt the integral part of the research process with scholarly strength and in accordance with the time frame;
- contribute innovatively to the original research that has broadened the boundary of knowledge through an in-depth dissertation, which has been presented and defended according to the international standards;
- make critical analysis, evaluation and synthesis of new and complex ideas;
- communicate effectively to promote technological, social and cultural progress through workshops, seminar presentations and refereed publications;
- display discipline, universal good values and ethics in the process of completing studies.

The contexts where students can develop these skills are in the preparation of lectures, in the lectures themselves (learning by doing) and after the lectures (through reflection on the activity).

## Juxtaposition of the case studies from Italy, Malaysia and Portugal

The case studies discussed here present the different national backgrounds that lie behind the global diversification of the curricula of PhD programmes related to adult education. The juxtaposition of these case studies represents the basis of the international comparative work that tries to "provide new insights into other countries and into new aspects and variations of new models. They also facilitate a better and more detailed understanding of the situation in one's own home country." (Egetenmeyer 2016, p. 19) While interpretation can be understood as a challenge, it can also be enriching (Egetenmeyer 2016, p. 19).

Following these last points, and having had the experience of the Winter School in 2016[10], this chapter shows a parallel between Italy, Portugal and Malaysia. The

---

10  "The Winter School was dedicated to the analysis and comparison of international and European strategies in lifelong learning. Based on social policy models, lifelong learning strategies in Europe were subjected to a critical analysis." (Egetenmeyer 2016, p. 13)

methodology adopted requires, after the description of these case studies, the identification of the main categories that can be used to draw a comparison. Indeed, indicators should not be too wide or too restrictive (Bereday 1964, p. 69; Leirman 1978; Jarvis 1992).

Adopting a methodology based on certain categories (Giorgi in Sità 2012), we identified some preliminary objective sub-categories, namely: "attendance to academic activities", "didactics", "contact between university and labour market" and "explicitly employability-oriented curricula". The aim was to find objective evidence of the approach of Italian, Malaysian and Portuguese universities to the development of soft skills, employability and transitions from academia to the labour market. After that, in the comparative phase of our analysis, we will highlight the similarities and differences among the three countries and the reasons behind them.

The following descriptive table tries to synthesize each country's approach to the social issue of the transition of PhD holders to the labour market.

*Table 1:  Comparison by objective sub-categories and by country (source: authors' own 2016).*

| | ATTENDANCE OF ACADEMIC ACTIVITIES | | DIDACTICS | CONTACT BETWEEN UNIVERSITY AND LABOUR MARKET | | EXPLICITLY EMPLOYABILITY-ORIENTED CURRICULA |
|---|---|---|---|---|---|---|
| | FORMAL COURSES (mandatory) | Participation in interactive workgroups, workshops, conferences, etc. | Didactical approach (space for reflexivity, interactive work...) | INTERNSHIP (or contact with the field work „Workplace or Experience") | CAREER SERVICES in the curriculum (for PhD students) | EXPLICIT aims of the curriculum: development of employability, teamwork |
| **Portugal** | 🙂 | 🙂 | 🙂 | 🙁 | 🙁 | 🙁 |
| **Italy** | 🙂 | 🙂 | 🙂 | 😐 | 😐 | 😐 |
| **Malaysia** | 🙂 | 🙂 | 🙂 | 🙁 | 🙂 | 🙂 |

The table above shows that while the universities in the countries analyzed adopt similar didactical approaches, they approach the labour market and the employability-oriented curriculum concept differently.

Indeed, looking at the table, we can observe a "smiley" in the column headed "Attendance of academic activities", which represents the presence of a common obligation to attend formal courses (lectures) and workshops at all the universities. Yet attendance is mandatory only in the first PhD year in Portugal; in Italy, it is mandatory during the whole PhD course. In both cases, formal lectures take place once a week, generally between October/November and June/July.

When considering the topic of didactics, one can say that a didactical approach in Portugal and Italy is usually developed not only according to the organization and aims of the course, but also in line with the respective professor's lecture and teaching style. Depending on the didactic approach adopted, students will have the possibility (or not) to have space for reflection and interactive work. Generally, PhD holders are seen as young researchers, so didactics are based on conversation and interaction.[11] In Malaysia, too, very specific attention is paid to the development of critical thought through didactics, as indicated in the official PhD national guidelines.

Regarding the contact between university and the labour market, we assigned a "light smiley" to the Italian case study in order to highlight the fact that PhD students are not required to develop workplace experience, yet some PhD theses can be developed in collaboration with businesses, especially those from the social economy and automotive industry, where some projects are shared (see SALM and PRIN EMP&Co. projects). Moreover, to ease the transition of PhD holders from higher education to the labour market, the University of Florence offers students access to career service activities, such as the Light Assessment Center and Business Incubator, although no ECTS credit will be given for attendance. In Portugal, we are starting to see some work in this field, but the relationship between the labour market and the university in the field of adult education is still weak ("non-smiley").

With reference to the last category, the "employability-oriented curriculum", we can assume that in Malaysia, the PhD curriculum in education is built with an explicit employability approach (Ministry of Higher Education Malaysia 2006). In contrast, Portugal and Italy do not seem to recognize the importance of developing an employability-oriented PhD curriculum, although national programmes and European strategies require this. Indeed, it was not possible to find any explicit

---

11  Debate, critical thought, discussions and reflection are fundamental tools for the development of the students' skills.

reference to the importance of the development of employability of PhD students either in the Italian or the Portuguese PhD programmes.

## Comparative analysis

The didactical approach adopted by the three universities observed presents both differences and similarities. All the universities consider the attendance of courses and workshops as important, and they share a very similar approach. Indeed, they offer a variety of learning options (conferences, workshops and discussions) focused on various topics to those PhD students who are willing to attend. In their opinion, this kind of activity is an important way of imparting knowledge to the students.

We observe that none of the PhD programmes indicates how the learning needs – which should lie at the basis of the PhD curriculum – have been recognized to cover soft skills. In other words, we have no assurance that the PhD programme has really paid any attention or listened carefully to the needs of civil society, as they have been stated by future employers, academia and PhD students.

None of the Mediterranean PhD programmes analyzed refers explicitly to these needs, nor do they define explicitly how employability can be built, used and implemented (Pegg, Waldock, Hendy-Issaac & Lawton 2012). Indeed, employability refers to complex learning that goes far beyond soft and hard skills and that can enhance the acquisition not only of one "graduate job", but of a multitude of "real jobs" and transitions in the long term (Yorke 2006b, p. 2; Boffo 2015, p. 153).

One reason can be found in traditional studies on employability and transitions. Indeed, if we look back to the history of pedagogy, we notice that studies on employability and transitions were first carried out in the UK forty years ago, while in Italy and Portugal, researchers have only been focusing their attention on these concepts for a few years. We can confirm that in the Mediterranean area, the study of employability is closely connected with the 2009 economic crisis and that only after that event did academia engage in the study of strategies, methods and practices on entry to the labour market.

## Final considerations

Comparing adult education at an international level is a methodological approach that helps to understand and form adult education itself.

This paper focused on the question of which soft skills are shown by adult educators and also how universities and PhD schools can help to further employability through their curricula. The study of the similarities and differences among the different approaches to employability helps us to reflect on the competences that PhD students working in adult education and lifelong learning will need in the future. Why do pathways towards professionalization in Italy, Malaysia and Portugal exhibit so many differences? What are the actual effects of these different approaches? Is there a common skillset at a global level?

Although employability is a very urgent issue, the strategies adopted vary strongly according to the geographical location, almost as if the nature of adult education has a different meaning in different places. According to the results collected, the different characteristics of each country lead to universities developing specific practices in the field of adult education; consequently, they impart PhD students in adult education with different skills.

The link between curricula, employability and didactics is very important and strong, yet it is not recognized in the same way. This results in the different construction of skillsets in the PhDs. Until similarities exist at a strategic and political level, PhD mobility around the world will be limited, since qualifications will not be recognized in the same way.

Until universities begin to discuss what the role of an adult educator at a global level is, they will not be able to draw up comparable curricula. As a consequence, the employability of PhD graduates on a global level will be impossible, and the professional identity of these specialists in adult education will not be recognized in the same way all over the world.

This will impact on the understanding of the paradigms of higher education in the context of a European common education space. Accordingly, we should observe PhD curricula from a different perspective, in order to allow PhD students to develop all the skills (such as reflection as well as critical and communication skills) that are needed for the future professionals of adult education on a global level.

There is some hope that PhD curricula will improve in the future, and that these changes will not only have a positive effect on the commitment of teaching staff, but also adopt a new political and strategic common approach. If this is the case, legislation may vary according to the European or Malaysian context, but there will always be a long-term vision for the construction of professionalization.

## References

Bennett, N. / Dunne, E. / Carré, C.: *Skills development in higher education and employment.* SRHE and Open University Press: Buckingham. 2000.

Bereday, G.Z.F.: *Comparative method in education.* Holt, Rinehart and Winston Inc: New York. 1964.

Boffo, V. / Federighi, P. / Torlone, F.: *Educational jobs: Youth and employability in the social economy.* Firenze University Press: Firenze. 2015.

Che-Ani, A.I. / Ismail, K. / Ahmad, A. / Ariffin, K. / Razak, M.Z.A.: "A new frame-work for University Kebangsaan Malaysia soft skills course: Implementation and challenges". *International Education Studies* 7(8). 2014, pp. 1–10.

Commission of the European Communities: *Communication from the Commission to the Council, the European Parliament, the Economic and Social Committee and the Committee of the Regions: Towards a European Research Area* (COM 6), 18 January 2000, retrieved from http://www.aic.lv/bolona/Bologna/contrib/EU/Toward_EResArea.pdf.

Egetenmeyer, R.: "Comparing adult education and lifelong learning in Europe and beyond: An introduction". In: R. Egetenmeyer (ed.): *Adult education and lifelong learning in Europe and beyond: Comparative perspectives from the 2015 Würzburg Winter School.* Peter Lang: Frankfurt. 2016.

Elias, P. / Purcell, K.: "Is mass higher education working? Evidence from the labour market experiences of recent graduates". *National Institute Economic Review* 190(1), October 2004, pp. 60–74.

European Ministers Responsible for Higher Education: *Communiqué of the Conference of European Ministers Responsible for Higher Education.* Leuven and Louvain-la-Neuve. 28 29 April 2009, IP/09/675.

Dorrell, L.D.: "Collaborative doctoral education: University-industry partnerships for enhancing knowledge exchange". *European University Association.* 2007, retrieved June 2016, from http://www.eua.be/Libraries/research/doc-careers.pdf?sfvrsn=0.

European University Association: "Doctoral programmes in Europe's universities: achievements and challenges". Report prepared for European Universities and Ministers of Higher Education, 2007 retrieved June 2016, from http://www.ub.edu/escola_doctorat/sites/default/files/internacionalitzacio/doctoral_programmes_europe_universities.pdf.

Fragoso, A. / Gonçalves, T. / Ribeiro, C.M. et al.: "Mature students' transition processes to higher education: Challenging traditional concepts?". *Studies in the Education of Adults* 45(1), 2013, pp. 67–81.

Gazier, B. / Gautié, J.: "The 'transitional labour markets' approach: Theory, history and future research agenda". *Journal of Economic and Social Policy* 14(1), 2011, pp. 1–26, retrieved May 2016, from http://epubs.scu.edu.au/jesp/vol14/iss1/6.

Harvey, L.: "Transitions from higher education to work". (Briefing paper – prepared with advice from ESECT and LTSN Generic Centre colleagues). Centre for Research and Evaluation, Sheffield Hallam University. 2003, retrieved May 2016, from http://www.qualityresearchinternational.com/esecttools/esectpubs/harveytransitions.pdf.

Holley, K.A.: "Doctoral education and the development of an interdisciplinary identity". *Innovations in Education and Teaching International* 52(6), 2015, pp. 642–652.

Instituto de Educação: *Education PhD program*, 2014–2015.

Knight, P. / Yorke, M.: *Learning, curriculum and employability in higher education*. RoutledgeFalmer: London. 2004.

Ministry of Higher Education Malaysia: *Development of soft skills for institutions of higher learning*. Universiti Putra Malaysia. 2006.

Muslim, N. / Yunos, N.: "The direction of generic skills courses at National University of Malaysia (UKM) towards fulfilling Malaysian qualifications framework". *Asian Social Science* 10(4), January 2014, pp. 195–202.

Pegg, A. / Waldock, J. / Hendy-Isaac, S. / Lawton, R.: *Pedagogy For Employability*. York. Higher Education Academy, 2012, retrieved February 2017, from https://www.heacademy.ac.uk/system/files/pedagogy_for_employability_update_2012.pdf

Orefice, P. / del Gobbo, G. (eds.): *Il terzo ciclo della formazione universitaria: Un contributo delle scuole e dei corsi di dottorato in scienze dell'educazione in Italia*. FrancoAngeli: Milano. 2011.

Schulz, B.: "The importance of soft skills: Education beyond academic knowledge". *Journal of Language and Communication* 2(1), June 2008, p. 146.

Sità, C.: *Indagare l'esperienza: L'intervista fenomenologica nella ricerca educativa*. Carocci: Roma. 2012.

Vieira, D. / Marques, A.: *Preparados para trabalhar? Um estudo sobre os diplomados do ensino superior e empregadores*. Fórum Estudante/Consórcio Maior Empregabilidade: Lisboa. 2013.

Yorke, M.: *Employability in higher education: What it is, what it is not*. The Higher Education Academy: York. 2006a, retrieved May 2016 from http://www.employability.ed.ac.uk/documents/Staff/HEA-Employability_in_HE(Is,IsNot).pdf

Yorke, M.: *Embedding employability into the curriculum*. ESECT and the Higher Education Academy: York. 2006b.

Kristina Pekeč, Dubravka Milhajlovič & Janiery Da Silva Castro

# Adult Education in Serbia and Brazil – Towards Professionalization

**Abstract:** This paper presents the results of a comparison of the main discourses in adult learning and education in Serbia and Brazil, with a focus on the current issues of professionalization in adult learning and education in both countries.

## Introduction

Professionalization is the burning issue in the current debates taking place in the field of adult learning and education. Bearing in mind that discussion on the need and possibilities of professionalization in adult learning and education has been taking place since the 1920s (Bierema 2011), it is legitimate to assume that an answer or solution to this discussion has still not been found. The main element of doubt, in our opinion, revolves around two questions.

The first question is whether adult learning and education is considered as a profession and/or whether adult educators can be seen as professionals. The reasons for raising this question are numerous, but for the purpose of this article we will mention the most important ones: employees in the field of adult education encounter very diverse and variable working environments – in terms of target groups, themes, subjects and educational goals, methods and approaches to adult education. Employees in adult education perform a wide range of working tasks and activities, which makes profiling them as experts even more difficult. Employees in adult education actually come from different occupations and professions, possess a variety of diplomas or qualifications and mostly have no expertise in adult learning and education (ALPINE 2010). In consideration of the above, a frequently raised issue concerns the education of adult educators themselves, which is rarely connected to education and even more rarely to adult education (Guimarães 2009; Jütte at al. 2011; Sava 2011). Bearing this in mind, we agree that there is without doubt a need for greater control and regulation in the field of adult learning and education, and we see professionalization as a means to achieving this goal.

The second question arises from two potential answers to the first question: if it is assumed at this stage of development in this field that we cannot talk about adult education as a profession, is it still possible for adult learning and education to become a fully developed profession? If there is agreement that the answer is positive, it is necessary to discuss conditions under which this can be achieved (e.g., competences for adult educators). These two questions on professionalization are, among others, to be answered in this article through the authors' own comparative research on adult learning and education in Serbia and Brazil.

## Methodological framework

### Research aim

Our aim is to compare the main characteristics of adult learning and education in two countries, Serbia and Brazil, with the emphasis on analyzing the current status of professionalization in this field.

Although it may appear that it is difficult to compare two very different countries, such as Serbia and Brazil, a deeper analysis of the characteristics of adult education in each country can lead to an implicit conclusion about the strength of the impact that international organizations (e.g., UNESCO, OECD) have on national policies. As no country can grow and develop without the influence of other countries (Savicevic 2003), it is now more than ever possible and necessary to extract and describe the differences in each country's pathway for adult education. Yet this is also very difficult, as it requires a full understanding of the holistic context in each country.

### Research questions

Starting with this aim, we have pointed out several questions for analysis that can be divided into two major groups: 1) Adult learning and education – an overall picture, which consists of the main characteristics of adult education in Serbia and Brazil and presents a good framework within the discussion of its professionalization; and 2) Adult learning and education and professionalization, which focuses on the problems of professionalization of adult education in each country. Each of these issues is examined through the following set of questions:

I. Adult learning and education – an overall picture:

- What are the main characteristics of adult learning and education in Serbia and Brazil?
- Where is the focus on adult learning and education according to the legislative frameworks in Serbia and Brazil?
- Which are the most important similarities and differences between adult education and learning in Serbia and Brazil?

II. Adult learning and education – towards professionalization:

- What are the main characteristics of professionalization in Serbia and Brazil (micro-, meso- and macro-level of analysis)?
- What is the current status of professionalization in adult education in Serbia and Brazil?
- Which are the main similarities and differences between Serbia and Brazil regarding the current status of professionalization in adult learning and education?

## Operational definitions

Operational definitions of key terms are given below (the main criteria for choosing these definitions is their operational value).

In this article, "adult learning and education"[1] is defined in accordance with UNESCO and includes all forms of learning, formal, non-formal and informal – "whereby those regarded as adults by the society in which they live, develop and enrich their capabilities for living and working, both in their own interests and those of their communities, organisations and societies" (UNESCO 2015, p. 10). There are two main points that made us to choose this definition among others. On the one hand, adult learning and education is seen as a core component of lifelong learning, and on the other, literacy is seen as a core component of adult education perceived in this way.

For the purpose of this research, an "adult educator" is defined as an employee in the field of adult learning and education who directs, helps and supports adults in their effort towards learning, self-development and growth in different learning contexts.

"Professionalization" is "a process of structural change of occupation induced by the continuous development of professional knowledge in the first place, and as a process sustained by some other elements" (Ovesni 2007, p. 22). These other

---

1   The terms "adult learning and education" and "adult education" will be used synonymously in this article.

elements, besides having a fundamental theoretical/professional knowledge in a particular field, are: higher education, professional associations, professional autonomy and authority, social control of profession and social sanction, monopoly on professional expertise, professional ethics and standards, public recognition, etc. We think that by having such a diverse field as adult learning and education, professionalization gains a new quality; for employees in this field, it is of the utmost importance that they recognize and perceive themselves first as adult educators (which is the quality they all share with each other), and only then as experts from particular fields of occupation (e.g., mathematician, biologist, gardener, artist).

"Profession" is an occupation that has fully developed elements that define the profession (as mentioned above) and for which the process of professionalization is completed.

## Research method

Moving through the problem area of this research, we aimed to understand and interpret the current adult education and learning discourse, as well as the process of professionalization in Serbia and Brazil. For this purpose, we used a comparative method. Comparison is a very important tool for knowing and learning, because "without comparison, it is difficult to comprehend and understand the dialectic of adult learning and education, to look more profoundly into dynamics of andragogical processes that are taking place" (Savicevic 2003, pp. 247–248). This is true not only in our own country, but also in other countries. The instrument used in this research is the *SERBRALE* (*Serbia and Brazil Adult Learning and Education*) protocol for content analysis, which is constructed especially for this purpose and consists of three parts:

1) *SERBRALE 01* contains a set of questions on the social, economic and demographic characteristics of Serbia and Brazil that provide a solid informative base for further understanding.
2) *SERBRALE 02* contains a set of questions aimed at examining and comparing an overall picture of adult learning and education in Serbia and Brazil, and providing answers for the first group of research questions.
3) *SERBRALE 03* contains a set of questions aimed at examining and comparing the current status of professionalization in adult learning and education in Serbia and Brazil, and providing answers for the second group of research questions. We chose these items because we consider them important elements of professionalism.

## Research results and discussion

Comparison of adult learning and education in Serbia and Brazil, with a focus on the burning issue of professionalization in this field, has been done using the *SEBRALE* protocol. Data obtained through implementation of this instrument are given in Table 1. The results of the comparison are presented and discussed according to the research questions.

*Table 1: SEBRALE protocol for content analysis (source: authors' own).*

| Questions for comparison | Serbia* | Brazil* |
|---|---|---|
| Social, economic and demographic characteristics – *SERBRALE 01* | | |
| Land area | 88,499 km² | 8,515,767 km² |
| Population (in millions) | 7.1 | 204.5 |
| Human development index / rank | 0.771 / rank in world: 66 | 0.755 / rank in world: 75 |
| Employment to population ratio | 40.8 % (ages 15 and older) | 65.6 % (ages 15 and older) |
| Gross national income (GNI) per capita (2011 PPP$) | 12,190 | 15,175 |
| Expected years of schooling | 14.4 years | 15.2 years |
| Overall picture of adult learning and education (ALE) – *SERBRALE 02* | | |
| Existing law on ALE (yes/ no) / year | Yes / 2013, but strategy for ALE has existed since 2006 | Yes, for youth and adult education / since 1988 |
| Areas of education and learning defined by law on ALE | All forms of ALE: formal, non-formal, informal | Primary education and secondary education |
| Target groups, defined according to a legislative framework | All persons involved in activities of ALE (all types of education) | Persons with no continuity in education at the right age |
| Main focus in ALE according to legislative framework | Adult literacy (second chance programmes) | Adult literacy (compensatory education) |
| Adult illiteracy rate (ages 15 and older) | 1.9 % | 8.3 % |
| Public expenditure on education (% of GDP) / on ALE | 0.1 / approximately 3% of the overall budget for education | 5.8 / 15% of the overall budget for education |

| Questions for comparison | Serbia* | Brazil* |
| --- | --- | --- |
| Recognition of prior learning (RPL) (yes/no) / current status | No / There is a legal framework, but with no implementation in practice for now | Yes / National Exam for Certification of Competences of Youngsters and Adults (ENCCEJA) |
| "Adult learning and education" in native language | Образовање и учење одраслих (Serbian) | Aprendizagem de adultos e educação (Portuguese) |
| Best known author in the field of ALE / contribution | Dusan Savicevic / established the Chair for Andragogy | Paulo Freire / creator of the concept of Critical Pedagogy |
| Transnational organizations with most influence on ALE | UNESCO, OECD, World Bank, EU bodies of influence | UNESCO |
| Towards professionalization in adult learning and education (ALE) – *SERBRALE 03* | | |
| Formal education for adult educators (yes/no) / title / duration / level | Yes / dipl. Andragogue / 4 years or more / tertiary education | Yes, partial / Some universities offer specialization in ALE |
| Training for adult educators (yes/no) / organizers / type | Yes / Institute for Pedagogy and Andragogy, Serbian Association of Andragogists / TOT | Yes, partial / Through the initiative of the Ministry of Education / courses |
| Defined competences for adult educators (yes/no) / explanation | Yes / Vocational competences required for working with adults are prescribed by law | Yes / Recent efforts towards guidance for young and adult educator profile |
| Professional association of adult educators (yes/no) / explanation | Yes / Serbian Association of Andragogists | No / But there are efforts toward professionalization |
| Social control of entering profession (yes/no) / explanation | Yes, partial / Fully for andragogists, but partial for educators with different initial education | No / Adult educators come from different fields and there are still no regulations regarding their qualification |
| Professional ethics (yes/no) / explanation | Yes / A code of ethics for andragogists has existed since 2011 | No / But there are efforts toward professionalization |
| Public recognition (yes/no) / explanation | Yes, partial / Fully for andragogists, not for others | No / Adult educators come from different fields |

*Statistical data are obtained from: Brazilian Institute of Geography and Statistics (IBGE), Statistical Office of the Republic of Serbia, International Human Development Indicators.

## Adult learning and education in Serbia and Brazil – an overall picture

With the first group of research questions, as stated above, we aimed to examine and to compare the characteristics of adult learning and education in Serbia and Brazil in order to provide a frame for understanding its current situation and to build a solid basis for discussion on professionalization in this field.

According to the research results (Table 1, *SERBRALE 02*), we noticed that some of the main characteristics of adult learning and education in Serbia and Brazil are similar. Both countries that we examined have a law on adult education and learning, which indicates that this area is regulated and supported by the government (at least in a legislative framework), although adequate financial support seems to be missing.

Data on the legislative framework indirectly allow us to conclude that the field of adult education is recognized as important from the national point of view. Also, in both countries, transnational organizations notably influence the national policies and practice of adult education. Brazil experiences the influence of UNESCO (which has been recognized as most influential), while Serbia, besides the organizations already mentioned, is strongly influenced by EU bodies such as the European Commission. The question of the nature of influences is very important, but fully understanding this nature requires more space and time, and should be undertaken separately; at this juncture, however, we can say that the influences are notable regarding different aspects and elements of education, e.g., directions for development of education and its role, goals, tasks and purpose.

When compared, data on public expenditure on education favour Brazil. The investment in education for both young people and adults, as well as in special education and indigenous education, comes from the overall budget for education. The share spent on adult education is 15%. The rest of the budget is mainly directed towards the primary and secondary education of children (National Institute for Educational Studies and Research "Anisio Teixeira" 2015).

We found that Serbia and Brazil's legislative frameworks on adult learning and education both put a common focus on adult literacy. With deeper insight into this matter, it is notable that most public funds go to "second chance" projects aimed at increasing the level of literacy among the young and the adult population who were left out of compulsory education. We can therefore agree that the main discourse in adult learning and education policies is very similar; at the same time, the major differences are becoming evident here, and we will explain why this is important.

The results show that the main differences between Serbia and Brazil manifest themselves in particular areas of the legislative framework and its implementation in the practice of adult learning and education.

The first major difference lies in forms of education that are defined by laws on adult education and target groups that are included by prescribed activities. Serbian law on adult education (2013) includes formal, non-formal and informal learning and education. In this respect, we found that activities in adult learning involve elementary and vocational education, continuing education and profesional development as well as all other educational activities focused on personal development, employment and/or the social life of adults. In contrast, the Brazilian law on youth and adult education (EJA)[2] provides compensatory educational activities in only a limited way. With the aim of expanding the concept of adult education, in 2000 the Brazilian Ministry of Education decreed that basic adult education should be integrated into vocational adult education (and at the same time established national curricular guidelines for adult education). Nevertheless, in terms of the law, the education of young people and adults in Brazil is almost exclusively compensatory education. There are other laws in Brazil that regulate the area of professional and higher education, but they do not correspond formally to the education of young people and adults.

According to the findings, we can conclude that there is a notable gap between forms and types of educational activities for adults that are included (or excluded) in the legislative frameworks in countries involved in our research. The reason for this probably derives from differences in the adult illiteracy rate, which is about four times higher in Brazil than in Serbia. Discussing this issue, we need to add that Brazil has made great progress in decreasing its illiteracy rate. A closer look at the data shows a decreasing illiteracy rate, from 17.2% in 1992 to 11.8% in 2002 and 8.3% in 2014. The fact that the illiteracy rate is much lower (twice as low in 2014 than in 1992) indicates that efforts in this field have produced significant results.

Bearing in mind the differences in educational forms and activities regulated by Serbian and Brazilian laws, it is expected that these activities involve different target groups. Our research results confirmed these expectations. While adult learners in Serbia are considered to be people over the age of 15 (for primary education), 17 (for secondary education) or age 18 and over (for all other

---

2    Regarding this, when we refer to data on adult education in Brazil, it should be noticed that they always specify *youth and adult education*, which is the legislative framework for adult education in Brazil.

programmes), adult learners in Brazil are only people that did not have access or continuity in primary and secondary education at the normal age – which is connected to the previously mentioned compensatory function of education in Brazil.

In order to find a possible cause for these differences, we must look deeper into the social-demographic history of Brazil and understand the broader context in which adult education takes place. From a historical perspective, Brazil was a country where access to education was selective, with deep socio-economic inequalities. Adult education was not constructed according to psychological characteristics, biological concepts or life stages (youth, maturity, old age), but around a social stigma against illiterate people in a literate society (Di Pierro 2005). In other words, the fact that adult education in Brazil was created to offer basic education for those who did not have the opportunity for schooling at the appropriate age was of crucial importance for defining its target groups.

The second major difference between Serbia and Brazil concerns the recognition of prior learning. The recognition of prior learning in Brazil is carried out according to the National Exam for Certification of Competences of Youngsters and Adults (ENCCEJA). The ENCCEJA is a policy formulated by the federal government and the National Institute of Educational Research "Anísio Teixeira" for youth and adult education, and it has two main objectives: 1) to be an alternative to compensatory courses that take place in Brazil as a way to complete primary and secondary schools (with an appropriate certificate or qualification), and 2) to support the continuation of education and increase the number of years spent at school. While both Brazil and Serbia have specified a system of recognition of prior learning in all major policy documents, only in Brazil can we find its implementation.

In our opinion, a possible reason for the difference observed in the implementation of activities regarding recognition of prior learning could lie in the differences in how the overall legal framework for adult education is set up. Although Serbia adopted the Strategy for the Development of Adult Education in 2006, it was not until 2013 and the Law on Adult Education that recognition of prior learning became part of the national agenda. So there is a gap of one decade (and more) between Serbia and Brazil in providing the legal basis for the implementation of adult education. We have reason to believe that once this has been done, it should be much easier to follow world trends and to begin with the process of assessment of knowledge, skills and competences acquired through the education, life or work experience of an adult (i.e., recognition of prior learning).

## Adult learning and education in Serbia and Brazil – towards professionalization

The second group of questions in this piece of research aims to provide a deeper understanding of the processes of professionalization in Serbia and Brazil as a particular issue in the field of adult learning and education. We formulated this set of questions in order to examine and to compare data regarding the elements of the profession that are most frequently mentioned in the relevant discussions and pieces of research in this field (see Bierema 2011; Guimares 2009; Ovesni 2007; Reischmann 2015; Zarifis & Papadimitrou 2015). The results of our comparison are organized around three levels of analysis: 1) macro-level, which involves professional ethics, public recognition and social control of entering profession; 2) meso-level, which involves formal preparation for becoming an adult educator and creating professional associations; 3) micro-level, which involves the professional competences required for adult educators. According to data on the comparison between Serbia and Brazil, one thing is notable: there are major differences in opportunities to engage in formal education for adult educators (Table 1, *SERBRALE 03*). As we will see in the discussion that follows, many other differences stem from this core divergence.

Analysis on the macro-level involves some of the frequently mentioned elements of the profession (see Despotovic 2010; Sava 2011), which are selected as indicators for examination of the process of professionalization: social control of entering the profession, public recognition and professional ethics. When talking about social control of entering the profession of adult education, the situation in Serbia and Brazil is the same as in the rest of Europe and the world. Serbia and Brazil employ educators (teachers, trainers and facilitators) from various occupations and professions, so we cannot say that entrance to profession is in any way controlled. Closely related is public recognition of the profession of adult education, which is mostly missing due to the broad range of professionals that work in this field. When comparing Serbia and Brazil at the macro-level, one significant difference becomes apparent: Serbia has a professional group of andragogists (this will be further discussed in the analysis at the meso-level). Therefore, the andragogists face social control when entering the profession, as well as social recognition of the profession, but this does not apply in the case of educators coming from other professions. The same applies to the existence of a professional code of ethics. While there is no obligatory ethical code for adult educators in Brazil, the code of ethics for andragogists in Serbia has existed since 2011.

Analysis at the meso-level includes comparison of the formal education and training of adult educators and professional associations. If we look at data on formal education for adult educators, the results show that while Brazil has no separate programmes for adult educators at the graduate level, some of its universities offer education with an emphasis on adult education within courses on pedagogy, and as further education (on the specialization, master or doctorate level). As we can see, the possibilities for specialization or further development in the area of adult education can be found under the umbrella of pedagogy. Meanwhile, Serbia established a chair of andragogy at the University of Belgrade in 1979 and, since then, students have had the chance to gain a university diploma in adult learning and education at the graduate, master and doctorate level. Although they are both in the same department, pedagogy and andragogy are two different study programmes, as they are two independent scientific fields. Serbia has a programme for the initial education of professional adult educators – andragogues – and because of this, we think that it is easier for Serbia to fulfil the challenges that derive from the process of professionalization in the field of adult education. This can also be seen in the fact that there is a Serbian association of andragogists; Brazil does not have such a professional association.

Nevertheless, we can notice some similarities in the characteristics observed of professionalization at the meso-level of analysis. According to our findings, both Brazil and Serbia have some forms of training for adult educators, and in both countries these activities are implemented under the jurisdiction of the government. Serbia has train-the-trainers (TOT) programmes that are accredited by the Ministry of Education, Science and Technological Development. These programmes provide an official certificate that qualifies adult educators to work in the field of formal and non-formal adult education. In Brazil, the Ministry of Education's Department of Continuing Education, Literacy, Diversity and Inclusion also offers courses in specialization in youth and adult education.

Finally, analysis at the micro-level concerns the professional competences of adult educators. The field of adult learning and education in Serbia and Brazil employs educators from various professions. In many cases, they possess little or no theoretical, methodological and didactical knowledge on how to support adults in their efforts towards learning and acquisition of a new skill or competence. They are not alone in this, as it is also the case within other countries (ALPINE 2010; Magoga & Perrude 2006; Soares & Simoes 2005). According to our findings, the competences of adult educators in Serbia and Brazil exhibit some major differences. In Serbia, regulation obliges adult educators in the non-formal sector to have the necessary competences for helping adults to learn. Prescribed vocational competences for adult educators refer to the main principles, characteristics and learning styles of adults; the motivation and management of the educational group; methods and techniques for interactive learning in adult education; methods and techniques for assessing achievements of adult learners; and planning, organization and individualization of the educational process (including people with disabilities) and evaluation of the educational process. We cannot find similar obligations regarding the competences of adult educators in Brazil, but there are notable efforts towards profiling the profession of adult educators.

## Conclusion

The results of the analysis of professionalization in Brazil and Serbia at the macro-, meso- and micro-levels allow us to draw conclusions using certain indicators that we have selected for our inquiry, but we must be very careful if we want to make generalizations. Although Brazil and Serbia partially share the problem of a lack of public recognition and social control of entering the profession, in terms of practice and practitioners in the field of adult education, we have observed differences regarding professional ethics, associations, formal preparation and the competences of adult educators. Nevertheless, it seems to us that both countries are investing great effort in the professionalization process. Reflecting on our findings, we believe that the perceived differences regarding the process of professionalization in Serbia and Brazil are due to the tradition of having the profession of andragogues in Serbia. The reason for such a conclusion lies in the fact that when there is a strong reservoir of andragogical knowledge, there is a solid foundation for answering almost every question or problem that arises from the practice of adult learning and education. Of course, it can be argued whether the strong legislative framework in Serbia is enough for drawing conclusions on certain aspects of a profession, especially when a very small amount of the overall budget for education goes to adult education (when compared with Brazil). In our opinion, the importance of formal preparation for adult educators lies not only in the professional knowledge and skills it provides, but also in the introduction to the culture of the profession and in developing a professional identity for adult educators. In this sense, despite the similarities that andragogy has with pedagogy, we believe that enabling independent, basic studies of adult education is an important step towards professionalization, because it is through this kind of study that a significant part of the professional socialization of adult educators occurs.

# References

Bierema, L.L.: "Reflections on the profession and professionalization of adult education". *PAACE Journal of Lifelong Learning* 20, 2011, pp. 21–36.

Brazilian Institute of Geography and Statistics: *National Survey by Household, Survey 1992/2011*, 2015, retrieved from http://seriesestatisticas.ibge.gov.br/series.aspx?no=4&op=0&vcodigo=PD171&t=taxa-analfabetismo-grupos-idade.

Brazilian Institute of Geography and Statistics: *Education: Illiteracy rate of persons 15 years or older*, 2015, retrieved from http://brasilemsintese.ibge.gov.br/educacao/taxa-de-analfabetismo-das-pessoas-de-15-anos-ou-mais.html.

Despotovic, M.: "Professionalization of adult education: Between public and scientific (non)recognition". In: *Adult education: The response to global crisis – strengths and challenges of the profession*. Department of Pedagogy and Andragogy, Faculty of Philosophy, University of Belgrade: Beograd. 2010.

Di Pierro, M.C.: *Annotations on the redefinition of the identity and the public policies for youth and adult education in Brazil*, 2005, retrieved from http://dx.doi.org/10.1590/S0101-73302005000300018.

Guimaraes, P.: "Reflections on the professionalisation of adult educators in the framework of public policies in Portugal". *European Journal of Education* 44(2) (Part I), 2009, pp. 205–219.

Jütte, W. / Nicoll, K. / Olesen, H.S.: "Editorial: Professionalisation – the struggle within". *European Journal for Research on the Education and Learning of Adults* 2(1), 2011, pp. 7–20.

Kothari, C.R.: *Research methodology: Methods and techniques*. New Age International: New Delhi. 2005.

Magoga, P.M. / Perrude, M.R.S.: "Professores da educação de jovens e adultos: Por onde passa sua formação?". In: M.R.S. Perrude / A.L.F. Aoyama (eds.): *Relatos de práticas e reflexões pedagógicas*. Moriá: London. 2006, pp. 99–105.

Ministry of Education: *Assembly of basic education: Resolution CNE/CEB nr. 1 establishes the national curriculum guidelines for youth and adult education*. National Council of Education: Brazil. 2000.

Ministry of Education, Science and Technological Development: *Law on Adult Education of the Republic of Serbia*, 2013, retrieved from http://www.mpn.gov.rs/dokumenta-i-propisi/zakonski-okvir/.

National Institute of Studies and Educational Research Anisio Teixeira: *Percentage of Total Investment in Relation to GDP by Education Level*, 2015, retrieved from http://portal.inep.gov.br/web/guest/estatisticas-gastoseducacao-indicadores_financeiros-p.t.i._nivel_ensino.htm.

Ovesni, K.: "Andragogical knowledge: A key to professionalization of the field of adult education". *Andragogical Studies* XIV (1), 2007, pp. 5–22.

Ovesni, K.: *Andragogical staff – profession and professionalisation*. Institute for Pedagogy and Andragogy, Faculty of Philosophy: Beograd. 2009.

Reischmann, J.: "Professionalization of adult education: Some aspects". *Andragogical Studies* 2, 2015, pp. 23–37.

Research voor Beleid: *ALPINE – adult learning professions in Europe: Key competences for adult learning professionals*. Research voor Beleid: Zoetemeer. 2015.

Sava, S.: "Towards the professionalization of adult educators". *Andragogical Studies* 2, November 2011, pp. 9–22.

Savićević, D.: *Comparative andragogy*. Institute for Pedagogy and Andragogy, Faculty of Philosophy: Beograd. 2003.

Soares, L.: "Educators of youngsters and adults and their education". *Educational Review* 47 2008, pp. 83–100, retrieved from http://dx.doi.org/10.1590/S0102-46982008000100005.

Soares, L.J.G. / Simões, F.M.: "A formação inicial do educador de jovens e adultos". *Educação e Realidade* 29(2), 2005, pp. 25–39, retrieved from http://seer.ufrgs.br/index.php/educacaoerealidade/article/view/25389/14723.

Statistical Office of the Republic of Serbia: 2016, retrieved from http://webrzs.stat.gov.rs/WebSite/

UNDP: *International Human Development Indicators for Brazil*, 2015, retrieved from http://hdr.undp.org/en/countries/profiles/BRA.

UNDP: *International Human Development Indicators for Serbia*, 2015, retrieved from http://hdr.undp.org/en/countries/profiles/SRB.

UNESCO Institute for Lifelong Learning: *Recommendation on adult learning and education: Final Report Draft*, 2015, retrieved from https://uil.unesco.org/adult-learning-and-education/unesco-recommendation/new-unesco-recommendation-adult-learning-and-0).

Zarifis, G.K. / Papadimitrou, A.: "What does it take to develop professional adult educators in Europe? Some proposed framework guidelines". *Andragogical Studies* 2, December 2015, pp. 9–22.

Fanny Hösel & Carlo Terzaroli

# Work Transitions in Adulthood: An Analytical Tool for Comparative Studies

**Abstract:** This paper analyzes work transitions in modern times. It discusses the pedagogical challenges involved in supporting adults, paying attention to the topic of professionalism in adult education. It proposes an analytical tool for investigating work transitions in a comparative perspective among countries or regions.

## From the societal and individual backgrounds of transitions to work pathways

Our modern times are characterized by a wide range of transformative processes and institutional changes, by the loss of old orientations and traditional safeties. Individuals are therefore increasingly responsible for choosing their own life path, a development explained by the so-called phenomenon of individualization[1] (Beck & Beck-Gernsheim 1994). On the one hand, the personal contribution required leads to more options; on the other hand, more freedom of action often produces feelings of uncertainty (Böhle & Weihrich 2009), more pressure and a need for orientation and guidance.

> As is now well established, the standard biography has been replaced by the 'elective biography' [...] This development has two corollaries. One is that in certain periods of life, many different tasks must be combined [...]. The second is that given the individualization of life courses, coordination of life and work on an aggregate social level becomes problematic.
>
> (Glastra et al. 2004, p. 295)

These trends become particularly obvious when examining the transitions people go through during changes in their life path. As Field has pointed out, the "reflexive modernization" theorists Beck and Giddens have argued strongly that transition and change are now routinely embedded in the social relations of contemporary life (Field 2013, p. 384). The transitions in modern times are characterized not only by

---

1  With knowledge of the non-empirical basis, individualization is for this purpose (only) used as a theorem and a theoretical substantiation for presumably ongoing processes of social change and "aspects of nonlinearity that seem to be characteristic of late modernity" (Field 2013, p. 386).

their high quantity but also by diversification, complexity, frailty, contingency and the risk created by the on-going dynamic development (von Felden & Schmidt-Lauff 2015, p. 11). It is therefore not just a question of how to change one's state or role through a simple transitional performance: if there is no more linearity within one's life path, and especially one's employment pathway, we are forced to deal with the permanent need to face transitions (Klingovsky & Pawlewicz 2015, p. 61).

A scientific discussion about transitions – especially in an internationally comparative view – needs common terms and a joint conceptual framework. In fact, from a traditional point of view the term "transition" can refer to both a change of status and a change of roles within the course of socialization or the time-related development of one's life path (Walther 2015, p. 36). This also involves an understanding of transitions as "a movement between institutional contexts [that] points to the ways in which institutions and practices shape the constraints and affordance that impact on transitions". (Ecclestone 2006, p. 6, quoted in Colley 2007, p. 430) Such an understanding largely represents a normative conception of status passages, which can be used to describe socially supported and regulated adaptive processes, but no dynamic and relational transitions (Welzer 1993, p. 7, quoted in Schäffter 2015, p. 21). Meanwhile, current literature – mainly German literature about adult education discourses – also has a wider understanding of transitions that focuses on "life trajectories" as a permanent movement into future-generating self-reflections within the scope of new contingent transitions (Schäffter 2015). The present paper therefore mainly focuses on who has to manage and shape the dedicated transition (in which the subject knows the end point) or the contingent transition (in which the end point is unknown and the transition is characterized by exploratory movement). For a holistically analytical conceptual approach, however, we must also consider how normative orientations influence and regulate the transitions and how institutions frame them (Klingovsky & Pawlewicz 2015).

With this theoretical framework, we can also point out elements at the level of the labour market that support this analysis. European workers' lives have been characterized by increasingly unstable pathways within the labour market (European Commission 2012). The economic crisis of 2008 sharpened unemployment rates and job security has ever more become a mirage. Policies have attempted to face this challenge by liberalizing working arrangements to be more flexible, a shift that has generated an increase in mobilization and the use of temporary contracts.

Thanks to these changes in the world of work, the challenges of profession-alization in adult education and lifelong learning have risen in consonance with the dimensions of transitions and employability (Yorke 2006; Boffo 2015). The next chapter investigates how educational actions could support transitions by providing learning opportunities for the individuals facing them. If "transitions of adult life are experiences from which we can learn and develop" (Merriam 2005, p. 7), it follows that learning processes may result from transitions and educational processes may bolster them.

## The pedagogical challenges of work transitions

The variety of work transitions calls for educational actions capable of support-ing the individuals facing them. It is not technocratic management proposals that are needed, but rather attention to the interactions of societal and individual perspectives, awareness of the pedagogical characteristics of work (Boffo 2012) and the realization that the participants' learning processes are crucial for find-ing effective pathways through transitions (von Felden & Schmidt-Lauff 2015, p. 15). In this sense, pedagogical professionalism could represent a supportive authority for coping with the issues of transformative life, work and employment situations. In fact, a merely external mediating authority, guiding participants through the status shifts in a quickly and seamless way, cannot be enough, and entails the risk of becoming a vicarious agent for economic or educational poli-cies (Klingovsky & Pawlewicz 2015, p. 62). This can only be prevented by "think-ing in transitions" (von Felden et al. 2014, p. 7), which means that professional experts have to accept the process logic of transitions, stress the promotion of learning and support individuals who are permanently in need of changing their role or state.

In this perspective, the educational actions should take into account the differ-ent elements of transitions and aim at assisting adults in making sense of their own lives (Biasin 2012, p. 46) at both a personal and a social level. Therefore, education for work transitions should create opportunities for self-development, facilitat-ing adults in re-interpreting their experience and transforming their transition (Dewey 1916) from a problem to a formative challenge for themselves and their destinies. Learning would therefore not just be functional and effective, provid-ing workers with tools and strategies, but rather serve as a broad path aimed at bolstering the whole person from the viewpoint of both identity and personal and social actions.

This educational process that educators could activate during the transition should firstly address the needs of the adult, helping the participant to build up a professional identity by starting with his or her already existing competencies and attributes; guidance could be an effective tool for accompanying adults in this process. In fact, the concept adopts a holistic view of the individual, his or her own responsibility of social realization, the centrality of professional activity in identity development and the social background of risk and uncertainty. In line with these aspects, guidance intends to reinforce the whole person by starting with their personal and professional needs, with the aim of developing the personal potential. Guidance here fulfils the crucial function of supporting people who are in the course of making decisions about themselves (Biasin 2012, p. 55). Therefore, its role cannot be limited to single actions but should be connected to a lifelong learning perspective (Field et al. 2009) with the aim of helping adults to understand the work context and their role and place within it.

This analysis suggests that education and guidance play an important role in helping adults to face work transitions. As these transitions involve not just the specific dimensions of the workplace, and its changes and challenges, but the deep relationship between the person and all everyday contexts, the supportive actions for transitions can clearly be classed as pedagogical tasks and not (only) psychological ones, and this process of learning and education could be developed not just during the transition from one workplace to another but also during the switch between different jobs within the same company. In fact, "support for transitions is becoming increasingly formalized and expected at all levels of the education system, leading to a growth industry in coaching and mentoring" (Ecclestone 2007, p. 8) that also offers opportunities for adult educators and their professionalization. Most commonly, adult educators offer biographical support that stresses self-awareness and self-reflexive processes (Ecclestone 2007): By reflecting on experience, "we can learn and develop" (Merriam 2005, p. 7). However, specific pathways are needed to transform a transition, which is a "neutral phenomenon" (Merriam 2005, p. 8), into a potential learning experience. Many authors have therefore strongly emphasized the importance of reflecting on work experience and work transitions – with such reflection, the participants can use the experience of the learning process to develop themselves.

Merriam particularly stresses her definition of the life path that involves identity, sociocultural aspects and the personal view of the self. The challenges of change are accordingly placed into the complexity and the ambiguity of the transition that demands that those affected "tolerate uncertainties and strength-en awareness of their own expectations"[2] (Biasin 2012, p. 61). In this sense, the aim of the whole process is not just to help adults to face a single transi-tion but to support them through a reflexive process, introducing the events of their working life into a broad framework that can help them understand their meaning. This support could be bolstered through educational actions (such as guidance, coaching and mentoring) that develop the participants' self-awareness about the transition phase, transforming the critical event into an opportunity to redesign their careers and lives in connection with personal structures of meaning.

## An analytical tool for planning and implementing educational actions for work transitions

In order to pay due attention to all of these pedagogical aspects, we propose using the "conceptual lenses" of identity, agency and structure highlighted by Ecclestone, Biesta and Hughes (2010, p. 1; also Ecclestone 2009) and to further supplement them with Andreas Walther's (2015) three modes of designing transitions in an analytical way: the discursive level, the institutional level and the individual level. Brought together as analytical categories, they can serve as a valuable tool for investigating transitions. Such an analytical instrument is also applicable in the context of international comparative research – pro-vided that the states involved share the theoretical background of the object of investigation.

Using the proposed approach to investigate specific aspects of the concept of (work) transitions provides researchers with the chance to "explore transitions in different ways, depending on the emphasis they place on each or all of the concepts" (Ecclestone 2009, p. 4). Figure 1 presents an overview of the relevant categories and the elements that could support researching work transitions for planning educational actions and implementing policies at different levels. The matrix also represents an analytical tool that can be used for comparative studies.

---

2   Personal translation from Biasin 2012.

*Figure 1: An analytical tool for analyzing work transitions (Source: authors' own elaboration from Ecclestone 2009 and Walther 2015).*[3]

| Categories<br><br>Perspective of design | IDENTITY<br>Construction of identity | AGENCY<br>Capacity for action | STRUCTURE<br>Contextual factors |
|---|---|---|---|
| DISCURSIVE LEVEL (normative)<br>Designation of social situations as transitions<br><br>Point of view: researchers | Transitions defined as the shift from one condition to another that could imply changes in personal and professional identity | Actions and requirements regarding the specific (normative) life roles and the necessary capacity to act (social expectations) | Present transitions as a process of change within the social situation; transition as a life chance and a chance to change one's role or status (e.g., from school to work) in different contextual and historical factors |
| INDIVIDUAL LEVEL<br>Biography work within the transition<br><br>Point of view: individuals | Identity as a projection of the individual into the future, focusing on being and becoming, to point out ways in which the self is represented and understood in dynamic, multidimensional and evolving ways | Self-portrait as "active agents" constructing, understanding and making sense of new experiences and challenges by drawing on various resources and actions at their disposal | Explicate structural factors (class, race, gender, economic and occupational conditions) for explaining individual action; identifying different access points to economic, social and symbolic forms of capital |

3    The figure represents a heuristic instrument for analytical research of transitions, based on two typologies of categories for the analysis of transitions. We, the authors, are attempting to implement relevant categories (the main aspects of transitions that have to be considered) and levels of analysis that represent the perspective of educational research. In this sense, for the specific context of adult education, we are adding to the classifications developed by Ecclestone (2009) and Walther (2015) on the level of educational professionals, since the aim of the research field is to provide pedagogical actions to support transitions.

| Categories<br><br>Perspective of design | IDENTITY<br>Construction of identity | AGENCY<br>Capacity for action | STRUCTURE<br>Contextual factors |
|---|---|---|---|
| INSTITUTIONAL LEVEL<br><br>Point of view: institutions and gatekeepers | In contrast with the individual level, it consists of the process of modelling identities through externally imposed models from school, family, the workplace and more in general institutions | Actions and programmes, at the macro- and meso-level, to support (but also to structure and limit) adults facing work transitions and passing from one stage to another | Identify key social divisions that frame possibilities and restrict social mobility throughout organizations. This process is regulated and controlled by institutional gatekeepers. |
| PROFESSIONAL LEVEL<br>Support for successful transitions<br><br>Point of view: professionals in adult education | Supportive reflections of self-being, supportive reconstructions of identity, supportive activities to resolve the difficult tension between individual and social identity | Educational actions developed at the workplace or in other contexts through formal, non-formal or informal learning processes to exercise autonomy | Understanding the global challenges of the world of work, the needs of workers facing transitions and their opportunities for new development within the labour market |

After describing the categories in general, the process should proceed to collecting data and classifying them with the analytical tool, in order to provide a broad insight into different dimensions of transitions and into factors to be analyzed for educational actions and policy making. This approach makes it possible to compare the results of different countries in a second step.

The first three concepts are to be understood as objects of research, classified according to research interests (horizontal). The modes of design (vertical) clarify the point of (research) view, which means that the results refer to different levels. If you are interested in "structure" (the contextual factors), for example, you can draw data from narratives of the individual level by asking individuals for subjective experiences with structural factors that influence their transitions. The possibilities vary by level: you can discuss structural factors in a theoretical and normative way (discursive level), analyze the gatekeepers (institutional level) or examine the professional perspective (professional level).

## Identity

Identity "can be defined as the ways in which the self is represented and un-derstood in dynamic, multi-dimensional and evolving ways". (Ecclestone 2009, p. 4) In this perspective, transitions are processes of subjective transformation in which the subjects change their situations. To analyze identity within transition, it is necessary to know something about the structure of identity: "[i]dentity is […] constructed through complex interactions between different forms of capital (cul-tural, social, economic and emotional), broader social and economic conditions, interactions and relationships in various contexts, and cognitive and psychological strategies" (Eccelstone et al. 2010, p. 9).

## Agency

Another important aspect of the individual approach to transitions concerns the role of agency, which is defined as "people's capacity to interact with others and with material conditions in order to shape their own destinies, both individually and collectively" (Ecclestone 2009, p. 5). Agency focuses on the choices and actions an individual takes that are related to personal, social and working circumstances. In this view, agency outlines "the choices and actions [people] take within the op-portunities and constraints of history and social circumstances" (Elder 1998, p. 4).

Walther's (2015, p. 47) *individual level* describes a similar concept, referring to how the subject copes and deals with transitions, including his or her strategies of management. In this perspective, the result of "doing transition" (in a normative view) is of less interest. It is much more important to look for the motivation in terms of biographical capacity to act. With this in mind, we can talk about biog-raphy work during the transition. It is therefore understandable that the manage-ment of transitions is strictly linked to potential learning processes, such as the development of required skills and the integration of role requirements into the subject's self-conception.

## Structure

Together with the concept of agency mentioned, it is the category of structure that has built the framing concepts of modern sociology as part of the so-called structure-agency debate (Ecclestone et al. 2010, p. 11; Raithelhuber 2013, p. 101). It is generally agreed that all agency is affected by structural factors like class, race, gender and economic and occupational factors. Moreover, the aspect of structure must also be taken into account (see Figure 1); indeed, labour market character-istics play a relevant role in influencing work transitions and career development.

That is why "many researchers argue that it is not possible to understand agency and identity without an account of how they are shaped, constrained and sometimes determined by the material conditions and normative expectations of different structural factors" (Ecclestone 2009, p. 6).

## Institutional regulation and the gatekeepers' level

This category concerns the institutions and how they regulate transitions. In contrast to the category of structure, which primarily describes the framing circumstances, this level stresses the importance of gatekeepers' regulatory measures. Such regulations consist of legal, organizational or ritualized conditions that have to be fulfilled and are controlled by gatekeepers (Behrens and Rabe-Kleberg 2000). In the formal sphere, gatekeepers can be found in companies' human resources departments as well as in the educational and social sectors. But there are also informal actors, maybe with differing resources and intentions, such as parents and peers (Behrens and Rabe-Kleberg 2000).

## Discursive level

The discursive level broaches the issue of transitions, which means the identification and the problematization of social situations as transitions (Walther 2015). In such a discursive way, transitions are addressed as a change of state, role or status by ordering them into a chronological sequence and marking them as biographically significant and far-reaching. The concept of status passage approaches the intended meaning.

## Professionals in the adult education level

According to these elements, the analysis could focus on the level of professionals in adult education, with the aim of providing an in-depth study of transitions for implementing educational actions for supporting work transitions (see Paragraph 2). In this sense, professionals should take into account all complex dimensions and factors, presented above, that could influence and undermine adults' transitions in their career pathways. This complex analysis reveals the interrelation of multiple elements that characterize adults facing transitions; in fact, the analytical tool reveals different aspects of identity, agency and structure at different levels for the implementation of educational actions (at the micro-level) and of policies and strategies (at the meso- and macro-levels). Therefore, the point of view of professionals in adult education, which aims at producing support and transformation for adults facing transitions, should take into account the composite framework (and different points of view) that can be identified for those facing changes in their work careers.

## Conclusions

Societal transformations at the mega- and macro-levels directly affect the lives of individuals, transforming their life paths and work conditions and forcing them to face multiple transitions during their lives. Moreover, the transformations of the economy and the labour market – whether they consist of increased flexibility, instable contracts or changes in the method of production – also impact adults' career pathways. In this perspective, the research in adult education aims not just at analyzing factors that characterize adults' work transitions, but at planning, implementing and providing supportive educational actions to bolster adults in those phases and prevent critical situations. In this sense, the analysis of transitions reveals different dimensions and levels in which the adult is involved. Any action (whether at the individual level or at the policy level) should consider many aspects of the phenomenon, to accompany and direct adults during work transitions, focusing on their identity and agency and also taking into account the structural factors in play; in fact, "it is only possible to understand transitions through a focus an agency and identity together with an account of how these are shaped, constrained and sometimes determined by the material conditions and normative expectations of different structural factors" (Ecclestone et al. 2010, p. 12).

Utilizing these various considerations, this paper has presented arguments and methodological instruments for a deep and comprehensive analysis of work transitions for designing and implementing policies at the institutional level through international comparison. Comparative studies of work transitions (among countries or regions, or between other types and levels of institutions) should consider more than a simple juxtaposition of specific measures, for while such a juxtaposition may serve as a good analytical exercise, we believe that it cannot reveal the broad and complex dimensions of personal, social and societal aspects that strongly influence an adult facing a work transition. Instead, the analysis should be capable of studying different dimensions and gathering data to create a broad framework of what individuals are facing, establishing both the implications for their lives and the context in which the change is taking place.

Our work has therefore tried to focus on this methodological issue to provide an analytical tool for academic research on work transitions. Since our final aim as researchers and professionals in adult learning and education is to develop educational actions that bolster adults' passage from one stage to another, we hope that our work can deepen our field's understanding of this level of analysis. Analyzing the impact of different aspects and levels in adults' (work) transitions could prove especially useful for professionals in adult learning and education, helping them to implement educational, supportive actions that always take account of the complexity of society, work and career pathways and the impact of those factors on adults that are "navigating difficult waters" (Cedefop 2014) of transitions.

# References

Beck-Gernsheim, E. / Beck, U. (eds.): *Riskante Freiheiten: Individualisierung in modernen Gesellschaften.* Suhrkamp Verlag: Frankfurt. 1994.

Behrens, J. / Rabe-Kleberg, U.: *Gatekeeping im Lebensverlauf – Wer wacht an Statuspassagen?* In: E. M: Hoerning, E.M. (ed.): *Biographische Sozialisation.* Lucius & Lucius. 2000, pp. 101–135.

Biasin, C.: *Le transizioni: Modelli e approcci per l'educazione degli adulti.* Pensa Multimedia: Lecce. 2012.

Boffo, V.: *A glance at work.* Firenze University Press: Firenze. 2012.

Boffo, V.: "Employability for the social economy: The role of higher education". In: V. Boffo / P. Federighi / F. Torlone (eds.): *Educational jobs: Youth and employability in the social economy.* Firenze University Press: Firenze. 2015.

Böhle, F. / Weihrich, M. (eds.): *Handeln unter Unsicherheit.* VS Verlag für Sozialwissenschaften: Wiesbaden. 2009.

Bonß, W.: „Die gesellschaftliche Konstruktion von Sicherheit". In: E. Lippert / G. Wachtler / A. Prüfert (eds.): *Sicherheit in der unsicheren Gesellschaft.* Westdeutscher Verlag: Opladen. 1997, pp. 21–42.

Cedefop: *Navigating difficult waters: Learning for career and labour market transitions.* Publications Office of the European Union: Luxembourg. 2014.

Colley, H.: "Understanding time in learning transitions through the lifecourse". *International Studies in Sociology of Education* 17(4), 2007, pp. 427–443.

Dausein, B.: *Sozialisation-Geschlecht-Biographie: Theoretische und methodologische Untersuchung eines Zusammenhangs.* Universität Bielefeld, Fakultät für Pädagogik: Bielefeld. 2002.

Dewey, J.: *Democracy and education.* MacMillan: New York. 1916.

Ecclestone, K.: "Keynote presentation". In: *Researching Transitions in Lifelong Learning Conference.* University of Stirling: Stirling, UK. 22–24 June 2007.

Ecclestone, K.: "Lost and found in transition: Educational implications of concerns about 'identity', 'agency' and 'structure'". In: J. Field / J. Galacher / R. Ingram (eds.): *Researching transitions in lifelong learning.* Routledge: London and New York. 2009, pp. 9–27.

Ecclestone, K. / Biesta, G. / Hughes, M.: *Transitions and learning through the lifecourse*. Routledge: London and New York. 2010.

Elder, G. H.: "The life course as developmental theory". *Child Development* 69(1), February 1998, pp. 1–12.

European Commission: *Labour market developments in Europe 2012*. Publications Office of the European Union: Luxembourg. 2012.

Field, J.: "Preface". In: K. Ecclestone / G. Biesta / M. Hughes (eds.): *Transitions and learning through the lifecourse*. Routledge: London and New York. 2010, pp. xvii–xxiv.

Field, J.: "Lifelong learning and the restructuring of the adult life course". In: W. Schröer / B. Stauber / A. Walther / L. Böhnisch / K. Lenz (eds.): *Handbuch Übergänge*. Beltz Juventa: Weinheim and Basel. 2013, pp. 378–393.

Field, J. / Galacher, J. / Ingram, R. *Researching transitions in lifelong learning*. Routledge: London and New York. 2009.

Glastra, F. / Hake, B. / Schedler, P.: "Lifelong learning as transnational learning". *Adult Education Quarterly* 54, 2004, pp. 291–307.

Hodkinson, P. / Bowman, H. / Colley, H.: "Conceptualising transitions from education to employment as career development and/or learning". In: *Constructing the future: Transforming career guidance*. Institute of Career Guidance: Stourbridge. 2006, pp. 35–48.

Klingovsky, U. / Pawlewicz, S.: „Übergang, Unsicherheit und Unterbrechung: Scheitern als Chance zur Differenzbildung". In: S. Schmidt-Lauff / H. von Felden / H. Pätzold (eds.): *Transitionen in der Erwachsenenbildung: Gesellschaftliche, institutionelle und individuelle Übergänge*. Barbara Budrich: Opladen. 2015, pp. 59–69.

Merriam, S. B. "How adult life transitions foster learning and development". *New Directions for Adult and Continuing Education* 2005(108), winter 2005, pp. 3–13.

Raithelhuber, E.: „Agency und Übergänge". In: W. Schröer / B. Stauber / A. Walther / L. Böhnisch / K. Lenz (eds.): *Handbuch Übergänge*. Beltz Juventa: Weinheim und Basel. 2013, pp. 99–140.

Schäffter, O.: „Übergangszeiten – Transitionen und Life Trajectories: Navigieren durch Bildungslandschaften im Lebensverlauf". In: S. Schmidt-Lauff / H. von Felden / H. Pätzold (eds.): *Transitionen in der Erwachsenenbildung: Gesellschaftliche, institutionelle und individuelle Übergänge*. Barbara Budrich: Opladen. 2015, pp. 19–34.

Schön, I.: "Adaptations to changing times: Agency in context". *International Journal of Psychology* 42(2), 2007, pp. 94–101.

Truschkat, I.: „Biografie und Übergang". In: W. Schröer / B. Stauber / A. Walther / L. Böhnisch / K. Lenz (eds.): *Handbuch Übergänge*. Beltz Juventa: Weinheim and Basel. 2013, pp. 44–63.

Von Felden, H. / S. Schmidt-Lauff, S.: „Transitionen in der Erwachsenenbildung: Übergänge im gesellschaftlichen Wandel, im Fokus von Forschung und aus Sicht pädagogischer Professionalität". In: S. Schmidt-Lauff / H. von Felden / H. Pätzold (eds.): *Transitionen in der Erwachsenenbildung: Gesellschaftliche, institutionelle und individuelle Übergänge*. Barbara Budrich: Opladen. 2015, pp. 11–16.

Von Felden, H. / Schäffter, O. / Schicke, H.: "Erwachsenenpädagogische Übergangsforschung: Lernwelten in gesellschaftlichen und biographischen Übergängen". In: H. von Felden / O. Schäffter / H. Schicke (eds.): *Denken in Übergängen: Weiterbildung in transitorischen Lebenslagen*. Springer VS: Wiesbaden. 2014, 7–18.

Walther, A.: "Übergänge im Lebenslauf: Erziehungswissenschaftliche Heuristik oder pädagogische Gestaltungaufgabe?". In: S. Schmidt-Lauff / H. von Felden / H. Pätzold (eds.): *Transitionen in der Erwachsenenbildung: Gesellschaftliche, institutionelle und individuelle Übergänge*. Barbara Budrich: Opladen. 2015, 35–56.

Walther, A. / Stauber, B.: "Übergänge in Lebenslauf und Biographie: Vergesellschaftung und Modernisierung aus subjektorientierter Perspektive". In: B. Stauber et al. (eds.): *Subjektorientierte Übergangsforschung*. Juventa: Weinheim and München. 2007, pp. 19–40.

Welzer, H.: *Transitionen: Zur Sozialpsychologie biographischer Wandlungsprozesse*. Edition Diskord: Tübingen. 2013.

Yorke, M.: *Employability in higher education: What it is – what it is not*. The Higher Education Academy: Helsington. 2006.

# Dimensions of Adult Education Professionalism

Sabine Schmidt-Lauff & Roberta Bergamini

# The Modern Phenomenon of Adult Learning and Professional Time-Sensitivity – a Temporal, Comparative Approach Contrasting Italy and Germany

**Abstract:** A temporal approach argues for a renewed understanding of time with respect to adult and lifelong learning in societies that are characterized by change and transformation. We promote the requirement of "quality time" for transformation, development and slow maturation as being a necessary component of a professional understanding of this phenomenon.

## Modern Conceptualization of Time – Transformation and Acceleration as Paradigms for Lifelong Learning Today

Our modern Western society is temporally complex, highly ambivalent and even paradoxical in its perspectives on time. These encompass flexibility, virtuality (e.g., synchronicity/a-synchronicity), acceleration, retardation, condensation, maturation and so forth. Time is directly interwoven with our existence and experience. From this point of departure, this article puts forward a new understanding of time in comprehending lifelong learning in societies characterized by change. It is therefore necessary to explore the influences and heterogeneous effects of these temporal, often contradictory, trends on adult learning and education. By questioning the effective "real times" for learning, one finds that time constraints are the main obstacle preventing adults from learning. This is true whether one lives in Italy or in Germany. Outcomes as a result of comparing chronometric criteria for participation may be surprising and reveal differences between the legal regulations concerning time in both countries. From a pedagogical point of view, it is helpful to consider some of the influences of these temporal trends on adult learning and adult education. How do transformation processes, often understood as modernization, affect the acceleration of social and biographical life courses? How could this be integrated into professional work with the sensitivity to time that is necessary?

The *Oxford Dictionary* (2011) defines time as "the indefinite continued progress of existence and events in the past, present and future regarded as a whole". We use clocks to measure the *quantity* of time and we divide time into units such as seconds, minutes, hours, days, weeks, months and years. From this position, we are able to structure time and to organize it in calendars, schedules and timetables. This has developed alongside the rise of a mainly linear conception and understanding of time within European culture (Leccardi 2013, p. 255). On the other hand, one recognizes another modality of time: the *quality* of time. One minute can seem very long while we are waiting and very short when we are busy with concentrated work. Time is therefore a relative and "relational" concept that depends on a frame of reference for its situational and personal experience[1].

As an observation of change, development or discontinuity, *transformation* is a recurring object. Whilst it is impossible to arrive at a single definition of transformation, the concept is often constructed as both a principle and a process of change over time. In our modern world, transformation occurs in such a highly dynamic way that its effects are obvious on all levels of society. According to Leccardi (2013, p. 255), "The linearity of life courses has been brought into question." Short circuits, 'just-in-time' reactions or 'on-demand solutions' are the new ideal, and thus "instants in succession take the place of temporal profundity" (ibid.).

(Lifelong) learning is often the answer. In cases where change and transformation are themselves becoming dynamic processes, learning over the lifespan emerges as an example of a successful (educational) biography. Thus, the idea of lifelong learning proves itself to be an expression of functional time interpretation. Consider, for instance, the notion that one must 'use your time sensibly for development and progress, such as by learning'. The concept of lifelong learning with normative pretensions can be seen as a manifestation of the temporalization of modern society, with "learning as adoption of infinite transformation" (Schmidt-Lauff 2012, p. 38). According to Kraus (2001, p. 115), there is a "correspondence between document-internal time perspective and the time period in which it arises".

A German example can be found in the recommendations of the *Committee on Innovation in Continuing Education* (BMBF 2008). The document states that "[g]lobalization and the knowledge-based society present people with great challenges" (BMBF 2008, p. 7). Decisions related to learning must react to these challenges quickly and flexibly in order to gain continuous "competencies that are acquired during voluntary activities and in everyday life" (ibid., p. 14). The implicit temporal influence on people today within globalization processes is pointed out very early, especially by Giddens (1991, p. 21), who states: "Globalisation concerns the intersection of presence and absence, the interlacing of social events and social

---

1    This dualism of quality versus quantity is often thought of as 'social' versus 'natural' time. There is a dichotomy between our individual memory and the sequential view of time as past, present and future (see Schmidt-Lauff 2012).

relations 'at distance' with the local contextualities." Globalization then means that "no one can 'opt out' of the transformation brought about by modernity" (ibid.).

Time sensitivity might be seen as an important priority for professional adult learning configurations. It is difficult to balance the right of an individual to determine his or her own present and future with the wider demand within society for ever-greater development, including achieving "economic growth" and "social cohesion" (EU Council Conclusion of 26 November 2012, p. 6). [2] De Haan (1996) establishes temporal points of reference for lifelong learning in the context of an awareness of an open future within the limitations of biological and cultural evolution. He writes that with the metaphor of "lifelong" learning comes the "intertwining of the present and future" (de Haan 1996, p. 160). This means that the problems related to careful consideration for the moment and the present must be balanced against concerns about continuity and responsibility for the future.

Transformation processes should be mastered individually (often declared as "management of transitions") as well as in a structurally adaptive way. "Transition" is a current buzzword and can be applied to the concept of "life-as-transition", that views time as a flow "in which human agency exists as a series of changing orientations" (Colley 2007, p. 431). Professional responsibility tries to balance and deal with such interrelations. [3] We are arguing for the need to challenge the ways in which time is understood in adult education and learning. Beyond the reductive and instrumental (didactical) conceptions of "time management" or "management of transitions", we want to emphasize time-sensitivity and temporal awareness as indispensable professional elements. It might also be interesting to ask how much time for learning is hidden in official work or during informal work activities.

## Contradictory Trends on Adult Learning: Hegemony of the Future, Shrinking of the Present and Loss of the Past?

The idea of time as an exceedingly complex concept within modern society leads to a review of the temporal dimension's past, present and future. When the future is given absolute priority and the present is marginalized, it might be the "end of 'long time', and the shrinking of the temporal that radically questions the concept

---

2   The economic perspective is especially stressed: 'Competence and skills levels...need to be continuously and thoroughly adapted to the changing needs of the economy and the labour market' (EU Council Conclusion of 26 November 2012, p. 6).

3   Here it might be interesting to ask: "How much time for learning during one's life is hidden within informal activities related either to official work or to informal work activities?"

of duration" (Leccardi 2013, p. 259). Very often, allowing the hegemony of the future results in the de-structuration of our past, our traditions and collective memories. How are the relationships among past, present and future changing? What does this mean for learning? How can professional adult education chart a course through modern conceptions of transition?

Firstly, the idea of learning throughout life and its "stabilizing" role leads to the core point of continuity and duration. The possibility to connect the past with the future – not firmly, but even through very small, continuous congruities – runs counter to the modern idea of full flexibility. Continuity, in contrast to radical change, is needed as a base for personal biography. *Bildung*[4] accepts the dual nature of modern times' need for continuity and the option of contingency. Time-sensitive professionalism handles contingencies as an open space of opportunity for transition, development and transformation of "meaning schemes" or "meaning perspectives" (Mezirow 2009). It therefore creates helpful processes of searching, questioning, latencies and (self-) reflection for learning's sake (Schmidt-Lauff 2016). Adult education then runs counter to an exaggerated belief in the future (linear learning) and it runs counter to purely utilitarian principles (instrumental learning).

Secondly, the pressure of the 'now and yet' increases and slogans such as 'the future is now' turn up. Again, to quote the German proclamation of the Committee on Innovation Continuing Education:

> *Knowledge, as well as the ability to use acquired knowledge, must be constantly adapted and expanded during the course of a person's life. Only in this way can personal orientation, societal participation, and employability be maintained and enhanced.*

(BMBF 2008, p. 7)

As Kraus (2001, p. 114) makes clear, it is of corresponding importance to implement change as a matter of educational policy "now under considerable time pressure" so that "the connection to developments is not lost, per the logic of this time structure". The prospect of learning throughout a lifetime represents a continuity-related answer to the erosion of temporal structures in a society that views itself as knowledge-based.

---

4   The term *Bildung* is one of the most controversial terms in German pedagogy. Its regard and discourse are important for a critical modern understanding of lifelong learning in an "accelerated" world (Schmidt-Lauff 2016). Since the beginning of the modern age, Bildung has aimed to explain human autonomy at the individual level, positing subjects as capable of self-development.

The future as "the new centre of human activity" is particularly important for our modern (Western) society (Leccardi 2013, p. 254). The hegemony of the future corresponds to habituation towards a problematic idea of time as a manageable resource. Capitalism modifies the economization of time as well. Time is defined as a scarce resource ("time is money"), which is the basis of concepts that influence our personal being and individual decisions in ways such as procrastination, punctuality, priority setting, output orientation and efficiency.[5] "The modern idea of the future we are accustomed to refers to a dimension separate from the present and distinct from the past, controllable and able to be planned" (ibid.). According to this interpretation, the ability to conceptualize time and "manage" it in a profitable way (individual but in the direction of contemporary capitalism) means that learning occupies an ambivalent role between slow maturation (e.g., stress reduction) and short circuit development (e.g., pursuing fast adaption).

Misguided belief in the ideology of progress and in the possibility to control the future should be overcome. Today we should know about the uncertainties generated by the future and the increasing presence of uncontrollable threats (Beck et al. 1996). "The future folds back into the present, it is absorbed within it"; but it is in fact the present "that is now associated with the principle of potential governability and controllability" (Leccardi 2013, p. 255).

These movements put the emphasis on (adult) learning in a specific form based on the understanding of learning as a (time-consuming) process (Schmidt-Lauff 2016). It gives learning a meaning of its own – always taking place in the present. Professional didactical orientations do not focus exclusively on outcomes and do not reduce the moments of receiving, reflecting and processing knowledge to short-term instances of updating information. If "things slow down", and learners have the opportunity to "immerse themselves in their learning", "valuable learning time" will unfold (Schmidt-Lauff 2008, p. 455ff; Schmidt-Lauff and Hösel 2015). What is needed for time-sensitive professional work, apparently, is didactically organized time, unburdened by the pressure of daily life (pauses, time to reflect, maturation, etc.), which in that respect creates a learning environment understood as an "oasis of deceleration" (Koller 2012, p. 119).

---

5   Structured and efficient time use is then so central to global functioning that there are recognized international organizations tasked with civil time, such as the International Atomic Time (IAT), the Coordinated Universal Time (UTC) and Greenwich Mean Time (GMT).

## Temporal Realities in Adult Learning and Education

These illustrations show that from a temporal-theoretical point of view, time aspects are of great significance for the specific life and learning phase of adulthood. Participating in formal and informal adult education and learning always involves making and taking time. In reality, how much time do adults spend on educational activities? To what extent do adults use their personal time resources for educational activities? What legislative background exists concerning time for adult education? What political actions and developments can be observed in Italy and Germany?

Studies show that "not having enough time" increasingly functions as an escape route for not participating in continuing education (CEDEFOP 2012; OECD 2011ff; German Adult Education Survey 2013). "Everyone has very little time" but the background and relations from which time rivalries result and which are opposed to lifelong learning are multi-layered (Schmidt-Lauff 2008). Since 2007, the Eurostat Adult Education Survey has repeatedly revealed that the main reason for non-participation in lifelong learning activities is a lack of time due to family responsibilities and conflicts with training and work schedules (Eurostat 2007). CEDEFOP (2012, p. 7) also declares, "The main obstacles that prevent adults from participating in lifelong learning are time constraints." In the 2014 OECD study *Education at a Glance*, a lack of time or temporal barriers to participation in adult learning activities are described as related to conflicts with work, family, inconvenient time offerings, lack of support and unexpected events. On average, 30% of the respondents declared "I was too busy at work" as the reason they did not participate in adult learning activities (OECD 2014, p. 359). In Italy, more than 35% of the respondents cited this while for Germany, no information was given.[6]

A further 15% of all respondents selected "I did not have time [to participate in adult learning activities] because of childcare or family responsibilities". Thus, for 45% of respondents, the burden of work or family precluded time for further learning activities. Factors related to how the learning activities were organized were also problematic. Of the overall sample, 12% felt that the primary issue was that "the course or programme was offered at an inconvenient time or place" (OECD 2014, p. 359). In Italy, this concern was indicated by less than 7% of respondents (ibid.).

---

6    We refer to the national percentage rate if a national specification has been given for Italy or Germany in the OECD data.

In addition, there are non-direct temporal limitations, such as "lack of employer's support", which 8% of respondents gave as their reason for not taking up a 'wanted learning activity'. Furthermore, some 4% said that "something unexpected came up", that interfered with further education or training (OECD 2014, p. 395).

Unlike school during childhood, in adulthood, where established temporal institutions for education are lacking, taking time for learning can generally be interpreted as an expression of individual learning interests and motivation. "In all countries surveyed, more participants than non-participants wanted to take up (further) learning activities" (OECD 2014, p. 359). There is clearly a demand for more individual time for learning. Non-participation in continuing education cannot be judged as a sign of disinterest in learning, as some studies argue (Schmidt-Lauff 2008, p. 355), or as an inability to manage personal time efficiently. As Sellin and Elson-Rogers (2003, p. 29) state:

> There is a clear need for more research into the relationship between the motivation to participate in CVET, the ways in which this is translated into real participation, and the impact of time as a resource in this process, both independently and in relation with other resources.

In this sense, it would be interesting to study the differences among (generational) learning times by analyzing the time reserved for learning for young adults versus that for working adults and elderly people.

## Legal Regulations Concerning Time as a Resource for Adult Learning (Macro Level)

At the macro-level, the development of adult rights to education is of high importance. For example, the first recommendation of the Committee on Innovation in Continuing Education (2008, p. 12) named "financial and time-related resources" as one of the basic conditions in need of improvement.

Legislative transnational regulations also matter, such as the ILO Paid Educational Leave Convention of 1974 (No. 140), which states in its preamble, "Human Rights affirms that everyone has the right to education." This convention argued for "protection of workers' representatives concerning the temporary release of workers, or the granting to them of time off, for participation in education or training programmes" (Article 1, ILO 1974, p. 1). As of today, 35 states have given their ratification by convention. At the same time, national laws and regulations also have to be considered. As Article 5 (ILO 1974, p. 1) points out:

*The means by which provision is made for the granting of paid educational leave may include national laws and regulations, collective agreements, arbitration awards, and such other means as may be consistent with national practice.*

In Italy, the development of adult rights to education began after the Second World War. At the same time, adult learning expanded in the field of education with the recognition of workers' rights to schooling (ISFOL 2008, p. 177).[7] The law 300/1970 (specifically Article 10), better known as the "Workers' Statute" (*Statuto dei Lavoratori*), expressed for the first time the right to obtain time to participate in educational courses. An amount of 150 hours per year and the possibility to obtain flexible working time for education has been specified by the D.P.R. 395/1988 (*Presidential Decree*). This decree applied the "Right of 150 Hours" per year for public workers. Law 53/2000, which has a specific focus on the right to care and education, states the right to education leave. It also declares the right to complete compulsory education or to obtain a secondary or higher education degree and the right to continuing education leave needed to increase knowledge and professional skills for a period not exceeding eleven months.

In Germany, an example of the concept of paid educational leave includes the "Länder Regulations", which deals with training leave (*"Bildungsurlaub"*, *"Bildungs- und Freistellungsgesetze"*). Every employee has the option to apply for approximately five days per year to participate in specific, accredited courses across a range of topics. These are mainly vocational but also include language courses, study trips, political topics, and so forth. Fourteen out of 16 federal states in Germany have these legislative options. Their primary objective is to grant employees enough time off to participate in learning outside the work environment in an area beyond their focus of employment. Some of the *Länder* have further instruments, including financial incentives, (e.g., *Bildungsscheck*) to encourage adults to take learning time.

## Comparison of Learning Times – Chronometric Criteria for Participation (Micro Level)

A comparative, empirical approach uses the functional part of time as an instrument to measure pedagogical impacts and participation. First, as per an OECD Indicator (*Education at a Glance*, annual study since 1996), chronometric measurements are used as an analytical instrument to evaluate school systems. Metrics

---

7    The following text was an outcome of the Students' Country Reports (Winter School 2016, Würzburg). Thank you very much to Carlo Terzaroli (Universita Degli Studi Firenze) and his translations of a report about "Participation in Adult Education in Italy: Time as a Mirror of Lifelong Learning Conditions".

of interest include time spent in a classroom, which is measured as the number of hours of teaching per year, or subject-related time for school pupils (OECD 2015).

For adults, the OECD study *Education at a Glance* (2012, p. 411) reports, "A participant in non-formal education receives 76 hours of instruction annually.[8] Four out of five of these hours are job-related." The time spent on non-formal educational activities represents an investment in the individual's skill development from both the employer and the individual (OECD 2011, p. 367).

*Table 1: The mean number of hours spent in non-formal education per participant and per adult (25 to 64 years of age) according to gender and age (2012) in Italy and Germany (source: OECD 2012, p. 412).*

|  | Men | | Women | | Women and Men | |
|---|---|---|---|---|---|---|
|  | Hours per participant | Hours per adult | Hours per participant | Hours per adult | Hours per participant | Hours per adult |
| OECD average | 74 | 24 | 81 | 26 | 76 | 25 |
| Italy | 47 | 9 | 48 | 9 | 48 | 9 |
| Germany | 78 | 36 | 74 | 30 | 76 | 33 |

Comparing the mean hours spent in non-formal education highlights the differences between Italy and Germany. While Germany almost mirrors the number of OECD average hours for participants as well as all adults, the time spent in non-formal adult education in Italy is nearly half this. Due to this overall lower participation rate in non-formal adult education, with Italy's rate standing at less than 30% and Germany's at approximately 46% in 2012, the difference between 'hours per participant' and "hours per adult" is much higher in Italy than in Germany (OECD 2012, p. 505). It would be also interesting to undertake further, comparative research to discover why in some countries (e.g. China), women spend less resp. more hours in non-formal education than men (without table).

Time is also used to forecast expected hours spent in non-formal education over a working life (ages 25 to 64). In all OECD countries, an individual can expect to receive 988 hours of instruction in non-formal education (OECD 2011, p. 364). The total investment in Italy is less than 400 hours, which is low compared to

---

8 Non-formal education is defined as "an organized and sustained educational activity that…may therefore take place both within and outside educational institutions and cater to individuals of all ages. Depending on country contexts, it may cover educational programs in adult literacy, basic education for out-of-school children, life skills, work skills, and general culture" (OECD 2011, p. 371).

Germany, where it exceeds approximately 1300 hours (OECD 2011, p. 365). The OECD (2011, p. 366) explains, "The expected number of hours of instruction is strongly related to the overall participation rate in non-formal education." On one hand, this might be a starting point for deeper comparative studies in the future, which are needed to understand these causes more effectively. On the other hand, it justifies professional action as a task to encourage more adults, such as in Italy, to participate in learning. Professional challenges for the future include building up temporally supportive structures and offering guidance and information, for example, about legal regulations and investments for adult learning (see 3.1).

For Germany, the Adult Education Survey (Bilger et al. 2013) provides a full chapter on "Time for Adult Education" (*Zeit für Weiterbildung*; Bilger et al. 2013, p. 48ff). In 2012, 31% of all learning activities lasted several days, with 24% lasting only several hours and 21% only one day (Bilger et al. 2013, p. 51). Surprisingly, 13% of all learning activities lasted a number of months. However, over the last few years, these long-lasting learning activities have tended to shrink.[9]

A differentiation between the segments of learning activities makes it obvious that, per year, vocational training takes place more often but with fewer hours of learning time. The participation rate of adults aged 18 to 64 is 35% in vocational training and 13% in non-vocational training (Bilger et al. 2013, p. 44).[10] The average number of hours spent on vocational training and learning is 74 hours while 108 hours are spent on non-vocational training annually (Bilger et al. 2013, p. 58). The latter includes general learning, including about culture, politics, health, and so forth. This difference between time spent on vocational and non-vocational training per year is very important but has had limited recognition in public debates. The average gross annual participation rate in non-vocational learning is nearly 1.5 times higher than vocational training hours. This is un-expected because in general, non-vocational learning activities mean that the learners themselves are giving up their private time, which could otherwise be spent on leisure, family, social engagements and recreation. Various studies in Germany have shown that there is a pronounced willingness for temporal self-reliant interaction for learning (Schmidt-Lauff 2008). This should not, however,

---

9   In Germany, such activities are, for example, a second chance for vocational or ..pro-fessional qualification, and state certified Master Craftsmen.

10  It should be noted that aging is becoming significant but until now this has not been reported in the statistics. According to an ISTAT (2013) forecast, in 2018, life expectan-cy in Italy should reach 78.8 years for men and 84.3 for women. People aged over 60 years would reach 28.9% of the population (ISTAT 2013). In Germany, it is becoming normal to work until the age of 67 or even 68.

be equated with "time sovereignty" as part of individualization but rather as a development towards "personal time competence" with an awareness of the necessity for collective structures.

## Implications of Modern Times on Adult Learning: More Research and the Necessity of Professional Time-sensitivity

Drawing on our time analysis about socially-conceived, time-related structures confronted by subjectively experienced time-quality, we believe that modern temporal phenomena are very important for adult education. During adulthood, time rivalries emerge between work, family and recreation on one hand and learning on the other. Often, the organization of explicit learning time comes into conflict with other activities. This underlines the need for professional time-sensitivity and support. On the micro-level, professional support means termination, seriation, sequencing, repetition, pauses and acceptance of synchronicity or asynchronicity during learning processes. Learning takes time, and professional programme planning at the meso-level must situate time slices for learning within different social and individual circumstances. On the macro-level, solutions may be achieved by establishing effective incentives and cost-sharing arrangements, including education voucher programmes, learning accounts or other schemes, "through which adults can accumulate both time and funding" (Federighi 2013, p. 68). In further research, there should be increased recognition about time, and not only money, as a resource for individual learning and as a temporal challenge for innovative professional interventions.

From a subjective point of view, learning times cannot be extended or accelerated endlessly. Reflection and (intentional) learning needs time (Alhadeff-Jones 2010). Where limitations emerge, compensation through informal variations such as 'learning en passant' is not a sustainable solution (Schmidt-Lauff 2008). "Explicit time for learning" encompasses presence-related phenomena and emphasizes the learning moment itself. This highlights the necessity of unburdened learning time, which is not "just there" but must be structured and sheltered. Learning time is then subjectively perceived as a special time quality, a time oasis and 'time well-being'. A new quality of learning can emerge as "a kind of standstill in time" in an accelerated world (Koller 2012, p. 119; Schmidt-Lauff and Hösel 2015). Participation in continuing education hints at the significance of explicit times for learning. Time for processes in which intended, reflexive learning can take place should exist as an essentially unburdened and exclusive time-space (Schmidt-Lauff 2016).

To understand the influence of temporality, it should be noted that it encompasses more than merely chronological, time-related attributes. There is great diversity among temporal elements as they exist in pedagogy, including time sequences during the (lifelong) learning process, problems of temporal limitations, such as work, family and recreation, the past-present-future relationship as a background for learning, and the didactical approach to synchronize learning processes. An inclusive educational model would promote lifelong learning that is temporally sensitive enough for modern times. It is therefore clear that adult learning and education does not take place in temporal isolation. In fact, a lifelong learning process derives insights from the past, implements the present and envisions the future. Rather than focusing only on the future or outcome-orientated results of learning, temporally sensitive professional understanding and support would value learning itself as a worthwhile, present-oriented and valuable process.

# References

Alhadeff-Jones, M.: "Learning to challenge time in adult education: A critical and complex perspective". In: Merill, B. (ed.): *Proceedings of the 40th Annual Standing Conference on University Teaching and Research in the Education of Adults*. Warwick University: Warwick, UK. 2010.

Beck, U. / Giddens, L. / Lash, S.: *Reflexive Modernisierung: Eine Kontroverse*. Suhrkamp: Frankfurt am Main. 1996.

Bilger, F. / Gnahs, D. / Hartmann, J. / Kuper, H.: *Weiterbildungsverhalten in Deutschland: Resultate des Adult Education Survey 2012*. wbv: Bielefeld. 2013.

BMBF: *Empfehlungen des Innovationskreises Weiterbildung für eine Strategie des Lernens im Lebenslauf.* wbv: Bonn and Berlin. 2008.

CEDEFOP: *Training leave: Policies and practice in Europe*. Publications Office of the European Union: Luxembourg. 2012, retrieved from www.cedefop.europe. eu/files/5528_en.pdf.

Colley, H.: 'Understanding time in learning transitions through the lifecourse'. *International Studies in Sociology of Education* 17(4), 2007, pp. 427–443.

Council of the European Union: *Council conclusion of 26 November 2012 on education and training in Europe 2020: The contribution of education and training to economy recovery, growth and jobs*. Brussels. 26 November 2012. REF 2012/C 393/02.

de Haan, G.: *Die Zeit in der Pädagogik – Vermittlungen zwischen der Fülle der Welt und der Kürze des Lebens*. Beltz: Weinheim and Basel. 1996.

Federighi, P.: *Adult and continuing education in Europe: Pathways for a skill growth governance*. Publications Office, European Commission: Luxembourg 2013.

Giddens, L.: *Modernity and self-Identity: Self and society in the late modern age*. Polity Press: Cambridge. 1991.

International Labour Organization (ILO): "Deferred examination of conventions: Paid educational leave convention, 1974 (no. 140) (short survey)". In: *Working party on policy regarding the revision of standards*. Geneva. March 2001, retrieved from http://www.ilo.org/dyn/normlex/en/f?p=NORMLEXPUB:12100:0:: NO::P12100_INSTRUMENT_ID:312285.

ISTAT: *La partecipazione degli adulti alle attività formative*. ISFOL: Roma. 2013.

Koller, H.C.: *Bildung anders denken: Einführung in die Theorie transformatorischer Bildungsprozesse*. Kohlhammer: Stuttgart. 2012

Kraus, K.: *Lebenslanges Lernen – Karriere einer Leitidee*. wbv: Bielefeld. 2001.

Leccardi, C.: "Temporal perspectives in de-standardised youth life courses". In: W. Schröer / B. Stauber / A. Walther / L. Böhnisch / K. Lenz, K. (eds.): *Handbuch der Übergänge*. Juventa: Weinheim and Basel. 2013, pp. 251–268.

Mezirow, J.: "Transformative learning theory". In: J. Mezirow / E. Taylor (eds.): *Transformative learning in practice: Insights from community, workplace, and higher education*. Jossey-Bass: San Francisco. 2009, pp. 18–32.

OECD: *Education at a glance 2011: OECD indicators*. OECD Publishing: Paris. 2011–2014, retrieved from http://dx.doi.org/10.1787/eag-2011-en.

Oxford Dictionaries (2011). *Time*. Oxford University Press: Oxford. 2016.

Schmidt-Lauff, S.: *Zeit für Bildung im Erwachsenenalter: Interdisziplinäre und empirische Zugänge*. Waxmann: Münster et al. 2008.

Schmidt-Lauff, S. (ed.): *Zeit und Bildung: Annäherungen an eine zeittheoretische Grundlegung*. Waxmann: Münster. 2012.

Schmidt-Lauff, S.: "Time as a reflective moment of transformative learning". In: A. Laros / T. Fuhr / E. Taylor (eds.): *Transformative learning meets Bildung: An international exchange*. Sense Publisher: Rotterdam, Boston and Taipei. 2016.

Schmidt-Lauff, S. / Hösel, F.: "Kulturelle Erwachsenenbildung: Ästhetisches, zeitsensibles und partizipatives Lernen". In: *erwachsenenbildung.at. Das Fachmedium für Forschung, Praxis und Diskurs* 25, 2015, retrieved from http://www.erwachsenenbildung.at/magazin/15-25/meb15-25.pdf.

Sellin, B. / Elson-Rogers, S.: "Engaging individuals in lifelong learning: Mobilising resources, time and money". CEDEFOP working paper: Thessaloniki (GR). 2003.

Kira Nierobisch, Hakan Ergin, Concetta Tino
& Ingeborg Schüßler

# Subjective Didactics – Effects of Individual Pedagogical Professional Action

**Abstract:** Subjective theories on adult teaching and learning regulate – although only implicitly – the didactic actions of teachers. This article presents a reflection of the subjective didactics of students of adult education as a way of developing their professionalization and the special role of comparative transnational analysis.

## Introduction

In response to the question of professionalism in adult education, Gieseke refers to the relevance of basic scientific knowledge that can be evaluated through experiences (c.f., Gieseke 2010, pp. 243–244). This also includes individual interpretations and diagnoses that determine pedagogical action. Accordingly, professionalism is "a differentiated approach regarding research findings, the use of instruments of action and their independent interpretation [and] the interpretation of action situations and flexible networked acting" (ibid.). This professional action, which relates to the micro- as well as to the macro-level, needs an academic education that not only depends on scientific bases, but also defines terms and concepts for this action (c.f., Gieseke 2012, p. 252). This includes the exploration of educational processes and work with empirical results (ibid.).

Using this understanding of professionalization, it is necessary to investigate the relationship between scientific knowledge and biographical experience in the study of adult education. What is the significance, for example, of socialization experiences, internships, part-time jobs, social commitments or major fields of study in the development of future adult educators? Citing a third element besides science and practice, Jütte, Walber and Behrens refer to the scope in which each system encounters and interacts with the other, and in which professionalization is experienced and negotiated (see 2012).

In this sense, the study of adult education can be understood as a reflective space of science and practice. Teaching and learning as key aspects of the professionalization of adult education are particularly important. On the one hand, it is important to deal with scientific theories; on the other, these theories should be applied and implemented in the course of individual seminar planning and holding or internships. Finally, students should refer back to these theories. In this interdependence of teaching and learning, subjective didactics arise. The theory of subjective didactics follows constructivist principles of self-control and self-organization, by which everyone develops their own structure and dynamic of learning (but also of teaching), and on which teaching and learning processes (c.f., Kösel 2008) should be expanded. Consequently, subjective didactics play a central role in the process of professionalization of (prospective) adult educators. They are – according to Nittel – also shaped by the cultural and social experiences of the subjects (c.f., Nittel 2000, p. 53), which determine their individual process of professionalization. This is involved in the respective national discourse on professionalization, and is also an expression of a discipline-specific discourse on professionalization. This aspect is taken up by the following article, which extracts the subjective didactics of students of adult education from Italy, Turkey and Germany, and analyzes these in terms of key components of individual but also discipline-specific professionalization.

This paper first states the importance of didactic knowledge in adult education and gives reasons for why examination with subjective theories about didactics forms the basis of understanding and dealing with scientific theories about learning and teaching (Part 2). Subsequently, key scientific theories about learning and teaching in the three countries are presented in brief, and didactic implementation within universities and in the practice of adult education is examined (Part 3). The genesis of the subjective didactics of students of adult education has been analyzed and extrapolated by empirical investigation. For this purpose, so-called "vignettes", whose methodology will be explained briefly, were used (Part 4). The main results of the countries involved are then presented and related to concepts of teaching and learning together with a brief outlook that refers to the relevance of subjective didactics for adult education (Part 5).

## Subjective didactics between experience-based and scientific knowledge

Adult education can be described as a field of practice relating to the processes of imparting and acquiring knowledge. It is for the adult educator to mediate between the subjective knowledge of participants, their ways of life and scientific knowledge. This requires an understanding of how learning processes can be encouraged and supported through teaching. Didactical knowledge is mentioned as the "basis of andragogic professionalism" (Siebert 1996, p. 3).

Mediation competence is identified as the "actual core of andragogic qualification" (Nuissl 1996, p. 33).

Thus didactical action extends to the following dimensions:

1) At the level of teaching and learning situations: micro-didactical detailed planning
2) At the level of planning seminars: i.e., planning courses, place of learning, period of learning, content and materials, depending on target group; selecting texts, regulating finance
3) At the macro-didactical level of programme planning: e.g., planning of training programmes in the field of further education in companies
4) At the organizational level of an institution or of a provider: questions about the educational mandate, content, target groups, organizational structure
5) Mediation tasks at the level of education policy: e.g., concerning legislation, regulation of minimum number of participants, conditions for the recognition of new establishments

This already shows that didactical action includes the mediation and planning of the tasks in which learning and teaching processes are integrated. As a result, didactical thinking on the macro-level is also relevant, because this also determines the organizational and learning culture in which the learning processes of institutions are embedded.

Didactical thinking is, in turn, influenced by biographical teaching and learning experiences achieved at school, in the parental home, at sports clubs or in institutions of child and youth welfare. Perceptions about good teaching or the "correct" way to learn, reinforce an understanding about didactics that extends from theories about everyday life. This understanding is called "subjective didactics", and the knowledge is based on experiences, reduced down from their actual complexity.

On the other hand, there is scientific knowledge. Almost all academic courses on adult education/further education address the essentials of the theory of learning; planning and designing lessons; and didactical and methodical action. This theoretical knowledge is substantiated with empirical findings, educational theories, learning theories and anthropological foundations.

It is important to apply these experience-based ideas and to contrast them with the scientific theories of didactics. For this reason, in a second step it is also necessary to know scientifically relevant theories about teaching and learning. To this end, the received didactic theories in Italy, Turkey and Germany are presented in brief below.

## Italy, Turkey and Germany: theories of learning and teaching

Participants in the comparative group emphasized that every professional who is involved in teaching and education must have a wide and solid theoretical background connected to the different theories of learning, e.g., behaviourism (e.g., Pavlov, Skinner), cognitivism (e.g., Piaget, Bruneror) or constructivism (e.g., Bruner, Vygotskij, Jonassen, Varela, Maturana).

Having this structure of knowledge is important in every educational context and, above all, when teaching and learning processes are developed in adult and learning education, because it guides teachers/educators to support learners in their personal development (Tramma 2011).

The three countries are included in the strategies of lifelong learning (Lima & Guimaraes 2011). The lifelong learning paradigm itself is based on the centrality of learners as an important condition of training processes aimed at learning in adulthood. Therefore, the roles of teachers and learners are renegotiated according to some key concepts: learner-centredness, learner responsibility, the learning contract and the role of the teacher as a facilitator of the learning and evaluation process.

However, compared to the Turkish academic context, the Italian and German ones have a larger explicit number of perspectives that teachers usually refer to within ALE courses. In fact, in Germany, *Bildung* is a characteristic theory known as a perspective based on Kant's idea of education, whose aim is the realization of the idea of humanity (humanism) within a democratic society, where a human being conceives the world through its understanding of the dialectic of theory and practice. In Italy, the development of the humanity of the individual in educational contexts is still important, but with globalization and the emphasis on productivity, another theory disseminated in Germany and in Turkey has begun to exert influence. This is the curriculum theory, whose main tenets are pragmatism and utilitarianism. In German contexts, another theoretical reference is the identity theory, known as a consequence of the crisis of modernity and associated with individualization. It is focused on concepts of "biography" and "identity". Learning, as a generative issue, is promoted by reflection on life experiences, through which individuals can reshape their actions and their life goals. In Italy, the approaches adopted that can have connections to this perspective are those focused on personal biography, through which learners explicate the experiences of their life or reflect on theories such as Mezirow's transformative theory (1990, 1991), Shön's model (1983), Boud's model (1994) or the phenomenological perspective (Husserl 1982).

Another theoretical perspective in German academic contexts is the empowerment didactics. This is based on the constructivism perspective, and it considers teachers as facilitators and not as generators of the learning process. In this sense, learners use their own most suitable method of learning and become masters of their knowledge destiny within a context of collaboration and interpersonal communication. In Italy, the reference theories of experiential learning can be connected to this approach, such as Kolb's learning cycle (1984) and the developmental cycle outlined by Jarvis (1996). The first holistic approach combines experience, perception, cognition and behaviour, and promotes learning as a result of the transformative process of experience. The second considers two essential elements of the developmental process: social interaction and the disjuncture that can occur during interaction and cause dissonance in any aspect. These include knowledge, skills, sense, emotions, beliefs and promoting learning. All the Italian perspectives have some connections with these empowerment didactics.

This section presents the theoretical perspectives connected to identity theory and empowerment theory in Germany, Italy and Turkey; they are based mostly on the constructivist theory of learning, which judges that adult learners are always responsible for their own process of learning. In fact, they are required to analyze their learning needs and subscribe to a learning contract (Knowles 1970); to be strongly involved within a cycle of transformation based on their experience (Jarvis 1996; Kolb 1984); to be autonomous within their learning process (Merriam & Caffarella 1999); to be able to develop reflective practices (Boud 1994; Mezirow 1990, 1991; Shön 1983); and to be able to activate a meta-reflective process in order to change their theories, assumptions, acquisition of new knowledge and learning results (Mortari 2012). On the one hand, this process of self-direction corresponds to what Orefice (2003) calls self-knowledge management, through which learners are able to regain possession of their learning through a deep appreciation of self. However, a broader reflection allows us to think about how little thought is given to the external variables that can influence learning, such as the didactical, social and political dimensions. Hence the questions are:

1) Does adult learning depend only on personal ability and responsibility?
2) What is the meaning of the theories that ALE mentioned for learning and training?

There will be an attempt to give a response to the first question in the final part of this paper. Important information has been gathered during the comparison work process to answer the second question. This phase helped the comparative group participants to reflect on the important aspects of a good approach to learning and teaching.

## Empirical design

The empirical design of the comparative group is thematically linked to a research project at the University of Education in Ludwigsburg, which investigates, in the context of the topic of professionalization, how attitudes towards the didactics of teaching and learning develop during study (Holm & Nierobisch 2016). For this purpose, a qualitative method using vignettes was employed, which was also used in the comparative group. Vignettes could be "short scenarios in written or pictorial form, intended to elicit responses to typical scenarios" (Hill 1997, p. 177), "concrete examples of people and their behaviours on which participants can offer comment or opinion" (Hazel 1995, p. 2) or "stories about individuals, situations and structures which can make reference to important points in the study of perceptions, beliefs and attitudes" (Hughes 1998, p. 381).

According to Hill (see 1997), the vignettes were used so that the participants[1] could explain a topic and reflect on it under the conditions of the guidelines. Consequently, the leading question of this study was: "What do you think: which aspects are important for learning and teaching in a good way? Please explain." In the evaluation of the genesis of subjective didactics, reference was made first to the country reports. Using these, we discussed the theoretical concepts of didactics that have been taught in the degree programme at university, the didactical concepts and teaching standards that are current practice outside of university, the biographical aspects that are relevant to developing an individual understanding or subjective theory of learning and teaching and, lastly, how learning and teaching are affected by society.

Based on the answers to all these vignettes, we developed different categories as references to the learning biography, fragments of learning theories, institutions of socialization, institutional contexts, framings of (education) policy and the economic and learning setting.

## Main results and conclusion

The analysis and comparison of vignettes brought to light that the most important aspect for learning and teaching processes is the learning environment, whose characteristics are the results of teachers' subjective didactics. This conclusion arises from the comparison process among the indicators considered at different

---

1    Every participant of the comparative group asked about five fellow students from their home university to complete a vignette. These vignettes were analyzed and evaluated in group work within the framework of the winter school.

levels: macro, mega, meso and micro. At the macro-level, there are three countries (Germany, Italy and Turkey) that have adopted European policies and the UNESCO concept of lifelong learning.

In Germany, awareness has grown that a response only to the labour market's needs cannot prepare the workforce to face current social and technological challenges; accordingly, the ideas of education and *Bildung* once more play an important role in solving economic problems successfully. In these terms, adult and continuing learning at the mega and macro-level are generally not based on a political state curriculum, so learners have the opportunity to make free choices and to follow their interests (vocational and continuing education and training; general, cultural and civic education; continuing and academic courses), thanks to the huge learning opportunities guaranteed at the macro-level and supported by the quality standard, whose framework is established by federal states. The key concepts of such a system are: "democracy, the right to further education, pathways not only for occupational aims". All this has implications at the macro-level, leading to a shortage of skilled workers, but also at the micro-level where, on the one hand, learners as voluntary participants are free to choose the pathway most suitable to them according to the principles of self-regulation and personal responsibility. On the other hand, teachers of ALE can implement subjective learning didactics based on different learning theories. This is a way to focus on the subjects and not on the content of the pathways. Comparison between the elements that create a learning environment within the different contexts focused not only on the didactical approaches that German teachers choose according to target-group participants, but also on two other aspects: infrastructure and personal and contextual conditions. In Germany, a large infrastructure with resources such as technological equipment and many free libraries is guaranteed. In addition, ALE institutions are readily accessible. The law foresees the creation of learning contexts with some important elements. For students, these include the right to learn and social equality. For teachers, the provisions are often a guaranteed job and a good salary. These are all elements that inevitably influence a learning environment.

In Italy, although changes in educational contexts have always been very difficult because of cultural heritage, from the 1990s onwards, important transformations have taken place within educational and public organizations. Organizations and their representatives have recognized new roles, tasks and responsibilities. This process, caused by the Italian economic crisis (at the meso-, macro- and micro-levels) and by the change within the European scenario (at the mega level), has come to involve adult and continuing education. In order to include adults in the education process, a system of recognition of non-formal and informal competences has also been implemented since 2013, but there is still a law governing participation in ALE/LLL. It is quite clear that, at the meso- and macro-levels, the will is there to evaluate and check results in order to reach European standards and to overcome current social challenges, including an economic crisis, unemployment and unqualified refugees. At the university level, still more needs to be done to support continuing education as well as teacher training. However, the content within courses and degrees in this area refers to different learning theories. This leads to the implementation of different didactical approaches based on traditional approaches, or ideas based on reflectiveness or active learning. However, the different approaches depend not only on the teachers' ideas of teaching and learning that stem from their own beliefs, and their own idea of their professionalism influenced by the legal salary and the lack of resources for training (personal, cultural and contextual aspects) – they also depend on the infrastructure available. In Italy, the conditions for implementing active didactics are often poor, because of the characteristics of the classroom (small with fixed chairs), or the large number of students in attendance. The content and the time of the course and the results to be achieved (norms) are other factors. In addition, the legal salary and lack of investment in teacher training intensifies the poor position of ALE. In this sense, personal and cultural teacher dimensions, or unsuitable environments and inadequate resources, contribute to the implementation of the teacher's own didactical methods, and to creating a kind of learning environment that is the result of many internal and external factors.

With reference to Turkey, it can be argued that the way adult and continuing education functions has changed due to the national (meso) and international (mega) policies of the governments in Turkey. This inevitably influences the approach and type of subjective didactic methods employed. Soon after the Turkish Republic was established in 1923, the early republican governments were required to disseminate the country's reforms, including secularism, republicanism and nationalism. Lecturers might therefore be employed to teach large numbers of people at the same time. Next, in the pre- and post-World War II period, teacher candidates at village institutes, which functioned like today's education faculties, were provided with both theoretical knowledge, such as how to teach literacy classes, and practical knowledge, such as how to farm. These teachers were sent to villages and asked to educate peasants in multiple ways, including economically and socially. Therefore, lectures, problem-solving, cooperative learning and practice-based approaches could be among the subjective didactics employed by these teachers. Following on from this, public education centres, which were opened in the 1950s and numbered almost a thousand around the country, became the main providers of adult and continuing education. Although these centres taught people literacy for a long time, they have recently focused on vocational courses. It would therefore not be surprising to see the use of role-play in a drama class or a practice session for a guitar class in a public education centre. Lastly, it should be noted that Turkey-EU relations have progressed adult and continuing education on the mega-, meso- and micro-levels. Accordingly, the government encourages collaboration with European countries, adult and continuing education centres envision making European connections and individuals aim at taking part in European projects and earning European certificates. The result is that a typical European project, which includes visits to another country, may well employ on-site visits, cooperative learning and training on the job among its subjective didactic methods.

The findings of this theoretical and empirical study show that the subjective didactics of students of adult education are particularly dependent on the balance of theoretical knowledge and practical experience. In the context of a university, theories about learning and teaching not only characterize professionalization in terms of curricular contents, but especially constitute knowledge that should be experienced in practice and also reflected pedagogically. Teachers and lecturers not only have the role of imparting knowledge, but also that of being a companion in this process. This includes subject-specific reconnection as well as personal presence in the sense of role-model functions and learning support. In addition to learning experiences in the context of a school, individual didactical experiences, such as internships and part-time jobs, are particularly influential in the process of professionalization. Nevertheless, pedagogical support and motivation to reflect on these experiences at university are essential so that students can pinpoint the theoretical concepts of teaching and learning. Developments in education policy, e.g., neoliberally anchored concepts of lifelong learning or questions concerning the shrinkage of education and its consequences, exert a great influence on adult education and the process of its professionalization. This is demonstrated by the findings of all three countries, and is so because these developments are reflected in individual concepts of subjective didactics. The vignettes analyzed also refer to the meaning and framing of (educational) policy for the professionalization of adult education. This is demonstrated, for example, by ministries imposing regulations according to the learning context that are neither pedagogically nor institutionally supported. These experiences lead not only to friction with learners in practice, but also influence the pedagogical process of the professionalization of students. The vignettes and the discussions in the comparative group indicate that scientific knowledge is not only a central component in the process of professionalization, but also that this process is framed by biographical experiences at the micro- and macro- didactical level. The process of self-reflection on one's own knowledge as it is applied in everyday life can be developed further to become professional didactical knowledge.

## References

Boud, D.: "Conceptualising learning from experience: Developing a model for facilitation". Published in *Proceedings of the 35th Adult Education Research Conference*, 20–22 May 1994. College of Education, University of Tennessee; Knoxville, Tennessee. 1994, pp. 49–54.

Gieseke, W. / Dietel, S.: "Professionelles Selbstverständnis der Disziplin Erwachsenen-/Weiterbildung". In: R. Egetenmeyer & I. Schüßler (eds.): *Akademische Professionalisierung in der Erwachsenenbildung/Weiterbildung*. Schneider Verlag Hohengehren: Baltmannweiler. 2012, pp. 247–257.

Gieseke, W.: "Professionalität und Professionalisierung". In: R. Arnold / S. Nolda & E. Nuissl (eds.): *Wörterbuch Erwachsenenbildung* (2nd edition). Bad Herbrunn. 2010, pp. 243–244.

Hazel, N.: "Elicitation techniques with young people". *Social Research Update* 12, 1995, retrieved 2.2.2016, from http://sru.soc.surrey.ac.uk/SRU12.html.

Hill, M.: "Participatory research with children". *Child and Family Social Work* 2(3), August 1997, pp. 171–183.

Holm, U. / Nierobisch, K.: "DidaktEB – Ansichten zum Lehren und Lernen: Individuelle Didaktiken von Studierenden der Erwachsenenbildung an der Pädagogischen Hochschule Ludwigsburg". In: S. Kuntze (ed.): *Der Blick auf Unterricht und Lernen – Reflexion forschungsmethodischer Ansätze in interdisziplinärer Perspektive*. 2016. In press.

Hughes, R.: "Considering the vignette technique and its application to a study of drug injecting and HIV risk and safer behaviour". *Sociology of Health and Illness* 20(3), May 1998, pp. 381–400.

Husserl, E.: *Ideas pertaining to a pure phenomenology and to a phenomenological philosophy* (Trans.: F. Kersten). Martinus Nijhoff: Haag. 1982.

Jarvis, P.: *Adult and continuing education* (2nd edition). Routledge: London and New York. 1996.

Jütte, W. / Behrens, M. / Behrens, J.: "Interaktive Professionalisierung in der Weiterbildung: Das Bielefelder Modell". In: R. Egetenmeyer / I. Schüßler (eds.): *Akademische Professionalisierung in der Erwachsenenbildung/Weiterbildung*. Schneider Hohengehren: Baltmannweiler. 2012, pp. 171–181.

Kösel, E.: "Lernkulturen als Lebenswelten von Lernenden und Lehrenden". In: U. Stadler- Altmann / J. Schindele / A. Schraut: *Neue Lernkultur – neue Leistungskultur*. Bad Heilbrunn. 2008, pp. 18–41.

Kolb, D.A.: *Experiential learning*. Prentice Hall: New Jersey. 1984.

Lima, L.C. / Guimaraes, P.: *European strategies in lifelong learning: A critical introduction*. Barbara Budrich Publishers, Opladen & Farmington Hills. 2011.

Merriam, S.B. / Caffarella, R.S.: *Learning in adulthood: A comprehensive guide*. Jossey Bass: San Francisco. 1999.

Mezirow, J.D.: *Transformative dimension of adult learning*. Jossey-Bass: San Francisco. 1991.

Mezirow, J.D. (ed.): *Fostering critical reflection in adulthood: A guide to transformative and emancipatory learning*. Jossey-Bass: San Francisco. 1990.

Mortari, L.: "Learning thoughtful reflection in teacher education". *Teachers and Teaching: Theory and Practice* 18(5), 2012, pp. 525–545.

Nittel, D.: *Von der Mission zur Profession? Stand und Perspektiven der Verberuflichung in der Erwachsenenbildung*. Bielefeld. 2010.

Nuissl, E.: "Erwachsenenpädagogische Professionalisierung 1995ff". In: K. Derichs-Kunstmann / P. Faulstich / R. Tippelt (eds.): *Qualifizierung des Personals in der Erwachsenenbildung* (Beiheft zum Report). Frankfurt am Main. 1996, pp. 23–36.

Orefice, P.: *La formazione di specie*. Guerini: Milano. 2003.

Schon, D.A.: *The reflective practitioner: How professionals think in action*. Basic Books: USA. 1983.

Siebert, H.: *Didaktisches Handeln in der Erwachsenenbildung. Didaktik aus konstruktivistischer Sicht* (2nd edition). Neuwied et al. 1996.

Tramma, S.: "L'educazione degli adulti davanti all'incrocio tra deindustrializzazione e invecchiamento dell'età adulta". In: M. Castiglioni (ed.): *L'educazione degli adulti tra crisi e ricerca di senso*. Unicopli: Milano. 2011, pp. 109–120.

Lilia Halim, Kamisah Osman & Wan Nor Fadzilah Wan Husin

# Core Competencies of Malaysian Science Centre Facilitators: A Delphi Study

**Abstract:** Science centre facilitators have a wide reach in the community. Acquiring the core competencies of an effective adult educator is, therefore, imperative. Malaysian experts highlighted competency related to the evaluation of learning as a particular priority, thus reinforcing the notion of learning for examination and employability.

## Introduction

Adult learning professionals, also commonly known as adult educators, are important for the realization of the lifelong learning agenda. They play an important role in providing opportunities and improving the quality of learning at all levels. Despite this, in his article *Profession and Professional Work in Adult Education in Europe*, Nuissl (2009) found that no country sees adult education as a profession, mainly due to the diverse nature of the adult education sector. Among others, this includes various target groups of adult learners and unclear institutional structures. Thus, Nuissl (2009) concludes that little is known of the jobs and skills that adult educators possess and need to improve.

One of the ways to bring focus to the adult education field and to create progress for the professional development of the adult educators is to identify the competencies needed by the educators to provide quality learning opportunities. Identifying competencies is one of the important stages towards the recognition of adult education and educators as a profession and professionals alike. Efforts to identify the relevant competencies are being pursued in both small- and large-scale research (e.g., Buiskool et al. 2010; Bernhardsson & Lattke 2009). These studies focus on the generic competencies of adult educators. At the same time, the researchers also recognize that competencies must dependent on both context and content.

This chapter deals with the competencies of adult educators in the field of science. Its particular focus is the competencies that are required for the teaching and learning of science in non-formal settings. The chapter first provides an overview of the professionalization of adult educators with special reference to the Malaysian context. Lifelong learning and continuing education have recently gained prominence in Malaysia with the launch of the national life-long learning (LLL) policies in 2014. This is followed by an empirical study to determine the competencies of adult learning professionals working in non-formal science learning agencies, and the implications of this work.

## Professionalism of adult educators

A common view of what counts as a profession is that specific knowledge and skills are required and must, therefore, be learned. Typical examples are law and medicine. Thus, one is said to be a professional when one has acquired the competencies required in the respective field. This perspective of professionalism is called the "competence theoretical approach" (Maier-Gutheil & Hof 2011). This understanding entails the identification of the desired competencies needed to do the job. As argued by Nuissl (2009), this theoretical approach is more geared to preparing an individual to gain access to the occupation. One can also acquire competencies during life and work. Thus, the mark of the professional is also achieved through ongoing learning derived from the experience of work (Maier-Gutheil & Hof 2011). In the context of adult education, it can be argued that competencies are probably acquired more through work experience, since educators may not have the formal education for the job they perform. This would be even more the case for those who work as volunteers in the adult education field.

In the Malaysian context, adult education encompasses education beyond the age of 15 and is conducted through formal and non-formal systems. The formal system refers to educational activity at an institution of higher learning that leads to a recognized certificate, diploma or degree (Azman & Ahmad 2006). Non-formal education is defined as any organized activity outside the established formal education system. The purpose of non-formal education is to enable individuals and the community to acquire the knowledge, skills and drive to meet change and development needs.

Adult education in Malaysia is provided by three major groups: government agencies, non-profit organizations and the private sector. These providers deliver educational activities to Malaysian adults, activities that range from the government literacy programme, personal development and citizenship education to ideological and religious studies. As a consequence, education is given by various kinds of "teachers", e.g., adult educators, trainers, health workers, community development assistants and semi-trained teachers.

Studies on adult educators (Sidin et al. 1996; Kamarudin & Jusoh 2008; Mohamed & Che Razali 2013) show that adult educators lack the following competencies: a) possessing certain qualities such as mutual respect, tact and treating participants as adults; b) communication skills; c) being good in their respective technical areas; d) the ability to present lessons using understandable concepts;

e) encouraging the participants to be active; and f) sufficient concern about the students' pace of learning. In addition, it was found that these adult educators only spent 20 per cent of their working time on teaching activities. The rest of the time was allocated for other tasks, such as attending meetings and handling administrative work.

It appears that the need for professionalization of adult educators persists throughout time. Both Sidin et al. (1996) and Kamarudin and Jusoh (2008) suggest that teachers must have an understanding of adult education philosophy, principles and delivery techniques. This must be combined with an awareness of learner needs and experiences, thus leading to a more effective training programme where adults are able to manage and determine their own learning.

Efforts to enhance the competencies of adult educators, according to the National Blueprint of LLL, are left to the discretion of the related ministries and agencies (MOHE 2011). Professionalization is done either as workplace training or by attending short courses conducted in-house by a given agency. Universities have, to some extent, provided short courses or accredited courses as part of CPD for adult educators.

Nevertheless, there is no explicit policy that indicates the need for adult educators or trainers to possess professional teaching certificates. The legislative blueprint does not specifically highlight the need for the professionalization of adult educators. While funds are largely allocated to lifelong learners, nothing in the blueprint mentions funds for the professionalization of adult educators. Our experience shows that funds are supplied by the employers of adult educators to the providers of the courses in question.

## Context of the study

While school is responsible for providing students with a foundation in scientific literacy, for the public, learning often occurs through non-formal science education, in places like science centres/museums, botanical gardens, zoos, aquaria, planetariums, industry and interactive exhibits. The role of non-formal science learning is beginning to form an important and complementary addition to formal education in engaging students in science learning (Mirrahmi et al. 2011). Falk and Dierking (2010) found that the major source of scientific knowledge is not school, but non-formal education.

As argued by Tran (2008) and Plummer and Small (2013), many studies have looked into the benefits of learning science in the non-formal context, but not many have examined the competencies of the facilitators. These facilitators are known as science communicators, science explainers or lecturers. As science facilitators in non-formal institutions, they fulfil various roles: a) as planner; b) as manager; c) as science tour guide; and d) as expert in a content area (Tran 2008; Kamolpattana et al. 2015). The nature of their work is similar to the field of adult education in any sector (Nuissl 2009). Like other adult educators in other sectors, science facilitators' backgrounds are varied and their educational training ranges from formal teaching certificates to no educational training whatsoever (Tran 2008). Agencies and organizations that are involved in non-formal science education also often employ volunteers.

The effectiveness of science education in non-formal learning depends on the learning process and also on the professionalism of the parties involved, especially the science facilitator. Science facilitators must not only be knowledgeable, but also be able to facilitate and build a very good rapport with visitors. They are required not only to transfer information or knowledge, but to enable students to discover and expand their scientific experiences.

Spencer and Spencer (1993) state that competency is an underlying characteristic of any individual, which is causally related to criterion-referenced effective and/or superior performance in a job or situation. Various definitions of competency suggest that the main components cover knowledge, skills and personal characteristics (Boyatzis 2008; Spencer & Spencer 1993; Siraj & Ibrahim 2012). A person with a high level of competence has always shown interest in influencing others, is able to take proactive decisions and adopts responsibility for actions taken. In addition, a competent person is also well accustomed to communicating verbally, and is able to instil a positive attitude and motivation in students.

Efforts in developing the core competencies of adult educators in major-scale studies are undertaken mostly in the western context. The International Association of Facilitators (2003) has developed a competency framework in Core Facilitator Competencies, which consists of six domains: i) Create collaborative client relationships; ii) Plan appropriate group processes; iii) Create and sustain a participatory environment; iv) Guide group to appropriate and useful outcomes; v) Build and maintain professional knowledge; and vi) Model a positive professional attitude. In Europe, Bernhardsson and Lattke (2011) divided the nine key competencies for the adult learner facilitator into three domains, namely: i) competence in personal development and development of the "professional self"; ii) competence in content and didactics; and iii) competence in assisting learners. In their study *A Model of Small Group Facilitator Competencies*, Kolb et al. (2008) developed a competency model that focuses on five important categories. These categories are: i) communication; ii) task; iii) relationship or climate; iv) organization; and v) professional ethics. In her article *High-Performing (and Threshold)*

*Competencies for Group Facilitators*, Stewart (2006) also proposed a model that consists of four competencies: i) interpersonal competencies – communication and further skills; ii) management process competency; iii) knowledge competency; and iv) personal characteristics.

Accordingly, this study focuses on the science facilitator's competencies specific to the non-formal context. The main aim of the study is to identify key competencies that can be used as a basis for professional development for staff working in the sector, and thus improve the quality of adult learning in the non-formal context. The findings reported here are part of a larger study.

## Methods

This research employed the survey method. In particular, the Delphi Technique was used to identify the competencies of science facilitators as seen from the experts' view. Experts involved in this study comprised senior science teachers, science educators and science officers in non-formal organizations. Panel experts were selected on the basis of their willingness and ability to express an opinion, and their experience and expertise on matters under discussion (Siraj & Ibrahim 2013).

There were two phases involved in the data collection process. Firstly, the five dimensions of the science facilitator framework were identified through documentary analysis and literature review. Secondly, a survey questionnaire (71 items) was distributed to the 15 experts in the first round of the Delphi study.

The number of rounds in the Delphi study often ranges from two to ten to ensure that the results meet the purpose and objective of the study (Bauder 1999). However, Brooks (1979) suggests that three rounds are usually sufficient to attain the high level of consensus required among experts on a particular question item.

This study involved two rounds of the Delphi study. The results achieved from the first round were analyzed to determine the mean and interquartile range. The level of consensus is based on Siraj and Ibrahim (2013) (see Table 1). Items with a high level of consensus are used in the second round of Delphi, whereas items that did not reach consensus are deleted.

*Table 1: Level of consensus (Source: Siraj &Ibrahim 2013).*

| Score of interquartile range | Level of consensus |
| --- | --- |
| 0–1 | High consensus |
| 1.10 – 1.99 | Moderate consensus |
| ≥ 2 | No consensus |

## Findings and discussion

Five core competencies were identified through the literature and documentary analysis, namely: personal qualities, subject knowledge, communication skills, learning assistance learning evaluation. These competencies are relevant for science facilitators, as Kamolpattana et al. (2015) have shown. The role of science explainers, lecturers or science communicators should differ from the role of teachers in a school. The competencies identified are relevant to the various tasks in which they are involved and to the various types of participants, ranging from school children to adults.

The findings of the compentencies are shown in Table 2.

*Table 2: Interquartile range analysis of the first round.*

| Dimensions | Score of interquartile range (item) | | | | | Total items | New items |
|---|---|---|---|---|---|---|---|
| | 0 – 1 (High consensus) | | 1.10 – 1.99 (Moderate consensus) | ≥ 2 (No consensus) | | | |
| | 0.0 | 1.0 | | | | | |
| Personal qualities | 2 | 19 | 0 | 1 | | 22 | 1 |
| Subject knowledge | 0 | 8 | 0 | 1 | | 9 | 3 |
| Communication skills | 4 | 8 | 0 | 1 | | 13 | 2 |
| Assistance of learning | 5 | 10 | 0 | 1 | | 16 | 1 |
| Evaluation of learning | 0 | 8 | 0 | 3 | | 11 | 2 |
| Total | 11 | 53 | 0 | 7 | | 71 | 9 |

Overall, the findings of the first round of the Delphi study show that items in these five dimensions achieve a high level of consensus. However, there are a few items that do not gain consensus among the panel of experts. These consist of one item in each dimension – personal qualities, subject knowledge, assistance of learning and communication skills, respectively – and three items in the dimension for evaluation of learning. The experts also recommended nine new items and these items are spread across the five dimensions. From this analysis, the questionnaire for the second round was developed where seven of 71 items in the first round of the Delphi study were removed and another nine new items were added (see Table 3). The new questionnaire had a total of 73 items for the second round of the Delphi study.

*Table 3: Interquartile range analysis of the second round.*

| Dimensions | Score of interquartile range | | | | Total items |
|---|---|---|---|---|---|
| | 0 – 1 (High consensus) | | 1.10 – 1.99 (Moderate consensus) | ≥ 2 (No consensus) | |
| | 0.0 | 1.0 | | | |
| Personal qualities | 9 | 13 | 0 | 0 | 22 |
| Subject knowledge | 3 | 8 | 0 | 0 | 11 |
| Communication skills | 7 | 7 | 0 | 0 | 14 |
| Assistance of learning | 5 | 11 | 0 | 0 | 16 |
| Evaluation of learning | 3 | 7 | 0 | 0 | 10 |
| Total | 27 | 46 | 0 | 0 | 73 |

Based on Table 3, all 73 items obtained high consensus from the experts, with 27 items with scores at 0.0 and 46 items with scores at 1.0. This means that all the experts agreed to a high degree of consensus and the next round of Delphi was not necessary.

The dimensions in the framework suggested are seen as equally important to the competencies of science facilitators for learning to occur. Figure 1 depicts the dimensions and examples of question items in each dimension.

*Figure 1:  Competency framework of facilitators for science centres (source: Halim et al. 2015).*

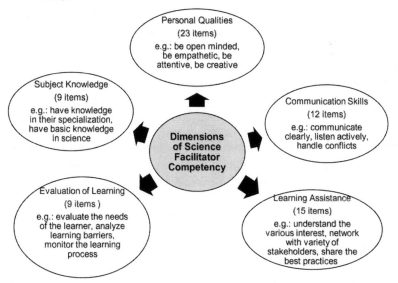

The framework suggested comprises dimensions that are generic in nature, namely personal qualities and communication skills. Chi-Chin (1995) and Kamolpattana et al. (2015) also found that personal qualities are important for creating a positive atmosphere for attracting visitors to hear their explanations. This study also found that Delphi experts stressed the need to develop education-related competencies (evaluation and learning assistance) among the science facilitators. The dimension of "evaluation of learning" is important to ensure that learning occurs in a free learning environment such as in science centres and science museums.

In a free learning environment, it is essential that the science facilitators are able to assist and engage the students in such an environment, and this requires facilitators to be competent in providing learning assistance to the students. A note of caution: similar to studies by Kamolpattana (2008) and Chi-Chin (1995), the emphasis on the evaluation of learning suggests that cognitive elements are being emphasized. In the Asian context, acquiring knowledge is seen as the main component of learning. However, developing the affective components of learning science – such as building a positive attitude towards science and encouraging an interest in science learning, which could be developed in the non-formal context – is equally important.

## Conclusion

Malaysia aims to be a developed country by the year 2020 and views economic progress as the key driver to achieve this status. Human capital development through education at all levels (pre-school to tertiary) and context (especially formal education) has always been given priority by the government as a means to achieving the country's economic advancement. Recent global developments such as the impact of globalization – namely the need to keep updating knowledge and skills so as to be relevant to the ever-changing demands of the workforce – has led Malaysia to promote the lifelong learning agenda in a concerted effort. Most noticeable has been the formulation of the national LLL policy in 2014. The LLL agenda focuses on continuous competency development for employability and, to a certain extent, learning for self-improvement. Examination of the LLL policy suggests that the issue of professionalization of adult educators is not being dealt with extensively. Thus, for an effective realization of the policy, ongoing conceptualization and research on the professionalization of adult educators is necessary, since it is still a contentious issue, as argued in the literature of adult education and continuing education.

The empirical study of this chapter is an effort to add to the existing knowledge of the competencies of adult educators, specifically science facilitators and in the non-formal context. In non-formal science education, the role of the science facilitator is very important, as it can encourage and facilitate science-centre visitors to explore science and thus develop scientific literacy. Being scientifically literate is one of the ways to empower society to deal effectively with the economic and environmental impacts of globalization. The five dimensions of science facilitator competencies identified will help the facilitators to improve their skills and knowledge. Science facilitators should be encouraged to reflect on their competency achievement and evaluate the extent of their proficiency in conducting daily tasks, so that they can do their job effectively. This could be done as part of an in-service training or a professional development course.

Identifying the competencies is a beginning to the professionalization of adult educators. Competencies can also be acquired at the workplace. Thus, future studies might measure the gap between acquired and expected competencies, so that planning for in-service training can be more effective. Identifying competencies at the micro-level related to the various tasks of science facilitators is also important. This would enable facilitators to follow a more focused professional development programme.

# References

Azman, N. / Ahmad, R.: "History, trends and significant development of adults' education in Malaysia". *HISTORIA: Journal of Historical Studies* 7(2), December 2006, pp. 66–82.

Bauder, S.M.: *A competency requirements analysis for digital television engineers.* University of Wisconsin-Stout: unpublished master's thesis in Management Technology. 1998, retrieved 20.10.2013, from http://www.sbe.org/pdf/Thesis.pdf.

Bernhardsson, N. / Lattke, S. (eds.): *Core competencies of adult learning facilitators in Europe: Findings from a transnational Delphi survey conducted by the project "qualified to teach".* QF2TEACH partnership: Bonn. 2009, retrieved from http://asemlllhub.org/fileadmin/www.dpu.dk/ASEM/events/RN3/QF2TEACH_Transnational_Report_final_1_.pdf.

Boyatzis, R.E.: "Competencies in the 21st century". *Journal of Management Development* 27(1), 2008, pp. 5–12.

Brooks, S.: *The challenge of cultural pluralism.* Praeger: Westport. 2002.

Buiskool, B.J. / Broek, S.D. / van Lakerveld, J.A. / Zarifis, G.K. / Osborne, M.: *Key competences for adult learning professionals: Contribution to the development of a reference framework of key competences for adult learning professionals.* Research voor Beleid: Zoetermeer. 2010.

Chin, C.: "Interpreters' perceptions about the goals of the science museum in Taiwan". Paper presented at the Annual Meeting of the National Association for Research in Science Teaching, 22–25 April 1995, San Francisco, CA.

Falk, J.H. / Dierking, L.D.: "The 95% solution: School is not where most Americans learn most of their science". *American Scientist* 98(6), 2010, pp. 486–493, retrieved 5.7.2013, from http://www.americanscientist.org/issues/feature/2010/6/the-95-percent-solution.

Halim, L. / Meerah, T.S. / Osman, K. / Samsudin, A.: "Developing the framework of core competencies needed by science facilitators in nurturing scientific literacy for the community". *Profile Book of Fundamental Research Grant Scheme (FRGS) Phase 1/2012.* Ministry of Higher Education: Malaysia. 2015.

Kamaruddin, K. / Jusoh, O.: "Adult computer literacy programme in rural areas in Peninsular Malaysia". *The Journal of Human Resource and Adult Learning* 4(2), 2008, pp. 142–152.

Kamolpattana, S. / Chen, G. / Sonchaeng, P. / Wilkinson, C. / Wiley, N., / Bultitude, K.: "Thai visitors' expectations and experiences of explainer interaction within a science museum context". *Public Understanding of Science* 24(1), 2015, pp. 69–85.

Kolb, J.A. / Jin, S. / Hoon, S.J.: "A model of small group facilitator competencies". *Performance Improvement Quarterly* 21(2), 2008, pp. 119–133.

Latif, L.A. / Fadzil, M. / Goolamally, N.: "Factors influencing the development of lifelong learning skills: OUM Tracer Study". *The 40th Anniversary of KNOU Future of ODL for "Knowledge Network Society".* Korea National Open University. 17–18 September 2012, retrieved from http://library.oum.edu.my/repository/791/1/Factor__LLL_Skills_Korea_LAL_PM_NOLI.pdf.

Maier-Gutheil, C. / Hof, C.: "The development of the professionalism of adult educators: A biographical and learning perspective". *European Journal for Research on the Education and Learning of Adults* 2(1), 2011, pp. 75–88.

Ministry of Higher Education (MOHE): *The blueprint on enculturation of lifelong learning for Malaysia (2011–2020).* MOHE: Putrajaya. 2011.

Mirrahimi, S. / Tawil, N.M. / Abdullah, N.A.G. / Surat, M. / Usman, I.M.S.: "Developing conducive sustainable outdoor learning: The impact of natural environment on learning, social and emotional intelligence". *Procedia Engineering* 20, 2011, pp. 389–396.

Mohamad, M.M. / Che Razali, C.M.: *Lifelong learning needs of instructors at training skills institute in Malaysia.* Faculty of Technical Education, Universiti Tun Hussein Onn Malaysia: Malaysia. 2013, retrieved from http:// eprints.uthm.edu.my/2851/1/613%2D623.pdf.

Nuissl, E.: "Profession and professional work in adult education in Europe". *Studi Sulla Formazione* 12(1/2), 2009, pp. 127–132, retrieved from doi: http://dx/doi. org/10.13128/Studi_Formaz-8591.

Plummer, J.D. / Small, K.J.: "Informal science educators' pedagogical choices and goals for learners: The case of planetarium professionals". *Astronomy Education Review* 12(1), December 2013, pp. 1–16.

Siraj, S. / Ibrahim, M.S.: "Competency standards of Malaysian teachers". *National Seminar Council of Malaysian Deans.* Faculty of Education, Public University: Johor Bahru, Malaysia. Paper presented October 2012.

Stewart, J.A.: "High-performing (and threshold) competencies for group facilitators". *Journal of Change Management* 6(4), 2006, pp. 417–439.

Spencer, L. / Spencer, S.: *Competencies at work: Models for superior performance.* John Wiley and Sons: New York. 1993.

Sidin R. / Salleh N.A. / Halimi, F.: *A review of non-formal educational research in Malaysia: A country report.* Faculty of Education: UKM Bangi. 1996.

Tran, L.U.: "Trained to interact: The professionalization of educators in science museums and centers". *Journal of Science Communication* 7(4), 2008, pp. 1824–2049.

Bolanle Clara Simeon-Fayomi

# An Exploration of Indigenous Adult Teaching Methods in Southwestern Nigeria and South Africa for Comparative Consideration

**Abstract:** This paper focuses on exploring indigenous teaching methods in comparison to other selected methods from around the globe. Using a tabulated information scale and extensive literature, the paper shows that indigenous methods comprise mostly informal components, as expressed in methods including the oral tradition, music and cultural activities.

## Introduction

Teaching methods are commonly known as tools for imparting knowledge. A number of teaching methods have emerged thanks to the continuous development in education. Conventionally, teaching methods refer to the general values, instruction and management approaches used for classroom instruction in a didactic situation. In an informal setting, indigenous teaching methods can be effective in stimulating students' interest in subjects; engaging students in the learning process; and cultivating critical thinking for sustained, inclusive and useful relationships. The methods remain a very active part of lifelong learning. This paper therefore seeks to explore the indigenous teaching methods in southwestern Nigeria in comparison with some selected teaching methods from South Africa, using a tabulated information scale and extensive literature.

## Literature review and theoretical framework

Robinson and Nichols (1998) refer to indigenous teaching methods as being holistic, imaginal, kinesthetic, cooperative, contextual and person-oriented. These are seen in sharp contrast to the teaching methods and orientation of western pedagogy. Indigenous teaching methods impart local knowledge that is considered unique to a culture or society. Such knowledge is passed from generation to generation, usually by word of mouth and by means of cultural rituals. Indigenous teaching provides the basis for agriculture, food preparation, health care, education and other activities that sustain societies in many parts of the world. Christie (1984) and Harris (1984) define the features of the indigenous teaching-learning process as observation, imitation, trial and error, real-life performance, learning the whole rather than the parts, problem-solving and repetition. These are explicitly framed as antithetical to western paradigms of schooling. Indigenous pedagogies tend to be anti-colonial, promoting resistance, political integrity and the privilege of indigenous voices (Rigney 1999). Langton (1993) observes that identity is not found, but produced through the dialogue between indigenous and non-indigenous people constantly defining and redefining each other through an ongoing exchange. In reference to cross-cultural theories, Harrison (2005) proposes that there is an informal discourse of negotiation at work in indigenous education, producing understanding about learning and identity that is seldom made explicit. Santoro, Reid, Crawford and Simpson (2011) raise awareness of this and refer to direct experiences of the informal and experiential learning and teaching that occurs between children, parents and elders in indigenous communities.

## Indigenous teaching methods and effective learning process

Callingham, Watson and Hay (2009) note that teaching methods that promote student involvement and which students find meaningful will retain the students' interest. Effective teaching methodologies that allow students to use their hands, eyes, ears and mind enhance effective learning and student achievement (Wachanga & Mwangi 2004). In addition, effective teaching methods emphasize high levels of thinking, focus on intrinsic rather than extrinsic motivation and help the students remember important information. Effective teaching methods produce a higher learning achievement and higher motivation (Li 2012).

*Figure 1: Indigenous pedagogy (Yunkaporta 2010).*

Yunkaporta's indigenous pedagogy framework contains some useful African indigenous teaching methods.

## Key African indigenous teaching methods

Song and dance: Songs have, for a long time, been a strong factor in making life meaningful. They are part of human experience for as long as we can recollect and recite them (Schoepp 2001). Songs have become so important that a wide variety of songs are appropriate to every human situation. There are lyrical tunes that are used in happy times and others used for more sombre moments. According to Gugliemino (1986), adults sing at religious services, in bars, in the shower and when they listen to the car radio. In traditional African and, in particular, southwestern Nigerian and South African societies, songs are an effective way of teaching children and adult learners to become responsible, cultured, well-mannered and active members of society. Lyrical methods are a kind of voice in pedagogy and andragogy. According to Herbst (2005), it is a voice that tends to "repeat", although not exactly, ideas in a true oral fashion, in order to gain more energy and direction. It is also a voice of peoples undergoing transformation as an important part of self-analysis, singing songs in acculturated verses validated by indigenous refrains. An ethnomusicologist, Masoga (2003), shared his experience from South Africa:

> Traditionally, novices in training for healing and divining had to use music, i.e. clapping of hands, drumming and dancing, to induce ancestral trances on a daily basis. Songs such as Khalel'nkanu, khalel'nkanu, nkanu y'baba b'yi buzi nkanu (I am crying for the healing horn, let my ancestral spirits bring the healing horn to me) were repeatedly sung by the novices led by their seniors in the sangoma lodges (izindomba). With drums beating in the background, novices danced and evoked their spirits to become active."

A dance, then, gives expression to a song. Dances show different forms, some of which are unknown in other cultures, and some similar to others, even when there are great distances between them. An example is the "Bata dance" in the southwestern part of Nigeria and the tap dancing found in many western world cultures. Each dance has a deeper connotation apart from the joy and exercise it shows externally. It is a symbol of practice and intimacy, as many people dance to the same songs in similar ways. Dances have names and are expected to be danced in certain ways. In many communities, they express moments of significance. In some cultures in Nigeria, for instance, the "dance of the virgins" is used for young women old enough for marriage, and a special dance is also performed by young brides who pass through the fattening room tradition before they wed.

Role-playing: Learning through experience is relatively more effective than learning through the western model, which is primarily based on a lecture format. Cherif and Somervill (1995) submit that teaching methods that use students' experiences can help generate enthusiasm for active involvement in the learning process. One effective technique that encourages such participation is role-playing, which provides an opportunity for "acting out" conflicts, collecting information about social issues, learning to take on the roles of others and improving students' social skills. In the African context, role-play is simply an assumption of one type of social behaviour, to which various roles and responsibilities are attached. Learners assume the roles, find personal meaning within the social worlds these demonstrate and resolve personal dilemmas with the assistance of a facilitator. In the social dimension, it allows individuals to work together in analyzing social situations, especially interpersonal problems, and in developing decent and democratic ways of coping in situations with which they are not familiar (Cherif & Somervill 1995). Whenever individuals project a kind of "what- if" scenario for the future, they are indulging in some type of role-play. They are projecting themselves into an imaginary situation where, although they cannot control the outcome, they can at least anticipate some or all of the conditions and "rehearse" their performance in order to influence the outcome, which ultimately contributes to their learning experience (Munyai 2011; Harbour & Connick 2005). Role-play has been used in traditional African settings to educate would-be leaders, hunters, farmers, artists and even husbands and wives, with a simulated life experience of what they will encounter in their future endeavours.

The use of proverbs and witty words: Africans in general have a very rich and diverse cultural heritage, which has been passed on from generation to generation and acts as a source of guidance. According to Malunga and James (2004), African cultural heritage forms the basis of self-identity, self-respect and self-confidence; it has enabled people to live in harmony with their physical, social and spiritual environments; and it also provides the foundation for leadership, guidance, problem-solving, decision-making, self-reliance and development (Malunga & James 2004). Experience, they say, is the best teacher; a wealth of experience from the past provides valuable lessons. Such past experience enables people to develop traditional sayings, proverbs and witty sayings that are very useful when trying to understand socio-economic, political and religious life. Proverbs are metaphors, which explain complex issues in simple statements (Malunga & James 2004). For example, people may be urged to be proactive about working and saving for rainy days when they recall an African proverb that reads: "Early in the morning, when a man wakes with nothing in pursuit of him, he must pursue something for the sake of the night."

There are many messages to be deduced from this powerful African proverb. For instance, it preaches against unwarranted complacency, laxity and procrastination. The metaphorical nature of this indigenous method of teaching creates a powerful mental picture in learners that is an effective way of ensuring that they will retain the material in a strong and lasting way.

Folk tales and storytelling: Folk tales and storytelling are another integral part of African teaching methods. They serve as sources of entertainment and enlightenment about the cultural orientation and traditions of African people. They are employed to educate people about cultural values, and are used as moral and character training. In Nigeria, for instance, telling tales by moonlight is a powerful community practice. Storytelling takes place at night, usually after dinner, when an elderly member of a family or clan is surrounded by a group of youngsters who listen to him or her narrating stories. At the end, the storyteller welcomes questions. This is to give some room for cross-fertilization of ideas among the children. The questioning session is facilitated and moderated by the storyteller who gives further interpretations of such issues as action or inaction in the tales, characters and consequences and their various implications. According to Amali (2014) and Samson-Akpan (1986), this is a lively process that is likened to an integrated classroom where children, teenagers and adults attend lessons. The children learn about existing issues in the human and animal world as reflected through folktales (Amali 2014). This oral tradition includes not only the history of the community, however, but also serves to "sustain morality, ritual, law, and sanctions against offenders" (Nsamenang & Tchombe 2011).

Dirges: Songs play an important part in Africans' lives. The traditional and cultural heritage of the continent leads to the expression of varying degrees of contexts using, for example, lyrical hymns or dirges. Dirges are songs composed and sung or performed at burials or at memorial events dedicated to a deceased person. In the traditional African setting, death is perceived as a transition to another life, referred to as "life after death" (Alembi, Gehman 1999). This is why in a funeral context, the mourners wail, sing and dance, saying "we are now escorting our sister" or "escorting dad in peace" (Alembi n.d.). Escorting the dead is obligatory and everyone is involved. Often, dirges are a kind of oral poetry that can come in many formats: odes, fables (with animal heroes, especially the tortoise), incantations, recitations, praises, etc. are used depending on the circumstances at hand and as the occasion calls for. These are expertly recited by adults while the younger ones listen attentively with the main purpose of learning life's lessons from the lyrics and internalizing the message for their own use later in adulthood, when most of the elders they have learned from will have passed on (Nsamenang & Tchombe 2011).

Festivals: Just as people in developed societies celebrate many different holidays, Africans commemorate different forms of many historical events that serve as symbols for the existence of a people in a particular community. Hence, festivals are a kind of cultural performance that is usually associated with religious traditions or local ritual celebrations premised upon an historical event. As Shalinsky (1985) rightly submits, these celebrations have other important functions: preserving heritage, fostering social cohesion, releasing tensions accumulating from daily life and inculcating pride and loyalty. Examples of traditional festivals include the "Ojude Oba Festival" among Ijebus in southwestern Nigeria and the "Yam Festival" among the easterners. Shalinsky (1985) further states that

> *community festivals provide an easily accessible resource for student "field" involvement and offer a unified focus for learning about history, community, social interaction, traditional values, and social change. Furthermore, numerous skills (observation, note-taking, analysis, and cultural analytical description) are involved in learning through community festivals (Shalinsky, 1985).*

At times, most festivals are ways of adoring and expressing gratitude to supreme beings. Such festivals, according to Omolewa (1981), provide the population with "courses" in the history of the locality; accounts of the origins, stories and legends of families; and the great men and women produced in that society.

Oral tradition/praise songs: These are songs that are composed to eulogize an individual or a family or clan. Praise songs normally comprise the oral tradition of family deeds, heroic feats and accomplishments passed down from one generation to another. They also give an insight into the traditional household craft or ancestral might of a people, as praise songs contain the names of the family's ancestors and their individual characteristics. The elders in African society use praise songs to awaken the positive spirit of a child and lead it towards a purpose, usually to taking a positive line in life. For example, a praise song among Yorubas of the southwestern Nigeria goes: "Omo agbolu aje; omo oberiri lookun; omo Osupa tigun ani ole; agbolu aje le eni owore to tun se…", meaning:

> *The son of whom carry the staff of wealth, he that dazzles in the night; the son of whom will say the moon is out but not yet full moon; the son of whom put the staff of wealth in the hands of those that can manage and make it better…*

As an African indigenous teaching method, praise songs provide historical compilations of the names, attributes and characteristics of the forefathers. They also serve as a way of motivating and directing young adults in society. It is an informal way of educating them to become part of a dedicated and patriotic citizenry.

Art works such as sculpture, painting and moulding: Although art works in the Western world are usually used as complementary tools, in the form of instructional aids to teaching and learning exercises, traditional African learning makes greater use of such objects. Sculptures, artworks and artifacts are symbolic. They are powerful pedagogical vehicles for engaging students in the process of forming imagery and historical thoughts and developing their imaginative as well as historical thinking (Suh 2013; Crawford, Hicks & Doherty 2009). They shower them with multiple perspectives, as they represent the physical and mental world of human beings that is not only personal but also associated with society in general (Suh 2013).

Rites of passages: In many African societies, rites of passage are important learning activities, as they bring an individual forward from one stage of life to another. In order to move from one phase to the next, rites are performed not necessarily as sacrifices, but as an ordination of the commencement of the next stage of life. Rites are performed at various cultural events such as the birth of a new baby, marriages and funerals. Commonly, all rites end with great feasts and music. As a teaching method, life assumes a higher dimension of presence. It is not taken simply as arrival and departure; the rites involved and the great expense incurred give a great measure of sanity and proper consideration to these phases of life. For instance, it is not easy to get married in an African culture within six months, as families must remain convinced even after the decision to marry has been made by the couple, for several months or years of courtship. The same applies to bringing children into the world.

*Table 1: Tabulation of the differences and similarities between types of indigenous teaching methods found in some parts of southwestern Nigeria and South Africa.*

| No. | Indigenous teaching methods | Nigerian indigenous teaching methods | South African indigenous teaching methods |
|---|---|---|---|
| | Songs and dance | Juju music and bata dance, cry of the bride | Adopted among the people of Mqatsheni in S.A. |
| | Role-playing | Dance of the hunter | In use in S.A. |
| | Proverbs and witty word usage | Work proverbs | Very common in S.A. |
| | Folklores | Story of Iyalode Efunsetan Aniwura, Iyalode Ibadan | Peculiar to S.A., especially in some rural settlements in the KwaSani Municipality, Sisonke District in KwaZulu-Natal Province |

| No. | Indigenous teaching methods | Nigerian indigenous teaching methods | South African indigenous teaching methods |
|---|---|---|---|
| | Storytelling | "Alo apamo and alo apagbe", i.e., stories for knowledge and stories for sing-along | Common practices |
| | Festivals | Odun ojude Oba, Osun festival | There are many festivals, such as "Cape Town International Jazz", a two-day festival held during March or April featuring some 40 international and African acts performing on five stages to an audience of 15,000. It also features photographic and art exhibitions. |
| | Oral tradition/praise songs | Oriki Agboluaje | In common practice |
| | Rites of passages in birth, age group and death | In common practice | In common practice |
| | Art works | Art works such as sculpture, painting and moulding are mostly for historical instruction. Some are for worship. | There are artworks in S.A. especially for decoration and identification, but with little use for teaching. |
| | Dirges | Song of the widow | Dirges are mostly used for totems and rites. |

## Comparative thoughts and discussion

With the foregoing discourse on the various southwestern Nigerian and South African indigenous teaching methods, it would be unethical and unscientific to call modern pedagogical methods undesirable, because many disciplines that have helped humanity to progress have adopted western methods and enjoyed remarkable success. The contention of this paper is to bring to the fore the various traditional methods at the disposal of Africans that are unique and useful tools if refined or adapted for better and more sound teaching and learning exercises. Essentially, teaching methods can be placed into these two categories: teacher-centred and student-centred approaches.

*Table 2: Comparison of characteristics of indigenous teaching methods and modern pedagogy.*

| Indigenous adult teaching methods | Modern pedagogy |
|---|---|
| Informal, non-formal | Formal |
| Community learning system | Individual learning system |
| Lifelong: from cradle to grave | Time long: from a period to a period |
| Collaborative efforts | Individual efforts |
| Lifelong and extensive: found in all aspects of life and situation | Restricted: often on one subject matter |
| Multilevel/multivariate | Single level |
| Multifaceted | Single faceted |
| Societal value | Individual value |
| Daily/continuous reinforcement | Intermittent reinforcement |
| Rapport non-verbal and verbal | Rapport mostly verbal |
| Balance character training | Varied/non-character training |
| Message, value, culture-oriented | Knowledge-oriented |
| Critical thinking models for complete life view | Critical thinking models for subject matters |

Table 2 shows the considerable and distinct features of the methods of teaching. It is obvious that indigenous teaching methods and similar approaches may, in the future, be essential to making education learner-centred, all-inclusive and catering to the individual needs. This is because the informal and non-formal setting is always a fair basis for education; it involves no certification, and it is flexible and controllable. Learning through traditional teaching methods is convenient and easy for learners.

As shown in Yunkaporta's (2010) indigenous pedagogical framework, indigenous African teaching methods are used both in sync and individually. They are flexible and learner-friendly. Like Katha in India, an indigenous southwestern Nigerian or South African teaching technique like storytelling is a process that is likened to an integrated classroom that children, teenagers and adults participate in. African indigenous teaching techniques may also be symbolic, such as the sculptures, artworks and artifacts among Nigerians that are powerful pedagogical vehicles for engaging students in the process of imagery and historical thoughts, and developing their imaginative as well as historical thinking (Suh 2013; Crawford, Hicks & Doherty 2009). It is important to state, also, that most African traditional teaching methods, as found in southwestern Nigeria and South Africa, foster collaborative efforts in lifelong training. The witty words and daily proverbs used by the elders are lessons that encourage young adults to develop their critical thinking and positive attitudes. Praise songs, such as Oriki among the Yorubas, are lyrical or poetic incantations to learners that reinforce active learning and good moral and character education.

## Conclusion

This paper reveals that the African indigenous methods found among southwestern Nigerians and South Africans are peculiar to them, as they are mostly found in informal learning. They are expressed in oral traditions, cultural activities and music. These methods are effective for teaching and learning. African indigenous teaching methods could be incorporated into many teaching methods of the western tradition to achieve better and more operative teaching, class participation and wholesome, productive interaction.

## References

Alembi, E.: "The Abanyole dirge: 'Escorting' the dead with song and dance", retrieved 31.1.2016, from https://www.folklore.ee/folklore/vol38/alembi.pdf.

Amali, H.I.: 'The function of folktales as a process of educating children in the 21st century: A case study of Idoma folktales". *Proceedings of the International Conference on 21st Century Education at Dubai Knowledge Village* 2(1), 2014, pp. 88–97, retrieved 31.1.2016, from http://www.21caf.org/uploads/1/3/5/2/13527682/amali.pdf.

Carmichael, C. / Callingham, R. / Watson, J. / Hay, I.: "Factors influencing the development of middle school students' interest in statistical literacy". *Statistics Education Research Journal* 8(1), 2009, pp. 62–81.

Christie, M.J.: "Formal education and Aboriginal children". *The Australian Journal of Indigenous Education* 1(14), May 1986, pp. 40–44.

Crawford, B.S. / Hicks, D. / Doherty, N.: "Worth the wait: Engaging social studies students with art in a digital age". *Social Education* 73(3), 2009, pp. 136–139.

Gugliemino, L.M.: "The affective edge: Using songs and music in ESL instruction". *Adult Literacy and Basic Education* 10(1), 1986, pp. 19–26.

Harbour, E.,/ Connick, J.: "Role playing games and activities rules and tips". 2005, retrieved 30.1.2016, from http://www.businessballs.com/roleplayinggames.htm [30 Jan 2016].

Harris, S. : "Aboriginal learning styles and formal schooling". *The Aboriginal Child at School* 12(4), September 1984, pp. 3–23.

Harrison, N.: "The learning is in-between: The search for a metalanguage in indigenous education". *Education Philosophy and Theory* 37(6), 2005, pp. 871–884.

Herbst, A. (ed.): *Emerging solutions for musical arts education in Africa*. African Minds: Cape Town, South Africa. 2005.

Langton, M.: "'Well I *heard* it on the radio and I *saw* it on the television...': An essay on the politics and aesthetics of filmmaking by and about Aboriginal people and things". NSW: Australian Film Commission: North Sydney, NSW. 1993.

Li, N.: "Approaches to learning: Literature review". *IB Review*. International Baccalaureate Organization: New York. 2012.

Malunga, C. / James, R.: "Using African proverbs in organisational capacity building". *The International NGO Training and Research Center* (INTRAC) *PraxisNote* 6. 2004, retrieved 31.1.2016, from http://www.intrac.org/data/files/resources/103/Praxis-Note-6-Using-African-Proverbs-in-Organisational-Capacity-Building.pdf.

Masoga, M.: "Establishing dialogue: Thoughts on music education in Africa". *Alternation* 10(2), 2003, pp. 334–347.

Munyai, N.N.: *Effect of role-play as a formative assessment technique on job performance, University of South Africa*. Unpublished M.Comm. thesis in Industrial and Organisational Psychology. 2011, retrieved 30.1.2016, from http://uir.unisa.ac.za/bitstream/handle/10500/6100/thesis_munyai_n.pdf?sequence=1.

Nsamenang, A.B. / Tchombe, T.M.S.: *Handbook of African educational theories and practices: A generative teacher education curriculum*. Human Development Resource Centre (HDRC): Bamenda, Cameroon. 2011, retrieved 31.1.2016, from http://www.thehdrc.org/Handbook%20of%20African%20Educational%20Theories%20and%20Practices.pdf.

Rigney, L.: "Internationalization of an indigenous anticolonial cultural critique of research methodologies: A guide to indigenist research methodology and its principles". *Wicazo Sa Review* 14(2), 1999, pp. 109–121.

Robinson, J. / Nichol, R.: "Building bridges between Aboriginal and Western mathematics: Creating an effective mathematics learning environment". *Education in Rural Australia* 8(2), 1998, pp. 9–17.

Samson-Akpan, E.S.: "Ibibio folktales in education". *Nigeria Magazine* 54(4), 1986, pp. 67–74.

Santoro, N. / Reid, J. / Crawford, L. / Simpson, L.: "Teaching indigenous children: Listening to and learning from indigenous teachers". *Australian Journal of Teacher Education* 36(10), 2011, pp. 64–76.

Schoepp, K.: "Reasons for using songs in the ESL/EFL classroom". *The Internet TESL Journal* 7(2), February 2001, retrieved 31.1.2016, from http://iteslj.org/Articles/Schoepp-Songs.html.

Shalinsky, C.: "Studying community festivals". Smithsonian National Museum of Cultural History. 1985, pp. 1–5, retrieved 31.1.2016, from http://anthropology. si.edu/outreach/Teaching_Activities/pdf/communityfestivals.pdf.

Suh, Y.: "Past looking: Using arts as historical evidence in teaching history". *Social Studies Research Practices* 8(1), 2013, pp. 135–159, retrieved 30.1.2016, from http:// www.socstrpr.org/wp-content/uploads/2013/09/MS_06372_Spring2013.pdf.

Wachanga, S. / Mwangi, J.G.: "Effects of the cooperative class experiment teaching method on secondary school students' chemistry achievement in Kenya's Nakuru District". *International Education Journal* 5(1), 2004, pp. 26–36.

Yunkaporta, T.: *Aboriginal pedagogies at the cultural interface.* Unpublished draft report for DET on an indigenous research project. James Cook University's School of Indigenous Australian Studies. 2010.

Maja Avramovska & Tania Czerwinski

# Professionalization in Adult Education: Curriculum Globale – The Global Curriculum for Teacher Training in Adult Learning and Education

**Abstract:** An international core curriculum for the training of adult educators worldwide has been developed and implemented by DVV International and the DIE to promote the professionalization of adult education that is being called for in all regions of the world. Examples from Uzbekistan and Macedonia show possibilities for implementation and lessons learnt.

## The development of Curriculum globALE

Adults learn in a variety of contexts, each with very different prerequisites, objectives and motivations. Supporting them in their learning is different from teaching children, and therefore requires a different set of knowledge, skills and competences. Adult educators all over the world often take up a teaching or training activity without undergoing any specific preparation for this work, which is very likely to impact the quality of the training they can provide. While such educators are highly knowledgeable when it comes to the subject they teach, there is frequently room for improvement in their adult education skills. In the Belém Framework for Action (2009), UNESCO therefore identified improving the training and professionalization of adult educators as a critical task for the future, and this same goal plays an important role within the Sustainable Development Goals (SDGs).

Curriculum globALE was developed on the basis of these requirements – a new global framework curriculum for the training of teachers in adult education. It was jointly developed in 2013 and revised in 2015 within a project headed by the German Institute for Adult Education, the Leibniz Centre for Lifelong Learning (DIE) and the Institute for International Cooperation of the German Adult Education Association (DVV International). It aims to support the professionalization of adult educators by providing a common reference framework, by supporting adult education providers in the design of their programmes and by implementing train-the-trainer programmes. It is meant to be suitable for use in all kinds of adult learning settings and contexts, and to serve on a global scale to foster knowledge exchange and mutual understanding between adult educators across countries and regions.

Curriculum globALE (CG) obviously cannot and does not provide a ready-made "one-size-fits-all" training programme. It makes a basic standard model available, which, for the purpose of implementation, is intended to be adapted individually to a variety of local needs. The basic element and unchangeable core of CG is a set of context-independent competences and learning outcomes that are relevant to all adult educators, regardless of the country or setting in which they practise. There are then many different ways in which these competences can actually be developed within a specific training programme, and users of CG are free to develop a format that is best suited to their particular needs. To support them in this task, CG provides a complete set of suggestions and examples as to how such a training programme can be organized, including proposals for the subject matter, didactic methods, formats and literature references.

As the global curriculum in adult learning and education, Curriculum globALE is organized in five core modules, plus one introductory module and two elective ones. The five core modules were identified as:

Module 0: Introduction

Module 1: Approaching adult education

Module 2: Adult learning and adult teaching

Module 3: Communication and group dynamics in adult education

Module 4: Methods of adult education

Module 5: Planning, organization and evaluation in adult education

The elective modules provide an opportunity for the participants either to deepen the knowledge and skills they acquired in the core modules, and/or to broaden their competence profile by acquiring knowledge and skills concerning a field or aspect that is relevant to their professional activity.

Practical experience and reflection are involved as essential elements for the competence development of adult educators. The learning formats therefore encompass taught sequences, as well as self-study, accompanied by practical work within real work settings, where the trainers can provide mentoring and guidance. CG is committed to the principles of competence orientation, practice orientation, learner orientation and learning sustainability. Cross-cutting issues that are to be considered throughout include: gender sensitivity, sustainable development, contribution to peace and democracy development.

As a basis for the further contextualization, each module is described in terms of:

- competences to be acquired,
- topics to be covered,
- linkages with other modules,
- literature for in-depth reading,
- suggestions for the implementation of the module,
- the role of practical application and reflection and
- recommended scope and workload.

To ensure a sustainable train-the-trainer concept, a curriculum must be localized and contextualized to suit specific local needs. Furthermore, the curriculum must be embedded within an existing context. When Curriculum globALE is introduced within a local context, it therefore has to be adjusted to the needs and specific institutional and professional contexts in order to support the development of that particular adult education system. The consequence of this is that CG can never exist as a "stand-alone" solution. It is recommended that the local curriculum be linked to pre-existing training schemes, to involve all possible stakeholders (government, international institutions, educational bodies, etc.), to align CG with national policy and local demands and to cooperate on a regional level. Such adaptations must be carried out by the local stakeholders themselves, as they know their context best.

Providing a global curriculum such as Curriculum globALE in the local language is one of the first steps towards implementation within the local context and with local stakeholders. Curriculum globALE has therefore been translated into nine languages (Arabic, English, German, Albanian, Bosnian, Serbian, Macedonian, Russian and Spanish).

Piloting is nevertheless an important instrument of verification to explore whether specific needs are being met, or whether adjustments need to be made. After Curriculum globALE had been piloted in a number of countries during 2013–2015, minor adaptations were made in order to improve further implementation in other countries. Within this article, we intend to present the implementation of Curriculum globALE in two different contexts, demonstrating the background, implementation and lessons learnt, especially in Uzbekistan and Macedonia.

## Training adult educators in Uzbekistan

### Background

During its 25 years of independence, Uzbekistan has experienced a series of economic reforms that have affected social and economic areas of life. Although
economic growth rates are high, several problems persist, including unemployment (especially in rural areas), labour migration and the lack of an ecologically
responsible, healthy lifestyle.

Modern processes in the development of adult education are taking place in the
country as rapidly as changes associated with scientific and technological progress,
democratization and the digitization of society, as well as related social changes.
Legislation relating to non-governmental educational institutions is developing.
There are new trends in training courses, e.g., in the frequency and also quality
of the training and retraining of the pedagogical staff. Consequently, there is a
need for experience exchange between different training providers and for a social
partnership between state and non-state players. "Education outside the formal
system" has not yet found its proper place in the established system of continuous education in Uzbekistan. For this reason, it is recommended that the next
stages of government policy on reforming the education system should focus on
developing special programmes aimed at nurturing non-formal adult education
and integrating it into the general system of continuous education. This will allow
formal and non-formal adult education to unite under one system – the system of
continuous education – and thus enable everybody to receive high-quality lifelong
education, regardless of social status, gender or place of residence.

The experience of DVV International in Uzbekistan shows that the region has
great potential for specialists with expertise in adult learning methodology. The
establishment of Curriculum globALE training courses in order to train highly
qualified staff specializing in adult education could improve the present situation,
among other things by closing the current knowledge gap in theory, history and
international trends in adult education.

Central Asia was the first region in which Curriculum globALE was tested.
Uzbekistan and other Central Asian countries, such as Tajikistan und Kyrgyzstan,
in which DVV International is working do not have any regulated training courses
for adult educators, only short-term options that furnish individuals with practical
skills. Most of the trainers in the field of adult education have therefore become
more professional mainly through their practical activities. Curriculum globALE
provides the opportunity to offer needs-based training in a flexible, modularized

system in order to professionalize adult educators who are working in different areas of adult education.

## Implementation

Curriculum globALE was initially launched with multiplier training courses. Through an open matchup, eighteen people from government and non-governmental educational institutions in Uzbekistan with a background in adult education were selected.

The complete training programme was organized by the DVV International Regional Office for Central Asia in Tashkent. The eighteen selected participants were initially enrolled in the programme, and fifteen of these attended the whole programme and sat the final examination. Whilst the group was very heterogeneous in terms of age, gender and professional background, all the participants had a good educational background (university graduates, many of them in educational sciences), but they had very different amounts of amounts of experience in working with adults. A few were virtual beginners as trainers, but had acquired experience during the implementation of the CG, whilst others already possessed more than 20 years of experience in adult education. This heterogeneity led to an interesting exchange among the participants and fruitful input during the courses.

All five core modules and the two elective modules were piloted from July 2013 to September 2014. Each module consisted of four- to five-day block seminars and training courses. The trainers were experienced professionals from Serbia, Germany and Russia. Many educational texts and presentations were translated into Russian and made accessible to the participants, as little relevant material is available in Russian. Their newly acquired knowledge was confirmed through tests and questions they reflected on within each module. After all the modules had been completed, the participants were able to put their practical skills to the test by planning and giving training themselves in a simulated training situation. A total of fifteen participants graduated from the course.

## Feedback and lessons learnt

At the end of the pilot, an evaluation workshop was held in Tashkent at which the practical experience was evaluated and documented together with the participants, trainers, DVV International and the authors of CG. This was an important step towards receiving sound, first-hand information for the revision of Curriculum globALE and making it accessible for future processes in other countries.

Six months after the piloting of Curriculum globALE had been completed in Uzbekistan, all fifteen graduates received a short questionnaire on the impact of this programme. The participants were asked to assess, on a ten-point scale, the effect of the CG training on various aspects of their teaching practice as well as on their own students' learning. The questionnaire also included some open questions in which participants were asked to describe in their own words the most important changes – including unexpected outcomes – that resulted from the CG training. The results were altogether positive. All in all, the participants stated that they were able to apply the contents from the CG training in their professional work as trainers to a large extent, and that their teaching practice had changed significantly and positively. But professional teaching practice was not the only dimension on which CG was seen to have had a major impact. Many participants felt that they had also developed personally as a result of the CG training.

The use of various methods as well as the more conscious decisions about the application of a particular method in their own training were an especially important aspect of professional teaching, as was the recognition of learners' needs and the adaptation of the teaching style to meet these needs. Not only that, but participants' roles as trainers also changed, as they reflected more profoundly on their own professional actions as trainers and, to some degree, felt more secure in the role as such. As a result, those learners who attend the CG-based adult educators' courses are more highly motivated to learn and participate actively and reflectively. Some participants also reported that they now feel more highly respected by their colleagues, their management, their clients and even their families. The answers also repeatedly referred to the participants' prospects on the training market. Various participants mentioned that they had managed to secure additional teaching assignments, for instance after having received recommendations from their former students. Others noted that they had become more selective in accepting teaching assignments, taking only those with a certain quality level and not solely seeking lucrative assignments.

The successes and positive effects of the pilot programme in Uzbekistan were quite clearly visible in 2015. The programme's graduates performed their duties as trainers several times during the year at various training courses in Uzbekistan and in the neighbouring countries of Kyrgyzstan and Tajikistan. The measures were based on individual CG modules that were adapted to suit their target groups. The participants were mostly multipliers from the VET system (members of the teacher training institutes, Master Trainers from AE Centres, etc.). The clients were DVV International as well as other German development cooperation organizations (GIZ, GOPA).

# Training adult educators in Macedonia

## Background

More than two decades have passed since Macedonia became an independent state following the collapse of the Federal Republic of Yugoslavia. During these years, Macedonia had to implement major reforms and establish its own institutions in all sectors, including the education sector.

*The quality of education was one of the positive assets which Macedonia inherited from the Federation. The literacy rate was about 94 per cent; the secondary school system was well developed, and there were two universities, in Skopje and Bitola, with a good range of faculties.*

(Pantaleev 2003: 9).

The adult education system had to be reorganized, decentralized and funded. In the first decade, however, the Macedonian authorities were mostly occupied with primary and secondary education reforms.

*In 2006, the General Assembly of the Republic of Macedonia adopted the National Programme for the development of education in the Republic of Macedonia 2005–2015. An integral part of this National Programme was the Programme for Adult Education in the Context of Lifelong Learning, as a strategic document addressing adult education as an integral part of the overall education system. In this Programme, the main goal of adult education was defined as being able to provide equal opportunities for all people to obtain quality education and to acquire sound knowledge, skills and competences.*

(Rizova 2015, p. 146).

A legislative adult education framework was adopted in 2008, aiming to initiate and maintain a positive and active approach towards lifelong education for people of all ages. One year later, in 2009, the public institution of the "Adult Education Centre" was established and tasked with promoting a system of adult education that would be functional, modern and in line with EU standards, a system that would provide high-quality learning opportunities that would lead to qualifications in accordance with the needs of the population, increase employment and develop entrepreneurship, meet the needs of the labour market and contribute to economic, social and personal development.

A variety of organizations and institutions in Macedonia offer adult education programmes. These include the open civic universities, private adult education schools, foreign language schools and civil society organizations. They all employ teachers/adult educators with different initial educational levels, and very often without any of the didactic-methodological knowledge and skills needed to teach adults. This de-professionalization of teachers in adult education was caused by the marginalization of the special knowledge and competences that are needed to work with adult learners, which allowed a number of people with no knowledge of the characteristics of educational work with adults – its principles, content, organization, forms and working methods – to operate in the adult education sector. Very recently, therefore, there has been a need for people involved in adult education at a professional level who lack the appropriate didactic-methodological knowledge and skills to obtain these through training, and to improve in this area. Furthermore, Article 21 of the Adult Education Act decrees that adult education programmes are to be implemented by teachers, professors, instructors in practical training and professional associates who have completed special training courses in working with adults. According to the Act, adult education teachers are entitled and obliged to undergo continuous professional training and training in working with adults.

Although this Act was adopted in 2008, apart from individual initiatives at a project level, there is still no system for imparting didactic-methodological knowledge and skills to teachers who work with adult learners. Until now, no flexible and modular programme has been developed and adopted by the relevant state institutions responsible for the further education of the personnel engaged in adult education providers.

## Implementation of Curriculum globALE in Macedonia

In 2014, in order to respond to the need to professionalize adult education in Macedonia, the Lifelong Learning Centre, as a partner of DVV International, made its first preparations to pilot and introduce Curriculum globALE to Macedonia. This project was launched and implemented in close cooperation with the Institute of Pedagogics at the Faculty of Philosophy at the "Cyril and Methodius" University in Skopje. The first step was to adapt the curriculum to the Macedonian context. This was carried out by a professor of the Faculty of Philosophy and discussed with experts from the relevant institutions. Once the Macedonian version of Curriculum globALE was available, participants were selected and the piloting started. Along with the piloting, the Curriculum globALE global framework was translated into Macedonian and Albanian. The initial group of 17 participants attended the series of training courses along the lines of modules (0 to 6) that were contained in the global curriculum. The selected group was somewhat heterogeneous, consisting of adult education professionals with a variety of educational and professional backgrounds and experience. Several of the participants were representatives of state institutions that were engaged in adult education; many of these were managers of adult education providers, and the rest were teachers and trainers in state and private providers and NGOs, with various levels of teaching experience.

This heterogeneity of the group was one of the challenges of the piloting process, which resulted in outstanding outcomes with regard to the participants' motivation throughout the entire process, with positive group dynamics. Not a single participant dropped out. The piloting process was conducted from April 2014 to December 2015 and completed by the participants sitting a final examination in February 2016. It is planned for these graduates to act as multipliers and train other teachers/adult educators in Macedonia.

As provided in the Adult Education Act, each teacher and trainer in Macedonia will have to be licensed in order to engage in educational work with adults. In order to comply with this precondition, and bearing in mind the lack of further education programmes for adult educators in Macedonia, the Lifelong Learning Centre sees Curriculum globALE as a great opportunity and tool to fill the gap left by the lack of such a capacity-building programme.

For that purpose, a programme is being developed in accordance with Curriculum globALE that will be submitted to the national authorities for state recognition. Approval of the programme would enable a state-recognized certificate to be issued to all participants. By attending a course and obtaining the certificate, participants would fulfil the precondition for performing educational work with adults. In this way, Curriculum globALE already plays, and will play, an even greater and more important role in supporting the capacity building of teachers and trainers in adult education and contributing to its quality and development.

## Feedback and lessons learnt

For the organizers, i.e., the Lifelong Learning Centre and the Faculty of Philosophy, the development of CG was a great opportunity, and sets the course for the future development and delivery of training programmes, as it offers a more structured and systematic approach. In this context, Curriculum globALE has contributed towards improving the implementation of trainer qualification. It is flexible and accommodates adjustments to the national context. Its modular structure enables and ensures the continuity of the participants throughout the entire cycle and the learning process.

The graduates of the first cycle of Curriculum globALE evaluated the impact of the programme by completing the same standardized questionnaires as Uzbekistan's Curriculum globALE graduates. As in Uzbekistan, their assessment of the outcomes and various quality aspects of the Curriculum was extremely positive. The majority of graduates stated that they were able, to a large extent, to apply the contents of the Curriculum globALE training in their professional work as trainers, and that they learned to structure the teaching process more effectively and to use new methods. One important outcome was their improved ability to identify and understand the needs of their adult learners and, hence, orientate the teaching/learning process towards meeting those requirements. Accordingly, their role in the teaching process with adults also completely changed. They now play a more facilitating and learner-centred role and plan their training sessions at a higher level of quality and according to the learners' needs. They stated that they knew more about learning theories and how adults learn, and are able to respond to the needs of learners and transfer their knowledge more efficiently using the most appropriate teaching methods. The first positive outcome of attending the Curriculum globALE training programme was also noticed by the students themselves who attended the courses and programmes run by the alumni of the CG training programme. The improved quality of the teaching/facilitating process has had a positive effect on student learning. Students are more highly motivated to work because they know what goals they are working towards, and are more interested in acquiring additional information and knowledge than was previously the case. The Curriculum globALE graduates have also gained knowledge and skills on how to integrate their students' previous knowledge and skills. This, in turn, has improved students' active learning.

Throughout the whole process, the participants became more self-confident, and their communication and presentation skills were enhanced. One important further result is that they gained a solid theoretical knowledge of international and national developments in adult education, which will allow them to engage in a more intensive exchange with colleagues from the region and other countries.

## Conclusions

In recent years, both Uzbekistan and Macedonia have passed through several reforms within the education sector. Nevertheless, non-formal adult education as well as lifelong education are still lacking in one way or another in both countries. The de-professionalization of adult educators, in particular in terms of knowledge and competencies needed to work with adult learners, and a proper system for didactic-methodological knowledge and skills, are still a challenge. Similar experiences have also been documented in other countries where adult education is not a high priority.

During the contextualization of the Curriculum globALE in all implementing countries, the experience has been that mostly national or regional information on adult education is missing, and only few materials are available in the local language, e.g., Russian or Lao, which are needed especially for individual study as well as for classes where a special focus is laid on different modules, depending on the background of the trainers participating. Due to the different potential stakeholders and implementing institutions in both the countries mentioned, Curriculum globALE has been implemented differently in order to be able to offer adequate training. In Macedonia, the implementation along with the University in Skopje provides a flexible and sustainable train-the-trainer programme that is officially recognized within the system. In the case of Uzbekistan, where the lack of an appropriate implementing institution led to direct implementation by DVV International, there is the challenge of offering the train-the-trainer programme within a system that, at this point, is not yet properly formed. This could present an opportunity to promote and show the necessity of such non-formal adult education.

The two different backgrounds and systems in Uzbekistan and Macedonia demonstrate that there is a strong demand in both countries for a flexible and modular programme for adult educators, and that providing this would create a great potential for professional adult educators. During the elaboration of Curriculum globALE, the aspects of flexibility and professionalization were very important, especially as the programme was based on existing train-the-trainer programmes from DVV International's work, national qualification systems and standards for adult educators as well as transnational competency standards.

After three years of piloting Curriculum globALE in various countries, and especially in the two countries presented above, analyzing the data and feedback received from the implementing organizations as well as from trainers and participants in the respective countries has allowed several general conclusions to be drawn:

Curriculum globALE has broadly achieved its goals, namely to enhance the professionalization of adult educators, provide a common reference framework, support adult education providers in the design and implementation of train-the-trainer programmes, nurture a culture of quality in adult education and foster knowledge exchange and mutual understanding between adult educators worldwide.

Since its launch in 2013, Curriculum globALE has been implemented or is being prepared for implementation in fifteen countries around the world. It is perceived in these countries as an instrument for the professionalization and further development of the adult education sector. The pilot project showed that it is possible and useful to develop a global curriculum framework that can be successfully adapted to national/local standards and implemented in various countries across the world, even countries with highly divergent adult education systems and standards, cultures and traditions.

These countries demonstrate a strong interest in implementing Curriculum globALE and setting it as a national quality standard for the delivery of training for adult educators. The pilot was launched simultaneously in several countries in which DVV International works and has offices along with a network of partner organizations and institutions. Even several organizations from other countries in which DVV International does not operate showed considerable interest in implementing the Curriculum.

The professionalization of adult education staff is still an issue in many countries, given the lack of institutions and organizations providing professional training in adult education. There is no other training opportunity for the professional development of adult educators in any of the countries in which Curriculum globALE has been/is being implemented.

The adaptation to the national adult education context and needs of the countries with regard to the application of national topics and culturally relevant methods, issues and developments was carried out in compliance with the quality standards of Curriculum globALE. The Curriculum was adapted successfully. Two countries adapted the Curriculum to the national/local context and to the needs of their participants, bearing in mind the process of further multiplication in the countries.

The analysis of the implementation and feedback of all the parties involved triggers the further development of supporting materials, handbooks and relevant tools that will make the process of implementing the Curriculum more efficient.

Several challenges were also identified regarding the implementation of Curriculum globALE. Adapting and implementing the Curriculum call for adequate funding, and some of the organizations involved in its implementation had problems allocating funds for this purpose. Another important aspect that is also connected with the financial issue is the matter of the availability of national trainers who can conduct the modules of the Curriculum. Most of the countries have no such trainers available. In some of the countries, such as Uzbekistan, international trainers were therefore invited to conduct the first cycle of training courses, whilst in other countries, trainers from neighbouring countries were also invited. The lack of sufficient adult education literature in national languages also poses a problem. In order to improve the situation, additional Curriculum globALE materials and handbooks will be developed in the near future that can be translated into the national languages.

A further issue that arose during the Curriculum globALE implementation process is the certification/validation of the Curriculum. The organizations responsible for the implementation in some of the countries are interested in validating the programme and issuing national certificates. The validation system for non-formal educational programmes is non-existent in some countries, but it nonetheless appears that most of the organizations involved consider the validation of the programme to be important. Further discussions with all the parties involved will show how the validation process develops in future.

## References

Avramovska, M. / Czerwinski, T. / Lattke, S.: *Curriculum globALE: Global curriculum for adult learning & education.* Institute for International Cooperation of the German Adult Education Association (DVV International): Bonn. 2015.

Government of the Republic of Macedonia, Ministry of Education and Science: *Adult Education Act (2008).* Official Gazette of the Republic of Macedonia: Skopje. 2008.

Pantaleev, T.: *Macedonia, adult and continuing education.* Institute for International Cooperation of the German Adult Education Association (DVV International): Bonn. 2003.

Rizova, E.: "Reforms and the system for adult education in the Republic of Macedonia". *International Journal for Education Research and Training* 1, January 2015, pp. 146–147.

UNESCO Institute for Lifelong Learning: *Confintea VI. Belém framework for action. Harnessing the power and potential of adult learning and education for a viable future.* UNESCO: Hamburg. 2010.

# Authors

Natália Alves, PhD in Education, associate professor, Instituto de Educação, Universidade de Lisboa, Lisbon, Portugal. Email: nalves@ie.ulisboa.pt

Philipp Assinger, research assistant, department for adult and continuing education, University Graz, Austria. Email: philipp.assinger@uni-graz.at

Maja Avramovska, senior desk officer Caucasus, Turkey, South East Europe and senior manager monitor and evaluation, Institute for International Cooperation of the German Adult Education Association (DVV International), Bonn, Germany. Email: Avramovska@dvv-international.de

Thomas Barany, M.A., Zentrum für Lehrerbildung, Schul- und Berufsbildungsforschung, Dresden University of Technology, Germany. E-Mail: thomas.barany @tu-dresden.de

Roberta Bergamini, doctoral student in education, University of Florence, Italy. Email: roberta.bergamini@unifi.it

Vanna Boffo, PhD, associate professor of general pedagogy, department of education and psychology, University of Florence, Italy. Email: vanna.boffo@unifi.it

Eunyoung Choi, doctoral student in education at Seoul National University, the Republic of Korea. Email: sarahchoiey@snu.ac.kr

Tania Czerwinski, senior desk officer East/Horn of Africa, Southern Africa, teamleader Curriculum globALE, Institute for International Cooperation of the German Adult Education Association (DVV International), Bonn, Germany. Email: Czerwinski@dvv-international.de

Julia Di Campo, doctoral student in pedagogical sciences for education and training. University of Padua, Italy. Email: julia.dicampo@phd.unipd.it

Catarina Doutor, doctoral student in education and research fellow at the University of Lisbon, Portugal. Email: catarinadoutor@gmail.com

Hakan Ergin, doctoral student in education, University of Istanbul/Turkey. Email: hakan.ergin1@yahoo.com

Regina Egetenmeyer, Dr. phil., university professor for adult and continuing education, Julius-Maximilian University of Würzburg, Germany. Email: regina.egetenmeyer@uni-wuerzburg.de

Gaia Gioli, PhD, postdoc, department of education and psychology, University of Florence, Italy. Email: gaia.gioli@unifi.it

Paula Guimarães, PhD in education, assistant professor, Instituto de Educação, Universidade de Lisboa, Lisbon, Portugal. Email: pguimaraes@ie.ulisboa.pt

Lilia Halim, PhD, university professor for science education (Physics), National University of Malaysia, Malaysia, Email: lilia@ukm.edu.my

Georg Hennig, B.A., Master student in education and learning culture studies, Dresden University of Technology, Germany. E-Mail: georg.hennig@s2011.tu-chemnitz.de

Fanny Hösel, doctoral student in adult education, Dresden University of Technology, Germany. Email: fanny.hoesel@phil.tu-chemnitz.de

Clara Kuhlen, research associate and doctoral student in adult/continuing education, Julius-Maximilians-Universität Würzburg, Germany. Email: clara.kuhlen@uni-wuerzburg.de

Dubravka Mihajlović, research assistant and doctoral student, Institute for Pedagogy and Andragogy, Faculty of Philosophy, University of Belgrade, Serbia. Email: dubravka.mihajlovic@f.bg.ac.rs

Balázs Németh, Dr. habil., professor of adult and lifelong learning, University of Pécs, Hungary. E-mail: nemeth.balazs@feek.pte.hu

Kira Nierobisch, PhD in education, research fellow, department of adult education and vocational education, University of Education Ludwigsburg, Germany. Email: nierobisch@ph-ludwigsburg.de

Kamisah Osman, PhD, university professor for science education (Chemistry), National University of Malaysia, Malaysia, Email: kamisah@ukm.edu.my

Kristina Pekeč, assistant to a professor and doctoral student, Chair of Andragogy, Department of Pedagogy and Andragogy, Faculty of Philosophy, University of Belgrade, Serbia. Email: kpekec@f.bg.ac.rs

Rute Ricardo, doctoral student in education, University of Lisbon, Portugal. Email: rutericardo_23@hotmail.com

Sabine Schmidt-Lauff, Prof. Dr., professor for continuing education and lifelong learning, Helmut-Schmidt-Universität Hamburg, Germany. Email: schmidt-lauff@hsu-hh.de

Ingeborg Schüßler, Prof. Dr., professor for adult and continuing education, department of adult education and vocational education, University of Education Ludwigsburg, Germany. Email: schuesssler@ph-ludwigsburg.de

Janiery da Silva Castro, doctoral student in education, University of Florence, Italy, Scholarship of CAPES/Brazil. Email: janiery.dasilvacastro@unifi.it.

Bolanle Clara Simeon-Fayomi, Ph.D., senior lecturer, Department of Adult Education and Lifelong Learning, Faculty of Education, Obafemi Awolowo University, Ile-Ife, Nigeria. Email: gbola202000@yahoo.com.

Shalini Singh, research fellow (RHEES-BURD) and doctoral student in adult education, Jawaharlal Nehru University, India. Email: contactingshalinisingh @gmail.com.

Carlo Terzaroli, doctoral student in adult education, Department of Education and Psychology, University of Florence, Italy. Email: carlo.terzaroli@unifi.it

Concetta Tino, doctoral student in education, University of Padua, Italy. Email: concettatino8@gmail.com

Nicoletta Tomei, doctoral student in education, University of Florence, Italy. Email: nicoletta.tomei@unifi.it

Ge Wei, joint PhD candidate, Peking University, China, and the University of Helsinki, Finland. Email: xdwg722@pku.edu.cn

Wan Nor Fadzilah Wan Husin, doctoral student in science education, National University of Malaysia, Malaysia, Email: wannor_fadzilah@yahoo.com.my

# Reviewers

Thank you very much for supporting the editors of this volume in the review process.

Dr. Clinton Enoch, University of Hannover, Germany

Prof. Dr. Paolo Federighi, University of Florence, Italy

Dr. Marion Fleige, German Institute for Adult Education

Dr. Daniela Frison, University of Padua, Italy

Prof. Giovanna del Gobbo, University of Florence, Italy

Prof. Dr. Paula Guimaraes, Universidade de Lisboa, Portugal

Prof. Dr. Bernd Käpplinger. University of Gießen, Germany

Prof. Dr. Ulla Klingovsky, University of Applied Sciences Northwestern Switzerland Susanne Lattke, German Institute for Adult Education

Prof. Dr. Licínio Lima, University of Minho, Portugal

Prof. Dr. Balasz Németh, University of Pécs, Hungary

Prof. Dr. Jost Reischmann, University of Bamberg, Germany

Prof. Dr. Silke Schreiber-Barsch, University of Hamburg, Germany

Prof. Dr. Ed Taylor, Penn State College of Education, United States of America

Prof. Dr. Alan Tuckett, University of Wolverhampton, United Kingdom

**Studien zur Pädagogik, Andragogik und Gerontagogik**

Begründet von Franz Pöggeler

Herausgegeben von Bernd Käpplinger und Steffi Robak

Die „Studien zur Pädagogik, Andragogik und Gerontagogik" widmen sich der theoretischen und empirischen Erwachsenenbildungs- und Weiterbildungsforschung. Sie reflektieren deren Internationalisierung in ihrer Wirkung nach innen und außen und begleiten diese kritisch. Sie sind ein transnationales Forum, wo Leitideen nationaler und internationaler Konferenzen fortgeführt werden. Es wird auch ein Raum für solche Grundlagenarbeiten offeriert, die der Konstitution und dem internationalen Vergleich der Erwachsenenpädagogik dienen.

In der Reihe kann auf Deutsch und Englisch publiziert werden. Manuskriptvorschläge sowohl etablierter Wissenschaftler/innen als auch ambitionierter Nachwuchswissenschaftler/innen können an die Herausgeber/innen gerichtet werden. Sie werden in Absprache mit dem Verlag begutachtet – oder peer reviewed – und ggf. zur Aufnahme in die Reihe empfohlen.

Kontakt:

Prof. Dr. Bernd Käpplinger (Humboldt Universität zu Berlin): bernd.kaepplinger@rz.hu-berlin.de / http://ebwb.hu-berlin.de/team/bernd-kapplinger
Prof. Dr. Steffi Robak (Leibniz Universität Hannover): Steffi.Robak@ifbe.uni-hannover.de/ http://www.ifbe.uni-hannover.de/robak.html

Band 67 Regina Egetenmeyer (ed.): Adult Education and Lifelong Learning in Europe and Beyond. Comparative Perspectives from the 2015 Würzburg Winter School. 2016.

Band 68 Tim Stanik: Beratung in der Weiterbildung als institutionelle Interaktion. 2016.

Band 69 Regina Egetenmeyer / Sabine Schmidt-Lauff / Vanna Boffo (eds.): Adult Learning and Education in International Contexts: Future Challenges for its Professionalization. Comparative Perspectives from the 2016 Würzburg Winter School. 2017.

Band 70 Bernd Käpplinger / Steffi Robak / Marion Fleige / Aiga von Hippel / Wiltrud Gieseke (eds.): Cultures of Program Planning in Adult Education. Concepts, Research Results and Archives. 2017.

www.peterlang.com